UNFORTUNATE DESTINY

UNFORTUNATE DESTINY

Animals in the Indian Buddhist Imagination

REIKO OHNUMA

OXFORD
UNIVERSITY PRESS

OXFORD
UNIVERSITY PRESS

Oxford University Press is a department of the University of Oxford. It furthers the University's objective of excellence in research, scholarship, and education by publishing worldwide. Oxford is a registered trade mark of Oxford University Press in the UK and certain other countries.

Published in the United States of America by Oxford University Press
198 Madison Avenue, New York, NY 10016, United States of America.

CIP data is on file at the Library of Congress
ISBN 978-0-19-063754-5

1 3 5 7 9 8 6 4 2

Printed by Sheridan Books, Inc., United States of America

CONTENTS

FIGURES

CONVENTIONS

1. All Pāli canonical and commentarial sources are cited from the Tipiṭaka (and commentaries) established at the Chaṭṭha Saṅgāyana or Sixth Buddhist Council held in Yangon, Myanmar, 1954–1956, and available online at www.tipitaka.org. However, as is customary, the bibliographic references given are to the standard Pali Text Society editions, as noted in the Abbreviations. Differences between the two that bear upon my translation of a passage are indicated in the notes (where the Chaṭṭha Saṅgāyana edition is referred to as CS).
2. All translations from Pāli and Sanskrit are my own, unless otherwise stated. The original Pāli or Sanskrit text is provided only when a significant word or phrase is involved.
3. Pāli terms and phrases are indicated by P., and Sanskrit terms and phrases are indicated by S. When discussing particular terms (rather than quoting them directly from a text), my decisions concerning which form to cite are somewhat haphazard and vary according to the context.

ACKNOWLEDGMENTS

Bits and pieces of this book have been presented over the years at the Minding Animals 3 Conference (Jawaharlal Nehru University, New Delhi), the Second Biennial Living With Animals Conference (Eastern Kentucky University), the Columbia University Seminar on Buddhist Studies, the 41st Spalding Symposium on Indian Religions (Cardiff University, Wales), the Five Colleges Buddhist Studies Faculty Seminar (Smith College), and the American Academy of Religion Annual Meeting (San Antonio). I am grateful to the audiences at all of these venues for helping me think through this material. John Strong (as usual) was a most perceptive reader of the entire manuscript, and Naomi Appleton offered her insightful comments on Chapters 3 and 4.

Chapter 6 is a revised version of a previously published article, "An Elephant Good to Think: The Buddha in Pārileyyaka Forest," *Journal of the International Association of Buddhist Studies* 35.1–2 (2012): 259–293. I am grateful to the anonymous reviewer of the original manuscript and to Nancy Lin for comments on the article as published. In revising the article for inclusion in this book, I am grateful to an anonymous reviewer at Oxford University Press for persuading me that aspects of my analysis in the article were unconvincing and needed to be revised. (Any elements of the analysis that remain unconvincing are, of course, my responsibility alone.)

Pieces of Chapters 5 and 7 were previously published in "Animal Doubles of the Buddha," *Humanimalia* 7.2 (2016): 1–34. I am grateful to the anonymous reviewer of that manuscript for comments that helped me to refine my language and analysis.

At Dartmouth College, I am grateful to the John Sloan Dickey Center for International Understanding and the Dean of Faculty Office for providing me with extra funding for travel to international conferences. I am also grateful to Cynthia Read at Oxford University Press for another pleasant and trouble-free publishing experience.

It is somewhat ironic for a person like me to write a book about animals, since I do not have a wealth of affinity for them. (I like them well enough, of course, but I am just not what most people might describe as an "animal lover.") Luckily, my sister Keiko does have such an affinity, and I have drawn more inspiration than she knows from her excellent writing, reporting, and editing of the now-defunct publication *The Bosque Beast*, which I eagerly devoured, cover to cover, every time it arrived. This book is dedicated to her, with love and affection.

It is also dedicated fondly to my own companion animals (the first two of whom went to their own "unfortunate destiny" during the writing of this book): Dusty Buster, Ukulele Ike, and the not-at-all-dangerous Captain Danger.

PREFACE

Early Buddhism in India was a profoundly human-centered tradition. Its founding figure, the Buddha, was neither a god nor a prophet of god, but a human being who soon became Buddhism's primary focus of worship and ultimate concern—*all* buddhas, in fact, must be human beings. Through his preaching of the Dharma, moreover, he taught a path of self-cultivation that was intended primarily for other human beings.[1] Even though the larger Buddhist cosmos was full of gods who vastly exceeded human beings in power, pleasure, and lifespan, Buddhism saw the human being alone, among all beings, as uniquely capable of bringing about an end to the perpetual suffering that all beings experience during their endless cycling through samsara. The ultimate goal of Buddhism—whether defined as nirvana or buddhahood—was open to human beings alone,[2] and those who found themselves in other states of existence had to wait for the rarity of a human rebirth in order to pursue this goal. Even if we put aside the ultimate goal of a permanent escape from samsara, one's movement throughout samsara itself—up and down the karmic ladder, to a better or worse state of existence—was likewise believed to be determined primarily by the actions undertaken while in a *human* rebirth. While the gods were mostly limited to experiencing pleasurable karmic rewards, and those in the lower realms of existence (hungry ghosts, animals, and hell-beings) were mostly limited to experiencing unpleasant karmic rewards, it was the actions undertaken when in a human rebirth that largely determined one's movement in either direction. It was human beings who had moral agency and were the masters of their own destinies. It was human beings who were able to benefit from the Dharma. Thus, only human beings could become members of the Sangha, the monastic community of monks and nuns around which Buddhism is organized. Buddha, Dharma, and Sangha—all three of the "Three Jewels" of Buddhism were profoundly humanocentric. Indeed, it would not be an overstatement to say that Buddhism constitutes one particular vision of the project of being human.

Human beings can only define themselves, however, in opposition to that which is nonhuman. Thus, in Buddhist literature from India, the vision of the human is constantly shaped and expressed through comparison and contrast with a variety of nonhuman beings—including gods, spirits, demons, ghosts, animals, hell-beings, and more. But while all of these categories can be fruitfully employed to highlight what it means to be human, the category of the *animal* is unique in being the only one that exists both at the level of representation and in the "real" world (see Figure P.1).

(A) (B) (C) (D)

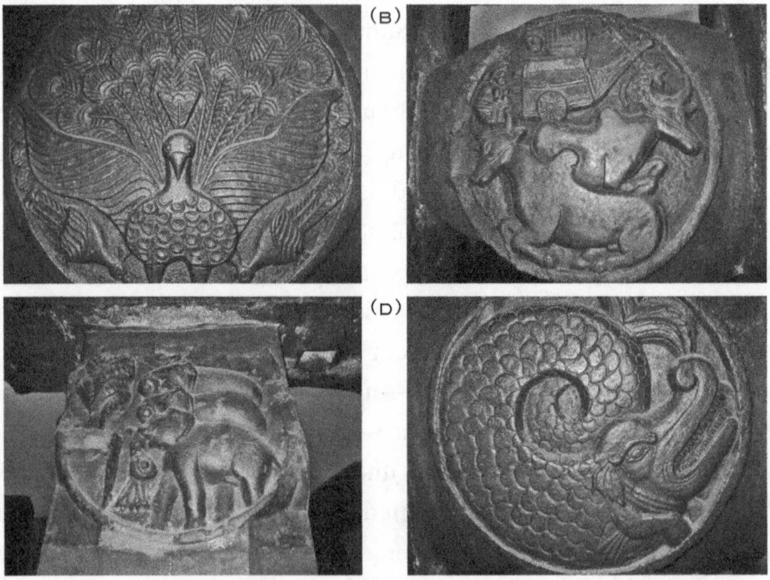

FIGURE P.1.

Animals used in decorative, nonnarrative contexts: peacock, oxen, elephants, *makara*. Railing medallions from the Bharhut *stūpa* (Madhya Pradesh, India), 2nd c. BCE. Indian Museum, Kolkata. (Photos by Anandajoti Bhikku, licensed under CC BY-SA 3.0.)

Representations of animals within Buddhist texts thus took shape in constant interplay and conversation with their authors' real-world encounters with actual animals in the wild. Buddhism in India was physically rooted within a natural landscape alive with the reality of nonhuman animals, and Buddhist monks, in particular, often built their monasteries on the outskirts of human settlements, as well as spending considerable time wandering or meditating in the wilderness. As a result, Buddhist texts display a high degree of knowledge of the characteristics, behaviors, and habitats of many different animal species. The phenomenological reality of the animals that monastic authors encountered obviously shaped and constrained—yet did not fix or determine—the symbolic representations of animals they employed in Buddhist texts. This constant interplay between animal representations and actual animals makes the animal a particularly potent symbolic resource for reflecting on the nature of the human. Animals, as Lévi-Strauss so famously noted, are not only "good to eat," they are also "good to think."[3] In fact, animals seem to hold a privileged place among the possible tools for thought: "They do not just stand for something, as a word stands for a thing ... they *do* something ... there is some added value in the fact that the blank screen for these projections is an animal."[4] This "added value" stems from the fact that the animal is *alive.* Animals are "symbols with a life of their own ... their animated gaze moves us to think."[5] Though amenable to serving us as tools for thought, their *aliveness* finally resists our complete control—and this makes them particularly compelling symbols with which to grapple. The animal alone, among all symbols, gazes back at us.

It is also the case, moreover, that human beings *are* animals themselves—in a way in which it is not equally possible to say that they *are* gods or spirits or hell-beings or plants. Because human beings *are* animals, yet continually define themselves in opposition to all nonhuman animals, there is a simultaneous *kinship* and *otherness, identity* and *difference*, and *attraction* and *repulsion* in humanity's relationship to the animal (a theme that runs throughout this book, and that I will return to in the Conclusion). Thus, animal representations—not only in Buddhism but perhaps universally—constantly display a human desire to both identify with and dominate over the animal realm, and to relate to animals through kinship and communion at one moment, and possession, abuse, and exploitation at the next. Animals are highly charged objects of meaning that often elicit multiple interpretations and feelings of dislocation and ambivalence.

This book is about some of the many ways in which animals are represented in early Buddhist literature from India. As should be clear by now, my interest is not in the animals per se—that is, the actual creatures—but rather in how these animals are represented within the world of Buddhist texts, and how, in particular, these representations are used to comment upon human beings, the nature of humanity, and the project of being human—as Buddhism sees it. I use the term "animals" broadly, moreover, to encompass a number of different things: animals as a specific realm of rebirth characteristic of Buddhist doctrine and cosmology; *animality* as a particular state, condition, or mode of being that is attributed with certain qualities and frequently contrasted with the state of being human; broader categories of animals, such as the "wild" versus the "tamed"; specific species of animals, such as horses, elephants, lions, and monkeys; and named and individualized animal characters who appear in Buddhist literature, such as the horse Kanthaka or the elephant Pārileyyaka. All of these phenomena, to one degree or another, are treated in the following pages. My treatment does not aim to be comprehensive, but only to bring forward those categories of animal representations that have been most striking to me and that I believe illustrate the predominant strains of early Buddhist thinking about the animal realm.

Not included in my treatment of "animals" are several types of beings that Buddhist authors themselves did classify as belonging to the animal realm, but that are better seen as purely mythical creatures. The most important among these are the *nāga* and its mortal enemy, the *garuḍa*. The *nāga* is a serpentine creature that might, in some contexts, behave like an ordinary snake. Nevertheless, *nāgas* are also described as having human heads and torsos, possessing many supernatural powers (including the ability to shapeshift into a human form), and residing in underwater kingdoms full of magnificent palaces—features that make them quite distinct from what we ordinarily think of as an "animal."[6] Likewise, the *garuḍa*—the traditional enemy of the *nāga*—may take on the general appearance of an eagle, yet its wings are golden and encrusted with jewels, the size of its wingspan extends over many miles, and it, too, is endowed with enormous strength and supernatural powers.[7] *Nāgas* and *garuḍas* also seem to appear in different narrative contexts than ordinary animals—in many Mahāyāna *sūtras*, for example, *nāgas* and *garuḍas* are regularly included among the audience listening to the Buddha preach, whereas the same is not true of ordinary animals.[8] In short, these creatures are so fantastic and so far removed from other animals that it makes little sense to treat them within the same context. I will therefore ignore these animal-like beings here.

Another important exclusion from my discussion is any sustained focus upon *animal ethics*, or Buddhist views on the ethical treatment of animals. In my view, animal ethics are distinct from (though obviously related to) the ways in which animals are represented and the ways in which animality itself is used as a comment upon the human. Since Buddhist animal ethics have already been treated at length—in fact, most of the existing scholarship on "Buddhism and animals" has focused heavily on this area—I have thought it better to refer the reader to the existing sources,[9] although I do discuss animal ethics briefly whenever it bears on the issue at hand. Buddhist views on the ethical treatment of animals are, of course, implicated throughout much of my discussion, but they are not one of my primary interests, and I have thought it better to maintain my focus by alluding to them only briefly and as necessary.

Regarding my sources, because I am interested in engaging in a close reading of textual passages and individual narratives, I have chosen to strictly limit the number and type of sources drawn upon for each chapter. The major sources I make use of throughout include Pāli canonical and commentarial literature and well-known Indian Buddhist texts in Sanskrit, such as the *Divyāvadāna, Avadānaśataka, Mahāvastu, Lalitavistara, Abhidharmakośabhāṣya, Mūlasarvāstivāda Vinaya*, and *Buddhacarita*. Since I lack the ability to read texts in Chinese, I have excluded Chinese translations of Indian Buddhist texts, except where

I found them to be absolutely necessary (particularly in Chapter 1)—relying, in these cases, upon short passages taken from the able translations of others. I describe my sources as being representative of "early" Buddhism in India only in the broadest of senses: all of my sources can confidently be dated prior to the sixth century CE. With a few exceptions, moreover, most of my sources derive from the Mainstream Buddhist tradition. This is fully intentional: since the Mahāyāna and Vajrayāna traditions likely developed some new and distinctive ways of thinking about animals—yet also shared with the Mainstream Buddhist schools a common heritage of animal representations that remained influential and relevant—I have chosen to focus upon those representations that were common to Indian Buddhism as a whole. The historical context for my discussion is thus broadly South Asian, relatively "early," and foundationally Buddhist.

The book is divided into three parts (which I will describe only briefly here, since each part also has its own Introduction that further describes the individual chapters contained therein). In Part I, I focus upon how the animal realm of rebirth is depicted in the humanocentric world of early Buddhist doctrine and cosmology, and how this depiction comes to shape Buddhist thinking about the animal's ability to make spiritual progress. In Part II, I turn my attention to the rich world of speaking and thinking animals found in the genre of the *jātakas* (previous-life stories of the Buddha), which offer a very different perspective on the animal than is evident in Part I. In Part III, I take a sustained look at three prominent animal characters within the life-story of the Buddha, whom I interpret as the Buddha's "doubles." While each part focuses on a different variety of animal representations (and draws on different sources), several themes run throughout the book and serve to tie the three parts together—for example, the simultaneous *kinship* and *otherness* in humanity's relationship to the animal, and the crucial role of *language* as a dividing line between human beings and animals. I return to some of these overarching themes in the Conclusion.

Finally, a word about terminology. Throughout this book, I will refer to "humans" and "animals" as if they were two mutually exclusive categories. In truth, of course, human beings *are* animals, and it would be more scientifically correct to refer to "human animals" and "nonhuman animals." I am aware, moreover, that our tendency to speak in terms of "humans" and "animals" as if they were mutually exclusive is not just an innocent verbal habit. It in fact has serious ideological consequences, unconsciously separating us from all other species and constantly reinforcing a human exceptionalism that has been disastrous for the other animals on our planet.[10] For this reason, many scholars working in the discipline of animal studies (to which this book seeks to make a modest contribution) have cultivated the habit of using phrases such as "human animal," "nonhuman animal," "other-than-human animal," the "more-than-human world," and even such neologisms as Lisa Kemmerer's "anymal" (used to refer to nonhuman animals without suggesting that humans are not animals).[11] While I am wholly sympathetic to the motivations underlying this terminology (and will use such phrases on occasion), I also—to be frank—find the constant use of these phrases to make for very tiresome and long-winded reading. After careful consideration, I have therefore made the decision to largely retain the language of "humans" and "animals," offering the partial justification that these two categories do appear to be more distinct within Sanskrit and Pāli terminology than they are in English. In Sanskrit, for example, the term *manuṣya* refers to human beings alone, while the term *tiryañc* refers to nonhuman animals. In order to bring humans and animals together into a single category, one would have to resort to a term such as *sattva* or *bhūta*, both referring to "living beings"—yet these terms also include a great variety of supernatural entities. Therefore, there does not seem to be, in Sanskrit and Pāli, a category of "animals (both human and nonhuman)" that excludes other types of beings. In any case, as the reader will see, the underlying recognition that human beings *are,* in fact, animals will be one of the major themes explored in the following pages.

UNFORTUNATE DESTINY

PART I

Unfortunate Destiny

Introduction To Part I

The most common Sanskrit term for designating nonhuman animals as a whole is *tiryañc*—suggesting a living being who "goes horizontally"—as well as its various extensions, such as *tiryag-yoni* and *tiryag-yoni-gata*, both suggesting "one born from the womb of an animal." These terms specifically exclude human beings (S. *manuṣya*) and are thus narrower than terms such as *sattva, bhūta, jīva*, and *prāṇin*—all of which refer to "living beings" or "sentient beings" more generally, including both human and nonhuman animals (as well as others). On the other hand, terms related to *tiryañc* are broader than a panoply of other terms designating smaller subcategories of animals, such as *mṛga* and *paśu* (wild animals and domesticated animals, respectively), *pakṣin* (birds), *matsya* (fish), and *sarīsṛpa* (reptiles). Terms related to *tiryañc* are thus very close parallels to the English terms "animal" or "nonhuman animal."

None of these terms are referenced, however, in the title of Part I. Instead, the title "Unfortunate Destiny" is an English rendering of the Sanskrit term *durgati*, which is used to designate all realms of rebirth (S. *gati*) that are "bad," "unfortunate," or "difficult" in nature

(S. *dur*)—including rebirth as a ghost, as an animal, or as an inhabitant of one of the many hells that populate the Buddhist cosmos. I have used this title in order to indicate that my interest in Part I is not animals per se, but rather, the animal realm of rebirth (S. *tiryag-yoni-gati*) as a specific feature of Buddhist cosmology, associated with particular karmic causes and carrying certain (largely negative) moral and ethical connotations.

Chapter 1 focuses on the depiction of the animal realm in early Buddhist doctrine and cosmology. It selectively brings together a number of crucial passages from Pāli canonical and commentarial literature, a few Sanskrit Buddhist texts (including the *Mahāvastu*, *Buddhacarita*, and *Abhidharmakośabhāṣya*), and a few Indian Buddhist *sūtras* and commentaries now preserved only in Chinese[1]—all of which might be described as "early" if we take "early" in the broad sense of pre-medieval or existing prior to the sixth century CE. Through these passages, we will see that early Buddhist doctrine and cosmology depict the animal realm as a most "unfortunate destiny," seeing animals as thoroughly immersed within a world of suffering (S. *duḥkha*) and granting them very little moral agency or opportunity for spiritual betterment.

With this rather hopeless scenario in place, Chapter 2 then looks at one particular method through which the miserable situation of the animal can be circumvented, and the animal can dramatically improve its karmic position in the universe, as well as its opportunities for further progress in the future. This is the method of giving rise to the mental state of "faith" (S. *prasāda*) when in the physical presence of the Buddha. The mechanism of *prasāda* takes full account of the lowly capabilities of the animal but offers a kind of karmic loophole by means of which these lowly capabilities are rendered irrelevant. Nevertheless, in stories that depict animals benefitting from *prasāda*, one also senses a lingering desire to place limits upon what the animal can achieve, as a way of safeguarding the privilege of being human. I see this subtext not only as a logical consequence of Buddhist doctrine and cosmology, but also, more generally, as a symptom of human anxiety when faced with the need to distinguish humanity from the animal. My analysis in Chapter 2 is limited to five narratives taken from the *Divyāvadāna* and *Avadānaśataka*, two Sanskrit texts dating to the early centuries CE and deriving from the Mūlasarvāstivāda and Sarvāstivāda traditions, respectively.

Put to the side and ignored in Part I are depictions of animals that seem to run counter to the lowly position they inhabit within Buddhist doctrine and cosmology, such as depictions of the Buddha himself, in his previous lifetimes as a bodhisattva, sometimes inhabiting the body of an animal who speaks, reasons, preaches the Dharma, cultivates the bodhisattva's perfections (S. *pāramitā*), and is morally superior to the human beings who surround him. To my mind, these depictions belong to a different category of animal representations within Buddhist discourse—one I will turn to in Part II.

CHAPTER ONE

UNFORTUNATE DESTINY

ANIMALS IN A BUDDHIST COSMOS

Monks, I could speak in so many ways about the animal realm, but it wouldn't be easy, Monks, to capture through speaking the suffering of the animal realm.

(*Bālapaṇḍita Sutta*)[1]

What does it mean to be an animal in a Buddhist cosmos? Let us ignore, for a moment, the use of animals in simile and metaphor, the appreciation of animal behavior in the wild, and the frequent depiction of the Buddha himself as a saintly and virtuous animal in one of his previous lives. Speaking strictly in terms of Buddhist doctrine and cosmology, *what does it mean to be an animal in a Buddhist cosmos?* The answer is clear and horrific: to be an animal in a Buddhist cosmos is to live a miserable and pathetic existence, to suffer intensely, to lack the intelligence that makes spiritual progress possible, and to die in a state of abject terror, with little hope of ever attaining a higher rebirth (let alone nirvana).

In Buddhist cosmology, the world of samsara consists of five (occasionally six) realms of rebirth (S. *gati*) into which one may be reborn, depending upon one's karma. Two among them—human beings (S. *manuṣya*) and gods (S. *deva*)—are considered "fortunate destinies" (S. *sugati*), brought about by positive moral deeds and involving pleasant and beneficial karmic rewards; whereas the other three—ghosts (S. *preta*), animals (S. *tiryañc*), and hell-beings (S. *nāraka*)—are considered "unfortunate destinies" (S. *durgati*), brought about by negative moral deeds and involving unpleasant and deleterious karmic rewards.[2] Rebirth as a ghost, animal, or hell-being is thus an unfortunate occurrence, something miserable, something to be avoided at all costs—or, as the common Buddhist phrase describes it, "a state of suffering (P. *apāya*), an unfortunate destiny (P. *duggati*), a state of ruin (P. *vinipāta*), hell (P. *niraya*)."[3] The final term in this phrase—hell—refers to the very worst rebirth of all and represents the culmination, endpoint, or most extreme case of the general misery suggested by the other three terms, yet the phrase as a whole is commonly used to describe all unfortunate rebirths. In practice, moreover, a great number of passages ignore rebirth as a ghost altogether and repeatedly hammer home the threat of being reborn as an *animal* or in *hell*. These two destinies in combination, in other words, are the very quintessence of a miserable lifetime full of suffering. Typical is this passage from the *Aṅguttara Nikāya*:

> Monks, the poor, destitute, miserable person who misconducts himself in body, speech, and mind, upon the breaking up of the body after death, is imprisoned in the bondage of hell or in the bondage of the animal realm (P. *tiracchāna-yoni*). Monks, I do not see any other single bondage that is as cruel and as terrible, or such an impediment to attaining peace from bondage, as the bondage of hell or the bondage of the animal realm.[4]

Being reborn as an animal, then, is just one step away from the excruciating torments of hell, and these two destinies seem to meld together, with rebirth as a ghost running a distant third in terms of misery.[5] In the *Mahāsīhanāda Sutta* of the *Majjhima Nikāya*, for example, we are asked, in a series of similes, to imagine a hot, exhausted, and thirsty man coming upon various different things that either increase or decrease his state of suffering.[6] *Hell* is like him coming across a deep pit full of blazing coals, while rebirth as an *animal* is like him coming across a deep cesspool full of shit. Rebirth as a *ghost,* on the other hand, is like him coming across a tree with thin foliage that provides only partial shade—which, in comparison, really doesn't seem so bad.

Even further: Which, we might ask, is finally worse, the pit full of blazing coals or the cesspool full of shit? The contrast between these two images suggests that while hell may be characterized by outright pain and agony—whose details may even be delightful to the human imagination, as evidenced by the many gleeful Buddhist descriptions of the varied tortures of hell—rebirth as an animal evokes something deeper and far more visceral: a natural human reaction of *revulsion* and *disgust* that comes about, in part, because of human kinship with the animal world. "In an aversion to animals," the philosopher Walter Benjamin has noted, "the predominant feeling is fear of being recognized by them through contact. The horror that stirs deep in man is an obscure awareness that in him something lives so akin to the animal that it might be recognized."[7] Although hell may be worse than the animal realm in terms of sheer suffering, the horrors of the latter are more intimately familiar to us and thus provoke a more visceral repugnance.

We see this sense of revulsion and disgust in the ample attention Buddhist sources pay to the details of animals' physiological lives—their modes of birth, locomotion, death, and, above all, eating and being eaten, all of which elicit disgust in one way or another. In the *Bālapaṇḍita Sutta* of the *Majjhima Nikāya*, the Buddha conveys the horrors of the animal realm not through any explicitly negative statements, but rather through a straightforward description of their physiological lives:

> Monks, there are animals that feed on grass. They eat by grinding fresh or dried grass with their teeth. And which animals, Monks, feed on grass? Elephants, horses, oxen, donkeys, goats, deer, and other such animals that feed on grass. Monks, a fool who has formerly, here in this world, indulged in objects of taste and committed evil deeds, upon the breaking up of the body after death, is reborn in the company of those beings that feed on grass.
>
> Monks, there are animals that feed on shit. Smelling the odor of shit from afar, they run up to it, thinking, "Now we can eat! Now we can eat!" Just as brahmins come running at the smell of sacrificial offerings, thinking, "Now we can eat! Now we can eat!," so also, Monks, do animals that feed on shit.... And which animals, Monks ... ? Chickens, pigs, dogs, jackals, and other such animals.... Monks, a fool who has formerly ... committed evil deeds ... is reborn [among their company].

> Monks, there are animals that are born in darkness, get old in darkness, and die in darkness. And which animals, Monks ... ? Bugs, maggots, earthworms, and other such animals.... Monks, a fool who has formerly ... committed evil deeds ... is reborn [among their company].
>
> Monks, there are animals that are born in the water, get old in the water, and die in the water. And which animals, Monks ... ? Fish, turtles, crocodiles, and other such animals.... Monks, a fool who has formerly ... committed evil deeds ... is reborn [among their company].
>
> Monks there are animals that are born in filth, get old in filth, and die in filth. And which animals, Monks ... ? Those beings, Monks, that are born, get old, and die in a rotten fish, or in a rotten corpse, or in some rotten food, or in a cesspit, or in a sewer, and other such animals.... Monks, a fool who has formerly ... committed evil deeds ... is reborn [among their company].
>
> Monks, I could speak in so many ways about the animal realm, but it wouldn't be easy, Monks, to capture through speaking the suffering of the animal realm.[8]

But he *has* captured the suffering of the animal realm—not by describing it explicitly, but merely by invoking the sheer diversity of animal species, all fecund and teeming with life. Animals are classified in endless ways in Buddhist sources: Among the 340 million different species (as counted by the *Saddharmasmṛtyupasthāna Sūtra*, preserved in Chinese, T. 721), some are aerial, some terrestrial, some aquatic; they have no feet, two feet, four feet, or many feet; they are born from eggs, born from a womb, born from moisture, or spontaneously generated; they are diurnal, nocturnal, or both; they are herbivorous, carnivorous, or both; they are wild or domesticated; they are quadrupeds, birds, fish, or insects.[9] And unlike, say, the Jain classification of animals according to the number of senses they possess (from one-sensed to five-sensed), which seems intended to devise a single, rational hierarchy of beings,[10] the Buddhist classifications are multiple, overlapping, and tangled. In the Buddhist cosmos, animal diversity is exhausting, overwhelming, and—through the theory of karma, which holds that different types of bad deeds lead to different species of animal rebirth[11]—a sobering reminder of the endless ways in which one can do wrong and things can go badly. "Monks," the Buddha says in the *Saṃyutta Nikāya*, "I do not see any other class of beings so diverse . . . as those in the animal realm."[12]

On top of this endless diversity is the embarrassing *physicality* of animal existence (equally evoked in the passage above)—their birthing and eating and sex and dying—which elicits within human beings both recognition and disgust. The maggot feeding upon a festering corpse is disgusting precisely because it reminds us—as all animals do—that we, too, eat, drink, piss, shit, bleed, vomit, have sex, give birth, grow old, and finally die. Animals manifest this physicality to an unsettling degree by also *eating and devouring each other*, causing our physical repugnance to bleed into a moral repugnance as well. This violence is emphasized in Buddhist texts as a particularly horrifying feature of the animal world (in spite of the fact that human beings are also animals who eat other animals). In the Sanskrit *Mahāvastu* (of the Mahāsāṃghika-Lokottaravāda school), when the monk Maudgalyāyana visits the various realms of rebirth, it is precisely the endless violence between predator and prey—and its negative karmic consequences—that are conspicuous in the animal realm:

> He saw beings reborn in the animal realm, experiencing all kinds of suffering. . . . They devoured one another; they drank one another's blood; they killed one another; they destroyed one another. They went from darkness to darkness, from state of suffering to state of suffering, from unfortunate destiny to unfortunate destiny, from state of ruin to state of ruin. They suffered thousands of different miseries, and only with difficulty did they endure the animal realm.[13]

Merciless, cruel, and lacking any compassion, "animals think only of harming one another," they "never stop practicing evil," they "live in the darkness of ignorance," they "commit acts that will lead them to hell," they "produce thoughts of anger," and they "do not take pleasure in virtue" (according to the *Mahāsaṃnipāta Sūtra* preserved in Chinese, T. 397).[14] Because of the violent nature of the animal realm, animals live in a constant state of terror. In the *Divyāvadāna*, the suffering most characteristic of the animal realm is the "suffering that comes from the fear of eating one another."[15] On the night of his Awakening, the Buddha, too, as he gained insight into the workings of karma and the various realms of rebirth, observed the violent cruelty of the animal world (as related in Aśvaghoṣa's *Buddhacarita*):

> Even though other kinds of suffering exist, the suffering of this realm is distinct: It comes from mutual hostility and subservience to others. For as soon as they meet one another, those who live in the sky are attacked by those who live in the sky; those who live in water, by those who live in water; those who live on the ground, by those who live on the ground.[16]

Animal violence involves a disturbing blurring of the boundaries, for animals don't just eat other types of animals; they also eat those of their own kind, in their own habitat. They lack any recognition of categories and distinctions.

Perhaps this is because they lack the fundamentally human characteristic of *language* and thereby fail to observe the social constructs and boundaries that language makes possible. According to the Sarvāstivādin *Mahāvibhāṣā* (preserved in Chinese, T. 1545),

> At the beginning of an eon, during an eon of evolution, all beings use the saintly language [i.e., Sanskrit]. But later, when they eat and drink, the division between beings becomes unequal; insincerity and hypocrisy grow; also, there are all sorts of languages, and a point is reached where there are some beings who are no longer capable of speaking.[17]

Such passages suggest that there was a time, in the far distant past, when animals spoke in the language of Sanskrit—but now, having lost the ability to use language and to recognize its attendant social categories, how can an animal behave properly? It is language that establishes social norms and boundaries, and without language, animals are reduced to the cruel and violent law of predator and prey, of "meat-eaters and grass-eaters,"[18] of the eater and those who are eaten.

One particularly repugnant result of the lack of language and its attendant concepts is the rampant promiscuity and even incest that animals mindlessly pursue. In a short *sutta* from the *Itivuttaka*, the Buddha says,

> Monks, these two good qualities protect the world. Which two? Shame (P. *hirī*) and conscience (P. *ottappa*). Monks, if these two good qualities did not protect the world, then one wouldn't distinguish one's mother, one's aunts, or the wives of one's teachers or gurus [from other women] here. The world would become promiscuous—just like goats and sheep, chickens and pigs, dogs and jackals.[19]

As the commentary on this passage makes clear, it is the linguistic and conceptual ability to classify certain female bodies as "mother," "sister," and so on that allows for shame and conscience to operate. For without this ability, "mothers would not be considered with respect and veneration, thinking 'this is my mother,' understanding 'this is my mother.'" Instead, there would only be promiscuity, or "the confusion and breaching of boundaries." And this situation is clarified through comparison to the animal world "because these beings do not recognize that 'this is my mother' or 'this is my aunt' with respect and veneration"—instead, "wherever they are born, they commit sin."[20] Animal reproduction thus calls to mind a nightmarish world of mindless lust, promiscuity, and incest. (Perhaps it is no surprise, then, that in Vatsyāyana's *Kāmasūtra*—that paradigmatic Indian treatise on sex—animal metaphors are abundantly used to describe sexual organs and sexual acts, and women, in particular, are envisioned as *becoming animals* during sex and thereby *losing language*, being reduced to animal-like sounds.)[21]

What future, then, lies in store for the hapless animal? Immersed in a perpetual maelstrom of immoral violence and sex, animals are destined to move endlessly "from darkness to darkness, from state of suffering to state of suffering." Cycling repeatedly through hell and the animal realm, with little opportunity to cultivate morally skillful deeds, how can such a being possibly turn things around and begin to change its karmic fate? Buddhist texts repeatedly hammer home the near impossibility of making it back to the human realm. Only the most hyperbolic analogy can convey just how unlikely this is—such as we find in the famous simile of the blind turtle, found in the *Bālapaṇḍita Sutta* (and repeated twice in the *Saṃyutta Nikāya*):

> "Monks, suppose that a man were to throw into the great ocean a yoke with a single hole in it, and suppose that the eastern wind blew it to the west, the western wind blew it to the east, the northern wind blew it to the south, and the southern wind blew it to the north. Suppose that a blind turtle there [in the ocean] were to rise up to the surface once every one hundred years. What do you think, Monks? Would that blind turtle ever put his neck through that yoke with a single hole in it?"
>
> "No, indeed, Lord. Or if he did, Lord, at some time or another, it would be after a very long period of time."
>
> "Monks, that blind turtle would put his neck through that yoke with a single hole in it more quickly and with less difficulty, I say, than a fool would regain the state of a human being, once he has gone to a state of ruin. And why is that? Because, Monks, in that realm, there is no righteous conduct, no tranquil conduct, no wholesome action, no meritorious action. In that realm, Monks, there is only mutual devouring and devouring of the weak."[22]

Moreover, the Buddha continues, even if, through some miracle, such a being does manage to regain the human state,

> then he is reborn into an inferior family—a family of outcastes, hunters, bamboo-workers, wheelwrights, or scavengers; a family that is poor, with meager food and drink, living wretchedly; a family in which it is difficult to get food and clothing. And he is ugly, unsightly, deformed, and sickly—either blind or lame or hunchbacked or crippled—and unable to get food, drink, clothing ... [etc.] He misconducts himself in body, speech, and mind, and having misconducted himself in body, speech, and mind, upon the breaking up of the body after death, he is reborn in a state of suffering, an unfortunate destiny, a state of ruin, hell.[23]

In other words, back down the karmic ladder such a being is sure to plunge to resume his endless cycling through the miserable realms of rebirth. This is compared to a gambler, on his very first turn, throwing an "unlucky throw of the dice" and immediately losing his wife, his son, and all of his possessions, as well as being reduced to utter servitude—a misfortune that is, in fact, "totally insignificant" compared to the disaster of a bad rebirth: "This, Monks, is the absolute fulfillment of foolishness."[24]

Throughout this hopeless litany of miseries that constitute the animal realm, we also see the human being's anxious impulse to *separate* himself as much as possible from this brutish and nasty world. In the *Mahāvastu*, the monk Maudgalyāyana, for example, after describing at some length the suffering of the animal realm, ends with a somewhat frenzied exhortation addressed to his fellow humans:

> Thus do those beings who are reborn in the animal realm experience all kinds of suffering, thousands of sufferings, and only with difficulty do they endure the animal realm. Therefore, we should strive for knowledge, gain [the goal], become enlightened, become fully enlightened, practice celibacy, and not commit any evil in this world—Thus I declare![25]

The *Mahāsaṃnipāta Sūtra* (T. 397) also reflects this anxious desire to separate the human being from the animal:

> Such are the torments [of the animal world], without measure and without limit. What man endowed with knowledge would like such a place? The man of wisdom, having seen what the animal destination is like, does not produce a single notion of pleasure in regards to it.[26]

Not a single notion of pleasure—no kinship, no communion, nothing but disgust and revulsion. The distinction between human beings and animals must be total and *categorical*.

The anxious desire to separate human beings from animals in a way that is definitive and categorical can be seen in a number of contexts. In the *Abhidharmakośabhāṣya*, there is a discussion of four different types of questions, one of which is "a question that should be answered categorically," and another of which is "a question that should be answered after asking another question." As an example of the latter, the text cites the question, "Is a human being superior or inferior?," and then explains why this question should be responded to by another question:

> If someone asks, "Is a human being superior or inferior?," one should answer after asking another question: "In relation to whom?" If they say, "In relation to the gods," one should answer, "He is inferior." If they say, "In relation to beings in an unfortunate rebirth," one should answer, "He is superior." [27]

In other words, the answer to this question—"Is a human being superior or inferior?"—depends on *whom* the human being is being compared to. Once we know whom the human being is being compared to, however, then the question *can* be answered categorically: A human being is *categorically superior* to any being within a painful realm of rebirth (including all animals), just as he is *categorically inferior* to any god—and it does not matter *which* human being, animal, or god we are talking about. Granted, this suggestion perhaps becomes problematic when we consider the saintly and heroic animals of the Buddha's previous lives, or when we consider the human being's ability (and the god's inability) to attain nirvana or buddhahood. Nevertheless, the basic claim being made here seems to be that in terms of the hierarchy of karma, animals are *categorically inferior* to human beings. As Paul Waldau puts it, the Buddhist view holds that "all non-human animals, from the simplest of karmic forms on up to the most complex . . . [are] fundamentally inferior to *any* human," and "humans are qualitatively distinct from all other animals."[28]

We might describe the Buddhist attitude expressed here as one of *speciesism*. The term *speciesism*, coined by Richard Ryder in 1970 and greatly popularized in Peter Singer's 1975 work *Animal Liberation*, refers, broadly speaking, to the assigning of different values, rights, or moral considerations to individuals based on species membership alone.[29] In *The Specter of Speciesism: Buddhist and Christian Views of Animals* (2002), Paul Waldau undertakes a thorough analysis of both Buddhism's and Christianity's "dominant attitudes" toward animals, and he concludes that both traditions' attitudes constitute a form of speciesism.[30] Waldau defines speciesism as "the inclusion of all human animals within, and the exclusion of all other animals from, the moral circle"[31]—or the realm of moral considerability. After analyzing various Buddhist sources (limited to texts of the Pāli Canon), he concludes,

> The early Buddhist tradition held *mere* membership in the human species to be a moral achievement. Further, this achievement was viewed as elevating members of the species to a status that entitled them to benefit from instrumental, obviously harmful uses of other animals. This special privilege, namely, the right to benefit from manifest harms to other sentient creatures, was deemed to be humans' prerogatives under the moral order.[32]

Waldau's conclusion may be surprising to those who are familiar with Buddhism's basic reverence for all sentient life—as reflected most strongly, for example, in the fact that the commitment to abstain from killing all living, sentient beings (P. *pāṇātipāta*)—"even down to an ant"—is the first of the five moral precepts, and thus the most important element of moral behavior (P. *sīla*), incumbent upon both monastics and laity, as well as the first of the ten wholesome ways of acting (P. *kusala-kamma*).[33] Nevertheless, without pursuing a long discussion of animal ethics in Buddhism (which others have already carried out),[34] I would have to agree with Waldau that many observers have greatly overemphasized the *continuity* between human beings and animals in Buddhist ethics and paid insufficient attention to their radical *discontinuity*.[35] To cite just one example, this discontinuity is readily apparent from the very different treatments of killing a human being and killing an animal in the code of monastic discipline incumbent upon all monks and nuns. In the Pāli *Vinaya*, for example, while the former constitutes a *pārājika* offense and results in one's permanent expulsion from the Sangha, the latter is merely a *pācittiya* offense requiring a simple act of expiation, and is placed within the same category as such seemingly trivial offences as tickling someone, playing in the water, or entering a village at the wrong time.[36] Human abuse and exploitation of animals, while certainly not condoned, is generally taken for granted in Buddhist sources and depicted as being routine and inevitable.[37] In fact, this abuse is often cited as one of the major types of suffering *inherent* to the animal rebirth. In the *Buddhacarita*, for example, while observing the animal realm on the night of his Awakening, the Buddha sees this exploitation and abuse:

> Because of the various deeds they did, arising from their turbulent minds, these other miserable beings are reborn from the wombs of various animals. In these states, they are pitifully killed for their flesh, hides, fur, and tusks, out of hatred, or just for thrills—even as their relatives watch. When they are oxen or horses, they are forced to work, their bodies wounded by whips, tormented by hunger, thirst, and exhaustion, even though they are helpless and powerless. And when they are elephants, even though they are stronger, they are burdened by the weaker, beaten by the heels of [men's] feet, their heads injured by hooks.[38]

This "subservience to others"[39]—human beings—is depicted not as something that demands to be condemned as soon as it is observed, but rather, as a natural, inevitable, and *karmically appropriate* feature of the animal rebirth.[40]

In any case, although some aspects of Waldau's claim of Buddhist speciesism are perhaps overstated,[41] I am less interested here in the issue of animal ethics than in the more basic idea of an ontological distinction between human beings and animals that is *categorical* in nature—or, as Waldau states, the idea that "*all* creatures outside the human species are *decisively* lower than *all* members of the human species in the universe's fundamental moral order," and that "human life is of a qualitatively *better* kind than is the life of any other animal"—a superiority humans have "by virtue of their mere participation in humanity."[42] Despite the much-vaunted continuity and fluidity of the karmic hierarchy (such that human beings can be reborn as animals, and animals as human beings), there is nevertheless a strong concern with keeping the basic *categories* of rebirth—the five or six *gatis*—distinct from one another and in proper hierarchical order.

We can see this concern, for example, in Buddhist scholastic sources' tortuous discussions of whether animals exist in hell and heaven. In heaven, for example, the gods are said to ride upon animal mounts, but how can there be animals in heaven if the animal rebirth is categorically (and karmically) distinct from a heavenly rebirth? According to the Pāli *Kathāvatthu*, the Theravādins held that heavenly animals (such as Sakka's elephant Erāvaṇa) were deities in animal form and not true animals, while the Andhakas held that they *were* true animals—a position that, from the *Kathāvatthu*'s perspective, does not make any sense, since it violates the necessary distinction between different *gatis*.[43] When faced with the conundrum of animal mounts in heaven, the *Mahavibhāṣā* (T. 1545) can only conclude that the "meritorious acts of the gods" must result in the "forms" of various animals appearing, "which are not counted among [real] beings—and the gods use them as their mounts."[44] In another passage from the *Mahavibhāṣā*, we find a similar explanation pertaining to what happens during a *kalpa* of dissolution, when each realm of rebirth is supposed to disappear in reverse order (from the lowest to the highest):

> If animals . . . are destroyed before human beings, how can the consumption of indispensable foods such as milk and yogurt, as well as the work of labor and transport, continue among human beings? Certain people explain: By virtue of the accumulation of the karma of human beings, *there is a manifestation of appearances of animals, which are not [real] beings*. They produce the milk, etc., and do the work [in question].[45]

Once again, we see an anxious concern to keep the realms of rebirth *categorically* distinct from one another—as well as an automatic assumption of humanity's natural and necessary right to consume and exploit animals for its own benefit.

In a Mahāyāna context, as well, the various buddha-fields (S. *buddhakṣetra*) or "pure lands" presided over by the buddhas and bodhisattvas of the Mahāyāna pantheon and praised as ideal utopias were thought to be incompatible with the presence of animals. Thus, in the *(Longer) Sukhāvatīvyūha Sūtra*, the very first of the forty-eight vows made by the bodhisattva Dharmākara is that he will not become a fully enlightened buddha "if anyone in my buddha-field could be reborn [there] . . . as an animal" or in any other unfortunate rebirth.[46] Although Amitābha's Pure Land of Sukhāvatī does have beautiful birds that sing out the Dharma six times every day, the *(Shorter) Sukhāvatīvyūha Sūtra* again assures us that these are not "real" animals:

> What do you think, Śāriputra? Are those beings born from the wombs of animals? You should not think thus. And why is that? Because, Śāriputra, in that buddha-field not even the *names* of the hells or of the animals or of the world of the dead exist—[let alone the actual rebirths]. Rather, those flocks of birds are magically created by the Tathāgata Amitāyus to utter the words of the Dharma.[47]

Not only the heavens of the ordinary cosmos, but also the purified buddha-fields of the Mahāyāna cosmos, are thus incompatible with the animal realm—or even the *name* of the animal realm. The blurring of boundaries to which animals themselves fall prey must never be allowed to infect the hard dividing line separating the human and animal realms of rebirth.

What is it, then, that finally lies at the root of the animal's categorical inferiority to human beings—and explains its far greater suffering, its miserable existence, its constant propensity to engage in evil, and its inability to cultivate virtue? According to a frequently cited passage from the Pāli *Milindapañha*, the most significant difference between human beings and animals is the animal's lack of *prajñā* (P. *paññā)*—usually translated into English as "wisdom" or "discriminative insight," but in fact comprising "intelligence, knowledge, discrimination, judgment" (according to Monier-Williams's *Sanskrit-English Dictionary*),[48] and glossed in the Pali Text Society's *Pali-English Dictionary* as "all the higher faculties of cognition, 'intellect as conversant with general truths,' reason, wisdom, insight, knowledge, recognition."[49] While "wisdom" might be the best translation of *prajñā* when the term is used in an explicitly soteriological context, when used to distinguish human beings from animals, I would translate the term with a broader sense as "higher mental faculties." According to Schmithausen and Maithrimurthi, the animal's lack of *prajñā* constitutes "the decisive difference between man and animals, and the one which, from a Buddhist point of view, constitutes the *essential* superiority of human existence over animal existence."[50]

Several passages that make this distinction will perhaps help to clarify what is at stake. The relevant passage from the *Milindapañha* (involving a dialogue between King Milinda and the monk Nāgasena) reads as follows:

> "Venerable Nāgasena, he who is not reborn—is it by means of systematic attention (P. *yoniso manasikāra*) that he is not reborn?"
>
> "Great King, it is by means of systematic attention, and the higher mental faculties (P. *paññā*), and [other] beneficial qualities."
>
> "But, Venerable One, aren't systematic attention and higher mental faculties the same thing?"
>
> "No, Great King, attention is one thing, higher mental faculties are another thing. Great King, sheep, goats, oxen, buffalo, camels, and donkeys all possess attention (P. *manasikāra*), but they lack the higher mental faculties (P. *paññā*)."
>
> "You are clever, Venerable Nāgasena."[51]

Thus, animals possess *manasikāra*—"attention," "thought," or the ability to direct one's mind toward some target—but they do not possess *paññā*—the "higher mental faculties" that enable reason, insight, knowledge, and wisdom. In regard to their possession of "attention," it is also worth noting, as Schmithausen and Maithrimurthi point out, that "the word *yoniso*, which had qualified *manasikāra* in the preceding discussion, is omitted in connection with animals."[52] In other words, animals possess only *manasikāra* (attention), not *yoniso manasikāra* (systematic attention), in addition to their lack of *paññā*. And this is why they are unable to attain nirvana and escape from being reborn.

While the *Milindapañha* passage discusses this distinction within an explicitly soteriological context—that is, what allows a person to stop being reborn?—a passage from the *Kuṭidūsaka Jātaka* (No. 321 in the Pāli *Jātakaṭṭhavaṇṇanā*)[53] will demonstrate the much broader significance of the animal's lack of *paññā*. In this story, a bird who is sheltering from the rain in a sturdy nest sees a monkey who is suffering out in the open. "Monkey," he asks, "your head and feet and hands are just like those of a human, so why do you have no shelter?" "Bird," the monkey replies, "my head and feet and hands are just like those of a human, but that which is best among humans—their higher mental faculties (P. *paññā*)—that I do not have." The word commentary on this verse glosses *paññā* with the synonym *vicāraṇā*, a verbal noun that connotes *examining, investigating, planning, arranging*, or *constructing*, and then notes that "the physical strength of heads, hands, and feet are irrelevant in this world"—and only *humans* possess the very "best" qualities of *paññā* and *vicāraṇa*.[54] And this is why the monkey cannot build for himself any shelter from the storm. Granted, this does not really explain why the bird *is* able to build a nest—but the basic point remains clear: Despite the obvious likeness between human beings and apes, they are finally distinguished from one another by the latter's lack of *paññā*—and that lack makes all of the difference, not only for the attainment of nirvana, but even for one's ability to construct a shelter from the rain.

The animal's lack of language and social constructs, its lack of the higher mental faculties, and its possession of a scattered (rather than systematic) attention ultimately result in a lack of moral agency and an inability to engage in spiritual cultivation. Paradoxically, we can see this lack of moral agency in the *Abhidharmakośabhāṣya*'s claim that animals, unlike humans, are incapable of committing the very worst sins of all—the five mortal transgressions that result in an immediate rebirth in hell (S. *ānantarya-karma*), which are matricide, patricide, killing an arhat, maliciously spilling a buddha's blood, and creating a schism in the Sangha.[55] Though freedom from these sins might seem to benefit the animal, this is hardly a redeeming feature of animal life, since the animal lacks the very recognition of mother as "mother" that would make the sin of matricide (for example) possible in the first place. Explaining why animals are not susceptible to either "restraint" (S. *saṃvara*) or "lack of restraint" (S. *asaṃvara*), the *Abhidharmakośabhāṣya* states,

> Those who inhabit an unfortunate rebirth possess neither the shame nor the conscience whose possession would lead to restraint, and whose destruction would lead to a lack of restraint. Indeed, the bodies of … those who inhabit an unfortunate rebirth are like salt-logged fields: neither restraint nor lack of restraint can grow in such a body, just as neither crops nor weeds can grow in a salt-logged field.[56]

In other words, animals are *so* lacking in moral capacity that they cannot even be truly immoral. Their inability to commit the five most heinous sins is simply the consequence of a lack of moral agency in general. It goes without saying, of course, that because they are incapable of both restraint and lack of restraint, they cannot follow (nor violate) the rules of the *prātimokṣa* (that is, the code of monastic discipline incumbent upon monks and nuns), and—as we learn in a famous story of the Pāli *Vinaya* in which a *nāga* attempts to become a monk—they cannot be ordained into the Sangha (nor can the *prātimokṣa* even be recited in their presence).[57] For animals, as the Buddha puts it, "are not capable of growth in this Dhamma and Discipline."[58] Indeed, rebirth as an animal is one of the eight "wrong times and wrong occasions for living a spiritual life."[59] The animal's lack of intelligence thus has moral repercussions as well, rendering the animal immune to moral or spiritual betterment.

If we compare the Buddhist view of the human-animal distinction to views that have been notably predominant in the West, there is perhaps less difference between them than many observers have supposed. Granted, the Buddhist view of animal sentience is very far away from, say, René Descartes's conception of animals as *machines* or mindless automata acting in a purely mechanistic manner. But how distant is it from Aristotle's conception of animals as categorically lower than humanity on the Great Chain of Being (*scala naturae*)? Or from Thomas Aquinas's view that "dumb animals and plants are devoid of the life of reason," and therefore "naturally enslaved and accommodated to the uses of others"?[60] Or from Immanuel Kant's claim that animals are devoid of "personhood" since they lack both rationality and autonomy?[61] We can even find statements made by prominent Western figures that seem like very close parallels to some of the Buddhist statements we have already looked at. In Erica Fudge's work on animals in early modern England, for example, she quotes from William Perkins ("the most widely-read and influential puritan theologian"[62] of his age, writing in 1596), who defines the difference between human beings and animals as follows:

> The proper subjects of conscience are reasonable creatures, that is men and Angels. Hereby conscience is excluded . . . from brute beasts: for though they have life and sense, and in many things some shadows of reason, yet because they want true reason, they want conscience also.[63]

Just as for Nāgasena, animals possess *manasikāra*, but not *yoniso manasikāra*—let alone *paññā*—so for William Perkins, they possess the "shadows of reason" but not "true reason" itself. Thus, they also lack the "conscience" that makes moral behavior possible—just as we saw (in several passages cited above) that animals lack the "shame" and "conscience" that allow for moral restraint. Perkins's focus on the animal's lack of "conscience" is equally comparable, we might note, to the Hindu view expressed in the *Hitopadeśa*: "Men are equal to animals as far as food, sleep, fear, and sex are concerned. They are distinguished only because of dharma: [A man who] lacks dharma is the same as the animals."[64]

Buddhist and Western views, of course, are both characterized by enormous diversity, such that it is difficult to engage in any wholesale comparison between them. Nevertheless, the tendency to present a far-too-sunny depiction of Buddhist views as a subtle means of condemning views predominant in the West (what Larry Lohmann calls "green Orientalism") should be resisted.[65] When Martine Batchelor, for example, states that "Buddhists . . . have never believed humanity superior to the rest of the natural world,"[66] or when Norm Phelps claims that Buddhism draws "no essential distinction between humans and animals" and "there is never a hint in Buddhist teachings that . . . any characteristic beyond the ability to suffer is relevant to moral standing"[67]—surely, they are vastly overstating the case. While Buddhism's *ethical* stance toward nonhuman animals may well be more generous than those predominant in the West, it seems to me that when it comes to the question of an *ontological* distinction between human beings and animals based on their mental faculties, moral agency, and spiritual potential, the Buddhist view is really quite similar to those that have predominated in the West.

In any case, putting such comparisons aside, perhaps we can now summarize what it means—doctrinally and cosmologically speaking—to be an animal in a Buddhist cosmos (a view, I might also add, that seems to have remained remarkably consistent as Buddhism traveled to other regions):[68] To be an animal is "a state of suffering, an unfortunate destiny, a state of ruin, hell." It is to live a short and brutish lifetime replete with suffering; constantly oppressed by "hunger, thirst, heat, and cold";[69] continually devouring and being devoured by others; mindlessly engaging in promiscuity and incest; tormented and enslaved by human beings; lacking in language, reason, intelligence, wisdom, and insight. The consequences of this condition for one's spiritual progress are also clear: Animals have little opportunity to engage in moral behavior and are thus doomed to cycle perpetually "from darkness to darkness, from state of suffering to state of suffering." They cannot practice "restraint" (or even "lack of restraint"); they have "no wisdom, no dignity, no honor, no thoughts of generosity," but only "suffering, tribulation, and great fear";[70] they are "not capable of growth in this Dhamma or discipline"; and they cannot be ordained into the Sangha or have the *pratimokṣa* recited in their presence. As the Buddha concludes in the *Bālapaṇḍita Sutta*, "in that realm, there is no righteous conduct, no tranquil conduct, no wholesome action, no meritorious action. In that realm, Monks, there is only mutual devouring and devouring of the weak."[71]

What hope is there, then, for the animal?

CHAPTER TWO

Catching Sight of the Buddha

Faithful Animals in the *Divyāvadāna* and *Avadānaśataka*

O Sage whose sight is so difficult to meet with, even in a thousand existences— Today, the sight of you has borne fruit!

(Śuka Avadāna)[1]

Devoid of reason and insight and lacking in moral agency, it is difficult—if not impossible—for an animal to engage in intentional self-cultivation or make deliberate progress toward achieving a spiritual goal. Stories in which animals are depicted as doing so are exceedingly rare in Buddhist literature, and those that do exist constitute anomalous exceptions.[2] In general, we do not see depictions of ordinary animals submitting themselves to forms of moral discipline, engaging in meditation, studying the Dharma, or even making merit. And yet the animal's situation is not hopelessly irredeemable. There are many stories, in fact, in which animals improve their karmic situations quickly and dramatically. The vast majority of these stories, however, adhere to a particular pattern. And this pattern seems concerned, first and foremost, with showing the animal's spiritual progress to be limited in extent, wholly passive in nature, and effected largely through the agency of another. In this way, compassion is shown toward the animal—yet not at the expense of eclipsing the uniqueness of being human.

The stories in question almost always involve the auspicious mental state known as *prasāda* (P. *pasāda*). Although this term is generally translated as "faith," its semantic range is significantly broader, suggesting "clearness," "brightness," "calmness," "tranquility," and "serenity of disposition,"[3] as well as "purity," "joy," "satisfaction," and "composure."[4] Generally, it is one's *citta* ("mind" or "heart") that is said to spontaneously give rise to the mental state of *prasāda* and thereby become *prasanna* ("faithful," "serene," "tranquil," etc.). The auspicious karmic result of giving rise to *prasāda* and becoming *prasanna*, if it occurs under the right circumstances, is often a highly favorable rebirth—usually, in the case of animals, rebirth as a deity in one of the lower heavens of Buddhist cosmology.

Should rebirth as a deity count as constituting "spiritual progress"? Granted, it is not equivalent to attaining any of the four soteriological goals that promise an eventual escape from all suffering—that is, stream-entry, once-returnerhood, nonreturnerhood, or nirvana itself—nor is it equivalent to becoming a buddha, a pratyekabuddha, or even a human being (especially a monk or nun) who experiences the ideal conditions for working toward one of these goals. Rebirth as a deity does, however, remove one from the downward spiral of the "unfortunate destinies" (S. *durgati*), often seems to lead one to a further series of fortunate rebirths (S. *sugati*), and gives one a heightened chance of eventually making it back to the realm of human beings—the only destiny from which the attainment of soteriological goals is really plausible. Given the low spiritual potential characteristic of the animal rebirth, this is presumably the best that an animal can hope for.

The conditions under which *prasāda* arises and the mechanics of its functioning have been thoroughly analyzed by Andy Rotman—at least as they appear in the Sanskrit *Divyāvadāna*, a collection of tales dating to the early centuries CE and drawn largely from the *Mūlasarvāstivāda Vinaya*. It will thus be useful for us to begin with a brief summary of his analysis.[5] Rotman describes what he refers to as the "seeing-*prasāda*-giving-prediction typology"[6] characteristic of many stories in the *Divyāvadāna*, as follows: Certain objects—the Buddha being foremost among them—are commonly described as *prāsādika*, meaning not only that they are "attractive" (the nontechnical meaning of *prāsādika*) but also that they are "agents of *prasāda*"[7] who spontaneously arouse *prasāda* in others. In the typical "seeing-*prasāda*-giving-prediction" scenario, a being *sees* a *prāsādika* object (such as the Buddha, one of his monks, or a *stūpa*), and this vision alone—irrespective of any teaching of the Dharma—causes *prasāda* to spontaneously well up within his *citta* ("mind" or "heart"), so that he becomes tranquil, serene, and faithful. This *prasāda* also results in a "compulsion to give,"[8] leading the being in question to make an offering to the *prāsādika* object. If that object is the Buddha, the Buddha then makes a prediction (S. *vyākaraṇa*) of the karmic rewards that will ensue from this encounter. It is a feature of the *prasāda* mechanism, moreover, that while the gift offered to the Buddha is generally something of little value—a lump of clay, for example—the predicted karmic rewards are extravagant: often, rebirth as a deity in heaven, or a long series of such rebirths, sometimes leading to buddhahood or pratyekabuddhahood in the far distant future. To cite just a single example, in the *Brāhmaṇadārikā Avadāna*,[9] a brahmin's daughter *sees* the Buddha, gives rise to *prasāda*, and *offers* him some barley meal as alms. The Buddha then makes a *prediction* that the brahmin's daughter will be reborn as either a god or a human being for the next thirteen eons and finally become a pratyekabuddha named Supraṇihita. Though nonreligious objects are also capable of arousing *prasāda*, it is in connection with specifically Buddhist *prāsādika* objects that such extravagant results are depicted as occurring.

Rotman focuses mostly on the human characters of the *Divyāvadāna* who benefit from the *prasāda* mechanism, but two related features of this mechanism are particularly important for its application in the case of animals. The first is the issue of what type of being constitutes the proper and appropriate beneficiary of *prasāda*'s effectiveness. Here, Rotman observes that the people involved are "generally individuals with little disposable income," and "the only people excluded are the wealthy and fortunate."[10] This becomes especially clear in the *Nagarāvalambikā Avadāna*,[11] in which a poor and leprous beggar woman attains great benefit by giving rise to *prasāda* in an encounter with the monk Mahākāśyapa. When the god Śakra tries to imitate her, however, he is admonished by Mahākāśyapa for being the wrong sort of *prasāda*-beneficiary—since he, as a deity, already possesses plenty of merit and good fortune. *Prasāda,* in other words, is reserved for the lowly: "Within the social logic of giving presented here," Rotman notes, "proper donors are not simply poor or unfortunate, but those whose meager stock of merit leaves them suffering."[12] While this requirement obviously pertains to lowly human beings like the beggar woman, it is even more relevant in the case of animals. As the inhabitants of an unfortunate destiny full of suffering (and with little disposable income to boot), animals thus constitute the perfect candidates to benefit from *prasāda.*

The second relevant feature—which is directly related to the first, and especially important in the case of animals—involves the *agency* of the *prasāda* mechanism. Rotman notes that "the arising of *prasāda* is represented as having less to do with an individual's personal efforts than with the force exerted by *prāsādika* objects. As 'agents of *prasāda*' it is they, and not the individual, that are the primary cause of the arising of *prasāda.*"[13] *Prasāda* thus involves a "lack of mental intermediation"[14] and its efficacy "does not rely on previously purifying the mind or cultivating proper intention but instead on being in the right place with respect to *prāsādika* objects."[15] All one has to do is to come within sight of a *prāsādika* object—whether intentionally or through mere chance—and *prasāda* can be expected to arise. *Prasāda* might thus be seen as a kind of "karmic intrusion" that involves "a bare minimum of personal effort and mental conditioning" and places no "burden on the individual to cultivate right thoughts and to perform proper actions."[16] In short, Rotman concludes, *prasāda* is "a wonderful refuge for the powerless."[17]

Clearly, this feature of the *prasāda* mechanism makes it highly relevant to the case of animals. Despite their lack of intelligence or the higher mental faculties, even the lowliest animals *are* capable of wandering into the presence of the Buddha and *seeing* his glorious form—whereupon the automatic efficacy of the *prasāda* mechanism can be expected to take over. The mental inferiority of the animal here becomes irrelevant, since the mechanism of *prasāda* appears to bypass the mind altogether. It seems, then, that one way of overcoming the many faults characteristic of an animal rebirth is to passively respond to the presence and charisma of the Buddha. This is precisely what we find, in fact, in several stories from the *Divyāvadāna* and *Avadānaśataka* (another collection of tales dating to the early centuries CE and belonging to the Sarvāstivāda tradition). In each of these stories, an animal *sees* the Buddha, spontaneously gives rise to *prasāda*, and thereby experiences a lofty reward. The external agency involved in *prasāda* and the passivity of the being it benefits are even further heightened in the case of animals by the fact that the "giving" element of Rotman's typology seems to disappear: None of these animals makes any offering to the Buddha (not even a meager one), yet *prasāda* still functions as it should. Animals are thus depicted as being even less capable and more lacking in agency than figures like the poor and leprous beggar woman, yet they are still able to benefit from the wonderful fruits of *prasāda*. One limitation placed upon animals, however, is that whereas human beings react with *prasāda* to a variety of different *prāsādika* objects, it may be the case that animals react in this way only through a visual encounter with the Buddha (or, sometimes, the bodhisattva). I am not aware of any animal stories in which an animal reacts with *prasāda* to someone or something other than the Buddha (in either his last or a previous life). Animals are thus severely limited in their opportunity to experience *prasāda* and must be lucky enough to find themselves in the physical presence of a living buddha. Their ability to benefit from *prasāda*, in other words, is dependent upon encountering the very greatest *prāsādika* object of all.

Below, I take a closer look at several stories involving animals giving rise to *prasāda* in an encounter with the Buddha. On the one hand, we will see that the *prasāda* mechanism functions as a kind of cosmic loophole that can mitigate the hopeless situation brought about by existence as an animal. On the other hand, human ambivalence toward the animal state and a lingering desire to limit the animal's potential in order to safeguard human prerogatives also make their appearance.

The Bull Saved from Slaughter

The *Aśokavarṇa Avadāna* (*Divyāvadāna* No. 11)[18] features a bull who is about to be slaughtered for meat by a butcher. "Frightened, trembling, and agitated,"[19] the bull runs around, looking for anyone who might save his life. Without plan or forethought, he happens to catch sight of the Buddha—and here, the text uses a stock phrase found repeatedly throughout the *Divyāvadāna* to emphasize the Buddha's great beauty, describing him as one "who was adorned with the thirty-two major and eighty minor marks of a Great Man, whose body was glorious, adorned with a halo of light, brighter than a thousand suns, shimmering like a mountain of jewels, wholly beautiful."[20] No effort, intention, or mental capacity is required of the bull, for as soon as he *sees* the Buddha, the *prasāda* mechanism automatically kicks into gear:

> And as soon as he saw him, his mind gave rise to faith (S. *cittam abhiprasannam*) in the presence of the Blessed One. With a mind full of faith (S. *prasanna-citta*), he reflected: "This distinguished being arouses faith (S. *prāsādiko*). He will be able to save my life. What if I were to approach him?"[21]

The bull breaks free from the butcher's restraints, falls at the Buddha's feet, and begins to lick them. After the Buddha has succeeded in ransoming the bull's life from the butcher, the bull "has even more faith in the Blessed One."[22] He circumambulates the Buddha three times and then remains close to him, "gazing upon the face of the Blessed One."[23] The Buddha then makes a prediction (by means of his smile, another stock element used throughout the *Divyāvadāna*): The bull will die in seven days—"his mind full of faith in the presence of the Tathāgata"[24]—and be reborn among the gods of various different heavens for the next ninety-nine thousand eons. In his final (human) rebirth, he will be a cakravartin king named Aśokavarṇa; then he will renounce the world and "directly realize the awakening of a pratyekabuddha and become a pratyekabuddha named Aśokavarṇa."[25]

No offering is made to the Buddha, no words are spoken between them, and no teaching of the Dharma takes place. All the bull needs to do is wander within the Buddha's sight line, and the mechanism of *prasāda* takes over. The bull's behavior is spontaneous rather than deliberate, seemingly brought about through the enormous charisma of the Buddha's glorified form. Moreover, in contrast to some of the other stories involving animals (as we will see below), the Buddha specifies in this case that the bull's spontaneous experience of *prasāda* will result in *both* the karmic goal of attaining a heavenly rebirth *and* the soteriological goal of becoming a pratyekabuddha. This is unusual: As we will see later, other stories seem more reluctant to attribute the latter sort of goal directly to *prasāda*, and thus put it within reach of the animal.

The *Aśokavarṇa Avadāna* does conclude, however, with a final note of ambiguity in the lesson the Buddha draws from the bull's example:

> And thus, Ānanda, even having a mind full of faith (S. *citta-prasāda*) in the Tathāgatas produces an inconceivable fruit—how much more does making a fervent religious vow (S. *praṇidhānam*)! Therefore, Ānanda, this is what you should learn: "Little by little, moment by moment, even for just a snap of the fingers, I should recollect (S. *samanusmariṣyāmi*) the figure of the Tathāgata." This, Ānanda, is what you should learn.[26]

Somewhat unexpectedly, the Buddha does *not* conclude from the example of the bull that his monks should also cultivate *prasāda* in the Buddha's presence. Instead, he concludes that, as unimaginable as *prasāda*'s rewards may be, *even greater* are the rewards of making a "fervent religious vow" (S. *praṇidhānam*)—a linguistic and conceptual practice that animals are presumably incapable of undertaking. In addition, monks should also "recollect the figure of the Tathāgata"—a clear reference to the practice of *buddhānusmṛti*, or recollection of the form and attributes of a buddha, another practice that seemingly lies beyond the mental capacity of the animal. The bull may illustrate the wonderful efficacy of *prasāda*, but he is an inappropriate model when it comes to the monks' own religious practice.

Why is this the case? In his discussion of the *prasāda* mechanism, Rotman cites two stories (including this one) to show that although monks are depicted as being capable of cultivating *prasāda*, there is also some suggestion that, in their case, such a practice is inappropriate, since *prasāda* generally results in a very long series of pleasant rebirths—ninety-nine thousand eons' worth, in this case—*before* resulting in an ultimate goal such as pratyekabuddhahood. Thus, just as an animal is doomed to wander perpetually "from darkness to darkness, from state of suffering to state of suffering," so the bull who has benefitted from *prasāda* is still doomed to wander from one heavenly paradise to another for the next *ninety-nine thousand eons* before finally attaining release. Is this an acceptable outcome for a *human* disciple of the Buddha? Certainly not for the monks of the *Cakravartivyākṛta Avadāna*, who exclaim (in regard to a similar case), "Who can pass so much time stuck in saṃsāra?"[27] Rotman concludes that "for those monks who desire to transcend more quickly the repeating cycle of birth, death, and birth again, cultivating *prasāda* isn't very effective."[28] Far better for a monk to engage in *buddhānusmṛti* and other practices that will lead to a quicker release—*human* practices lying beyond the diminished capacity of the animal. Thus, *prasāda* may be "a wonderful refuge for the powerless," but it also fails to take full advantage of uniquely human capacities.

The Talking Parrot

In the *Śuka Avadāna* (*Avadānaśataka* No. 56),[29] the Buddha is passing through a forest on his way to visit King Bimbisāra when he comes across a parrot endowed with human speech. The parrot begs the Buddha to spend the night in the forest, and the Buddha complies. The following morning, the parrot begs for the Buddha's forgiveness—for, "having been born from the womb of an animal,"[30] he does not have any goods to offer to him as a gift. In lieu of such a gift, the parrot offers to fly ahead and alert King Bimbisāra of the Buddha's impending arrival. Once the Buddha has arrived in Rājagṛha and been hosted by the king, the parrot gazes at the Buddha with admiration, whereupon he is "thrilled, satisfied, and delighted," and "gives rise to the highest joy and gladness."[31] At that very moment, he is snatched up and killed by a hawk—but just before dying, "he gave rise to faith (S. *cittaṃ prasādya*) in the presence of the Blessed One, died, and was reborn among the superior Trāyastriṃśa gods."[32]

Several features distinguish this tale from the other tales involving animals in the *Divyāvadāna* and *Avadānaśataka*. First, while most of the animal characters are devoid of human speech, the parrot is unusual in being able to speak. But this is likely due to the fact that he is a *parrot*—an animal well-known for mimicking human speech—and perhaps carries no greater significance. Second, the parrot does not give rise to *prasāda* as soon as he sees the Buddha, but only on the following day, when he perhaps has a greater opportunity to gaze upon and admire his form. Nevertheless, the basic *prasāda* scenario still obtains: The parrot *sees* the Buddha, gives rise to *prasāda,* and as a result is reborn as a god in heaven.

The story now continues with a stock passage shared in common with all of the animal stories in the *Avadānaśataka* (and seemingly replacing the "prediction" element commonly found in the *Divyāvadāna*): Instead of the Buddha giving a prediction of the parrot's future, the text itself actually depicts the parrot being reborn as a god in the Trāyastriṃśa heaven, remembering its former birth as a parrot, and then deciding to go and visit the Buddha at the Jetavana Monastery. Once there, the Buddha preaches to the parrot-turned-god "a discourse on the Dharma penetrating the four noble truths,"[33] whereupon the parrot-turned-god attains the goal of stream-entry. He lets forth three "solemn utterances" (S. *udāna*)—again common to all of the animal-related tales in the *Avadānaśataka*—that attribute his good fortune directly to the agency of the Buddha:

> This wasn't done for me, Venerable One, by my mother, my father, the king, the gods, my cherished relatives and kinsfolk, my ancestors, renunciants, or brahmins—this was done for me by the Blessed One alone! The oceans of blood and tears have dried up, the mountains of bones have been leapt over, the doors to unfortunate destinies (S. *durgati*) have been slammed shut, the doors to heaven and liberation are held wide open—for I am established among gods and humans![34]

Several things are worth noticing in this account. First, in line with Rotman's discussion of the *prasāda* mechanism, it is clear that the parrot's good fortune comes about not through his own agency, but rather through the agency of the Buddha. The parrot doesn't need to *do* anything—in fact, he even laments his inability, as an animal, to give the Buddha an appropriate gift. All he needs to do is gaze upon the Buddha, and the mechanism of *prasāda* takes over: "O Sage whose sight is so difficult to meet with, even in a thousand existences, today, the sight of you has borne fruit!"[35] It is his *eyes* rather than his *mind* that seem to be crucial. Second, when it comes to attaining the soteriological goal of stream-entry, the story makes it clear that this had nothing to do with his life as a parrot. For when the monks ask the Buddha, "Which acts did he do to be reborn among the gods and to obtain a vision of the truths?,"[36] the Buddha replies that his rebirth in heaven was the result of giving rise to *prasāda* as a parrot, but his attainment of stream-entry was the result of *keeping the moral precepts during a long-ago life as a human layman.*

It is significant, I think, that while the monks' original question had lumped heavenly rebirth and stream-entry together and sought a single karmic explanation for both, the Buddha's response consciously and clearly pries the two apart: the attainment of stream-entry was *not* a result of the *prasāda* he experienced as an animal; instead, it was the result of keeping the moral precepts during his long-ago life as a human being. What I discern in this complicated presentation of karmic cause-and-effect is a lingering reluctance to allow the animal to obtain any soteriologically significant goal merely through *prasāda* alone. To explain the achievement of a soteriological goal such as stream-entry, the narrative *bypasses the animal rebirth* altogether and finds its origin within a long-ago lifetime as a human. Thus, even a parrot endowed with human speech is ultimately limited in what he can achieve *within an animal's body*—and even that comes about not through his own agency, but through the agency of the Buddha. In this way, the uniquely human prerogative to engage in intentional self-cultivation is carefully preserved.

The Flock of Geese

We can deal more quickly with the *Haṃsa Avadāna* (*Avadānaśataka* No. 60),[37] since it follows the same general pattern as the story of the parrot. In this tale, King Prasenajit is visiting with the Buddha at the Jetavana Monastery when he receives a gift of five hundred geese from another king and decides to set them free right there, on the monastery grounds. The Buddha and his monks offer food to the geese, whereupon the geese are "satisfied, with their senses content"[38]—however, no mention is made of them giving rise to *prasāda*. The Buddha then preaches the Dharma to the assembly, and the geese are said to "come into the presence of the Blessed One and listen to the Dharma"[39]—but again, no mention is made of *prasāda*. Shortly thereafter, they die and are reborn among the Trāyastriṃśa gods. Following the pattern typical of these stories in the *Avadānaśataka*, they remember their former lives as geese, decide to come and visit the Buddha at the Jetavana Monastery, listen to him give a sermon on the four noble truths, and attain the goal of stream-entry.

Once again, the monks inquire into the geese's karmic history, and the Buddha makes it clear that because, as geese, "they gave rise to faith (S. *cittaṃ prasāditam*) in my presence, they were reborn among the gods."[40] Despite the lack of any mention of *prasāda* earlier in the story, the Buddha thus makes it clear that *prasāda* did arise in them at some point—and presumably, it was the arising of *prasāda* rather than listening to the Dharma that resulted in their heavenly rebirths. Once again, however, while the monks are seeking a single karmic cause for both rebirth among the deities and the attainment of stream-entry, the Buddha takes care to separate the two attainments: their winning of the goal of stream-entry was *not* brought about by the arising of *prasāda* when they were geese, but rather, by their keeping of the moral precepts in their long-ago lives as human monks. Once again, therefore, distance is placed between the animal and the ultimate goal, and stream-entry is attributed to actions undertaken as a human being.

In these stories from the *Divyāvadāna* and *Avadānaśataka*,[41] we see that the mechanism of *prasāda* and the presence in the world of *prāsādika* objects such as the Buddha offer a wonderful karmic loophole that can allow a being to circumvent the hopeless situation brought about by existence as an animal. Nevertheless, the animal is stripped of all independent agency within this process, and can only benefit from *prasāda* because *prasāda* is aroused through someone else's agency and functions in the same instinctive manner as the animal itself. What the animal can achieve *as an animal,* moreover, seems to be the object of anxious concern, and it is limited and circumscribed accordingly. Not only are the fruits of *prasāda* generally limited to a divine rebirth in heaven, but in all of these cases it is the Trāyastriṃśa heaven that is specified. I believe this is significant. The Trāyastriṃśa heaven is the second-lowest of the twenty-six heavens contained in the standard Buddhist cosmos, and one of six heavens contained in the lowest realm of the universe—the *kāma-dhātu*, or Realm of Desire. While these heavens are attainable through ordinary good deeds, the higher heavens that make up the upper two realms of the cosmos—the Form Realm (*rūpa-dhātu*) and the Formless Realm (*ārūpya-dhātu*)—are generally seen as resulting from the cultivation of various transic states of meditation (the four *dhyānas* and the four *ārūpya-dhyānas*). Because the higher heavens are associated with intentional acts of self-cultivation, I suspect that there is reluctance to depict an animal achieving one of these higher heavens through actions undertaken within the body of an animal. Finally, even when the animal-turned-deity goes on to attain a soteriological goal such as nirvana or stream-entry, care is taken to trace this accomplishment back to actions undertaken long ago as a human being. When it comes to those attainments that promise a final release from all suffering, it is human agency alone that matters.

The Black Snake and the Fierce Buffalo: De-animalizing the Animal

Two final animal stories from the *Avadānaśataka* offer an interesting twist on the basic *prasāda* scenario, and it will be useful to look at them in tandem. In the *Kṛṣṇasarpa Avadāna* (*Avadānaśataka* No. 51),[42] a venomous black snake who kills everyone that comes into his garden is pacified by the Buddha, gives rise to *prasāda,* dies, and is reborn as a deity in the Trāyastriṃśa heaven. Similarly, in the *Mahiṣa Avadāna* (*Avadānaśataka* No. 58), a fierce buffalo rushes toward the Buddha to kill him but is instantaneously tamed by the Buddha's performance of several miracles.[43] He, too, gives rise to *prasāda*, dies, and is reborn as a deity in the Trāyastriṃśa heaven. In both cases, the Buddha again makes it clear that the animal's rebirth as a god in heaven is a direct result of its experience of *prasāda*. Both stories thus adhere to the basic *prasāda* paradigm—although in both cases, the animal, being fierce, requires an initial step of taming or pacification before *prasāda* can arise.[44]

What is unique in these two cases, however, is the manner in which the animal's *death* is brought about. We should first observe from the stories examined above that a relatively quick death immediately following the experience of *prasāda* seems to be an essential factor of the *prasāda* mechanism in the case of animals[45]—something, we might note, that does *not* seem to be required in the case of human beings.[46] Thus, the bull of the *Aśokavarṇa Avadāna* dies within seven days of the arising of *prasāda* (although the reason for its death is not specified); the talking parrot of the *Śuka Avadāna* is in the process of being killed by a hawk when he experiences *prasāda*; and the geese of the *Haṃsa Avadāna* die shortly after their encounter with the Buddha (again, the reason is unspecified). A quick death seems to be the price that the animal must pay in order to experience *prasāda*'s benefits—which already suggests an important distinction between human beings and animals in the functioning of *prasāda*.

But what happens if a sudden death does not naturally occur? In the cases of both the black snake and the fierce buffalo, we are treated to the spectacle of *animals committing suicide*. The animal at last seems to exercise some agency—but only in the form of its own annihilation.

Since both stories proceed in a similar manner (with multiple identical passages in each case), we can focus more closely on the story of the black snake to represent what happens in both.[47] In its previous lifetime, this snake was a miserly rich man who was overly attached to the hoard of treasure buried within his garden. Thus, he was reborn in that very same garden as a black snake with a "venomous glance" (S. *dṛṣṭi-viṣa*),[48] who continued to stand guard over this treasure and kill anyone who came close to it merely by his glance. The Buddha, upon being

FIGURE 2.1.
The Buddha taming the black snake of Rājagṛha (*Avadānaśataka* No. 51). Gandhāra school, 3rd c. CE. Lahore Museum. © Kunst- und Ausstellungshalle der Bundesrepublik Deutschland (Bonn).

asked by King Bimbisāra to pacify the snake, enters the garden and emits rays of benevolence (S. *maitrī*) toward the snake (see Figure 2.1). What follows is worth quoting in full:

Then the venomous snake began looking here and there, wondering, "Whose majesty causes this delight to my body?" Then he saw the Blessed Buddha, endowed with the thirty-two major and eighty minor marks of a Great Man, whose body was glorious, adorned with a halo of light, brighter than a thousand suns, shimmering like a mountain of jewels, wholly beautiful. As soon as he saw him, his heart gave rise to faith (S. *cittaṃ prasāditaṃ*) in the Blessed One's presence, and when his heart was full of faith, the Blessed One taught him the Dharma pertaining to his birth and future destiny:

"Good Fellow, you alone acquired this wealth which has brought about your birth as a venomous snake. Very well, then! Give rise to faith

> in my presence and turn your heart away from this treasure, lest when you die here, you arrive among the beings of hell!"
>
> When the Blessed One reminded the snake of his birth, the snake began to weep.
>
> Then, on that occasion, the Blessed One spoke some verses:
>
> "What can I do for you, now that you have been born
> as an animal and met with misfortune?
> Why are you weeping in vain?
> Very well, then!
> Give rise to faith in the Greatly Compassionate Conqueror.
> Detach yourself from the animal realm here,
> and then you will go to heaven."
>
> Then the Blessed One put the snake into his bowl and brought him to Veṇuvana.... Then the venomous snake, despising his own nature, succeeded in starving himself. Giving rise to faith in the Blessed One's presence, he died and was reborn among the superior Trāyastriṃśa gods.[49]

This is followed by the usual stock passage in which the god remembers its former birth, goes to visit the Buddha, hears a sermon on the four noble truths, and attains the goal of stream-entry. At the end of the story, the Buddha informs his monks that because the snake gave rise to *prasāda*, he was reborn as a god—and because, in a long-ago lifetime as a human layman, he kept the moral precepts, he attained the fruit of stream-entry.

But here, of course, an additional element is present: the spectacle of the animal bringing about its own death by willfully depriving himself of all food. What particularly strikes me about the passage I have quoted (much of which also appears in the story of the fierce buffalo)[50] is the high degree of *agency* attributed to the animal, which stands in marked contrast to the passivity of the other animals we have looked at. The Buddha uses three imperative verb forms altogether, telling the snake to "give rise to faith in my presence," to "turn your heart away from this treasure," and once again, to "give rise to faith in the Greatly Compassionate Conqueror."[51] The other animal stories, however, are completely lacking in imperatives addressed to the animal.

The Buddha even asks the snake (rhetorically), "What can I do for you?"—suggesting that it is up to the snake alone to eradicate its own misfortune. Both the snake and the buffalo are asked to *do* something, rather than just reacting willy-nilly to the sight of the Buddha. Both animals are finally granted the agency to bring about their own spiritual betterment.

The *cost* of this agency, however, is the animal's denial of its own animality. When the Buddha reminds the snake of his existence as an animal, we are given a poignant image of the *animal becoming conscious of its own animality*—which is, of course, precisely the phenomenon of self-consciousness that is so often said to distinguish human beings from animals and that animals are said to utterly lack—and weeping out of grief in response. This "reminding," moreover, is indicated by the word *smārita*, the causative past-passive participle of the verbal root *smṛ*—the same verbal root from which *smṛti* (mindfulness), *buddhānusmṛti* (recollection of the Buddha), and other technical terms suggestive of spiritual cultivation are derived. The animal, in a sense, is being asked to *meditate* on his own existential condition as an animal—and, as a result, he soon comes to "despise his own nature" (S. *svāśrayaṃ jugupsamāno*) and starves himself to death. At last, we are given the image of an animal engaging in intentional self-cultivation—but only for the purpose of eradicating its own animality. Through the process of abstaining from food, the animal gradually *erases* its physical existence as an animal. Only within this context of self-eradication is the animal depicted as exercising some kind of autonomous agency.

How should we interpret the "suicides" of the snake and the buffalo? The ethics of suicide in early Buddhist discourse have been much debated over the years, with some arguing, for example, that Buddhism seems to condone suicide for those who have attained arhatship, but not for those who are "ordinary beings," and others arguing that suicide is never condoned for anyone.[52] In the present case, we might note that the Buddha neither criticizes nor praises the actions of the animal who starves himself to death—although the tone of both stories is generally upbeat. In any case, keeping in mind the larger discourse surrounding animals characteristic of Buddhist sources, I would prefer to see the actions of the snake and the buffalo less as a matter of individual suicide and more as a matter of the symbolic erasure of animality itself. The fact that both the snake and the buffalo begin as *fierce* and *violent* animals perhaps further suggests that it is the state of animality itself—and everything that it stands for—that must be negated in order for agency to be exercised. The snake and the buffalo are not really akin to individual human personalities whose motivations in committing suicide we can ponder and question—as we can, for example, in the cases of the monks Chaṇṇa, Vakkali, and Godhika (three monks who commit suicide in the Pāli Canon). Instead, I see the suicides of the snake and the buffalo as a symbolic assertion of the total incompatibility of the animal state with moral agency, self-cultivation, or the final release from suffering. Both animals serve as testament to the fact that the absolute precondition for any of these phenomena is the negation of animality itself.

The *prasāda* mechanism appears to be one way in which Buddhist doctrine compassionately provides for the spiritual betterment of lowly creatures who are otherwise described as incapable of exercising any moral agency or pursuing any spiritual goals. Through the *prasāda* mechanism, animals are capable of catapulting themselves up the karmic hierarchy to become deities in heaven, and may even make progress toward the final goal of release. Nevertheless, while providing this loophole, these stories are equally careful to preserve the distinction between human beings and animals and to ensure that individual moral agency remains a human prerogative alone. The only animal who exercises such agency is one who, "despising his own nature," is in the process of eradicating animality outright.

PART II

WHEN ANIMALS SPEAK

Animals in the Pāli Jātakas

Introduction To Part II

If a lion could speak, we could not understand him.
(Wittgenstein, Philosophical Investigations)[1]

All species of animals, my friend, do indeed speak,
but not in front of people.
(Pañcatantra)[2]

The doctrinal view of animals (Chapter 1) and the consequences of this view for the spiritual development of animals (Chapter 2) are both important, yet they do not exhaust the discourse surrounding animals in South Asian Buddhist literature. No discussion of this discourse can suffice without taking account of the pervasive presence of animals within the genre of the *jātakas* (previous-life stories of the Buddha), and especially within the massive Pāli *jātaka* collection, where animals appear on virtually every page. In fact, it is precisely the need to take account of the animals appearing in the *jātakas* that has made it impossible for scholars to elucidate any single "South Asian Buddhist view of animals"—since the roles played by animals within the *jātakas* are not only highly varied, but also frequently stand in stark contrast to the standard doctrinal view. When, for example, the Buddha himself, in a previous lifetime, is born in the lowly form of a hare who not only preaches a sermon to other animals in the forest, but also cultivates the bodhisattva's "perfection of generosity" (S. *dāna-pāramitā*) by compassionately sacrificing his own life in order to feed a hungry wanderer,[3] this seems to utterly contradict what we would expect, given the low spiritual potential of animals in Buddhist doctrine. Rather than trying to reconcile such stories to the standard doctrinal view, I believe (for the reasons stated below) that it is essential to treat them separately, as a different strand of the Buddhist discourse on animals.

Part II of this book is thus devoted to animals as they appear in the *jātakas*. For the sake of coherence—and because it gives me more than enough material to work with—my treatment of animals in the *jātakas* will be limited to the Pāli collection alone—that is, the *Jātakaṭṭhavaṇṇanā* or *Jātakaṭṭhakathā*, a massive collection of 547 *jātaka* tales in verse and prose, of which only the verses are considered canonical (constituting the tenth book of the *Khuddaka Nikāya* of the Theravāda canon), while the prose portions are commentarial. The canonical verses are known to be considerably earlier than the prose commentary, which only reached its final form in fifth-century CE Sri Lanka. Nevertheless, the verses are often unintelligible without the help of the prose, and it is clear that the stories themselves draw on much older narrative traditions (with depictions of some *jātakas* already appearing in Buddhist art as early as the second century BCE). Moreover, while recognizing that the *Jātakaṭṭhavaṇṇanā* is a distinctly Theravāda collection in nature and part of the "Pali imaginaire" (to use Steven Collins's phrase),[4] many of its stories exist in parallel versions in Sanskrit Buddhist literature, as well as Chinese and Tibetan translations, and the collection as a whole—at least in regard to its depiction of animals—is not markedly out of step with the larger context of early South Asian Buddhism.

Animals are pervasive, omnipresent, and central in the Pāli *jātakas*. By my count, out of the 547 *jātakas* included in this collection, 117 of them (or just over 20%) feature the Buddha himself appearing as an animal (always male) in a previous rebirth, with the most frequent animals represented being the monkey, deer, goose, lion, parrot, and elephant, but also including many lowly or generally disfavored animals, such as the lizard, mouse, frog, pig, dog, and jackal (see the Appendix for a full accounting). We cannot limit ourselves to these tales alone, however, for many additional tales in this collection also focus substantively upon animals, even without the bodhisattva himself being one of them. By my estimation, there are slightly more than 200 tales altogether (close to 40% of the total) that feature animals in a substantive manner and might reasonably be referred to as "animal tales." This includes those tales in which the bodhisattva himself is an animal, but it also includes many other tales that focus upon animal characters, but in which the bodhisattva appears as a human being, tree-spirit, or some other kind of being. In my view, the question of whether or not the bodhisattva is an animal is less important than the overall focus of the tale upon animal characters. My discussion in the following chapters thus draws from this larger body of "animal tales."

While it is clear that many of the Pāli *jātakas*—perhaps especially those involving animals—are drawn directly from pre-Buddhist Indian folklore and then adapted to Buddhist ends, I do not subscribe to the view that such stories should be labeled "non-Buddhist" and thereby considered dismissible. For regardless of their origin, these stories were passed down over time (and the verses associated with them made canonical) for a reason. Moreover, when we consider the enormous popularity of the *jātakas* over time, the multiple versions in which they appear, their frequent depiction in Buddhist art, and their everyday use to teach a moral lesson or illustrate a point (in contemporary Southeast Asia, for example), it makes little practical sense, I think, to attempt to distinguish those *jātakas* adopted from existing Indian folklore from those that might be "genuinely Buddhist" (whatever that may mean). Since the historical audiences for these tales never made such a distinction themselves, it can only be of limited scholarly interest. My discussion in the following chapters, therefore, takes these animal tales as a whole and does not attempt to judge the degree of "Buddhist-ness" of any particular tale.

Animals as Allegorical Human Beings

Why are the animals of the *jātakas* worthy of separate treatment? The primary feature that distinguishes the animals of the Pāli *jātakas* from the animals of Chapters 1 and 2 is their highly anthropomorphized depiction. Animals in the *jātakas* are generally represented as thinking, speaking, planning, and reasoning in much the same manner as human beings. Perhaps most important is their frequent use of *language* and the fact that they *speak,* not only to each other but also (in many cases) to the human beings they encounter. While the animals featured in Parts I and III often *think*—and the texts do not hesitate to relate to us the exact content of their thoughts—they generally lack the faculty of intelligible speech (a rare exception being the parrots found in one tale from the *Avadānaśataka* and another tale from the *Divyāvadāna,* whose speech is explainable as a result of the fact that they are parrots).[5] The ability of the animals in the *jātakas* to speak serves as the foundation for their highly anthropomorphized depiction, since speech leads inevitably to planning and reasoning, as well as discussing, conspiring, and arguing with other beings (both human beings and other animals). The ability to speak also leads to a depiction of animals as constituting a kind of *society,* complete with family and kinship relations, distinctions of *jāti,* allies and enemies, and features of governance (for example, the lion as king of all beasts). In all of these ways, the animals of the *jātakas* are more like human beings than animals.

Several scholars have pointed to the importance of drawing a distinction between the highly anthropomorphized animals found in so many of the *jātakas* and the more realistic and naturalistic animals found elsewhere in Buddhist literature. Ian Harris, for example, states,

> Some care is needed in the proper interpretation of the *Jātaka* and other animal-oriented stories. Certainly, animals [in the *jātakas*] are often displayed in a positive light.... However, it could be argued that the

> often highly anthropomorphic character of the essentially pre-Buddhist folk-tradition of these narratives is largely devoid of "naturalistic" content. . . . Indeed, the animals are not really animals at all, for at the end of each story the Buddha reveals that the central character was none other than himself in a previous life, with his monastic companions playing the supporting roles.[6]

Similarly, Padmanabh Jaini, in an important article on the spirituality of animals in India, observes that "in almost all fables where the Bodhisattva appears as an animal-manifestation, he not only leads an exemplary life in practicing the perfections of charity and moral-discipline, but even preaches the dharma to human beings." Yet, "magnificent as these stories are, they do not refer to the fate of ordinary animals, but only to the *bodhisattva* in the guise of an animal."[7] Jaini then contrasts the exemplary animals of the *jātakas* with other, more naturalistic depictions. Finally, Florin Deleanu similarly draws a distinction between "the apparently deliberate usage of animals as characters in parables and fairy tales, mainly occurring in the *Jātaka*,"[8] and other uses of animal imagery and animal characters in Buddhist literature.

What all three of these scholars seem to suggest is that the speaking and thinking animals we find in the Pāli *jātakas* are not really "animals" at all. Instead, they can be seen as allegorical human beings. This is especially true, of course, because of the conventions of the *jātaka* genre, which dictate that each animal character is closely linked to a specific human character by his or her status as a previous birth of the Buddha or one of his contemporaries. When we learn, for example, that the evil jackal of a particular tale was a previous birth of the Buddha's nemesis Devadatta,[9] we come to think of the jackal as "really" being Devadatta or at least serving as a karmic foreshadowing of Devadatta's character. But even putting aside this particular feature of the *jātaka* genre, the speaking animals who populate animal fables around the world have often been interpreted as allegorical human beings—such as we find, for example, in Aesop's Fables (some of which have close parallels among the Pāli *jātakas*). Such fables are clearly intended to illustrate the faults, virtues, and qualities of human beings rather than animals, and they ask their human readers to identify with the animals depicted. Thus, the animals are not really animals; they are stand-ins for human beings.

In his classic essay "On the Use of Animals in Fables" (1759), the German Enlightenment writer and critic Gotthold Ephraim Lessing (1729–1781) elucidated the rhetorical effectiveness of employing animal characters within simple didactic tales.[10] Lessing observed that due to "the widely known constancy of their characters," the mere mention of a particular animal immediately brings to mind certain qualities and features that are "able to be recognized . . . by everyone, without exception," thus lending both great economy and universal accessibility to the tale. Lessing offers a particular example:

> We hear "Britannicus and Nero." How many of us know what we are hearing? Who was this one? Who the other? In what relations do they stand to one another? But then we hear: "the wolf and the lamb." At once we all know what we are hearing, and we know in what relation the one stands to the other. . . . [If] we were to place Nero in place of the wolf, and Britannicus in place of the lamb, the fable at once would lose what had made it a fable for the entire human race.

Daston and Mitman, in their introduction to a collected volume on anthropomorphized animals, put it this way:

> In [traditional] fables animals are humanized, one might even say hyper-humanized, by caricature: the fox is cunning, the lion is brave, the dog is loyal. Whereas the same stories told about humans might lose the moral in a clutter of individuating detail of the sort we are usually keen to know about other people, substituting animals as actors strips the characterizations down to prototype. Animals simplify the narrative to a point that would be found flat or at least allegorical if the same tales were recounted about humans.[11]

In a specifically Indian context, Thomas Forsthoefel observes of the *Pañcatantra* that although this collection of tales presents itself as an attempt to educate princes in the art of government, its moral lessons are, in fact, intended for everyone, regardless of class or caste. He notes that the use of animal characters "allows for universal appropriation, whether by princes or peasants."[12] Anthropomorphized animal characters thus allow for both simplification and clarity of the moral lesson the tale conveys, as well as its universal accessibility to everyone (which perhaps explains why such tales are so often told to children).

On an emotional level, moreover, animal characters facilitate the human reader's interaction with the tale by allowing one to engage in simultaneous identification and distance between oneself and the protagonists of the tale. Lessing emphasizes the importance of distance, noting that in the story of the wolf and the lamb, for example, "we sympathize with the lamb, but this sympathy is so weak that it has no noticeable impact upon our intuitive knowledge of the moral principle."[13] If the lamb were replaced by a human being, on the other hand, our sympathy for our fellow human being would be great enough to excite our "passions" and thus get in the way of our learning the lesson. Although Lessing's point might well be objected to by some animal lovers, it is no doubt the case that animal characters do allow for a degree of emotional distance that facilitates the moral effectiveness of the tale. Forsthoefel, on the other hand, emphasizes the interplay between identification and distance—and here he is speaking specifically of both the *Pañcatantra* and the Pāli *jātakas*. Animal stories thus allow for "a certain safety, a certain non-identification: 'these characters are not me.'" And yet, precisely because of this ontological distance, "the reader feels less of a need to establish one's moral superiority in advance; consequently disarmed, the reader nonetheless finds himself or herself identifying with the animal characters in any case . . . 'I am like this after all.'"[14]

In light of the rhetorical and didactic functions they fulfill, then, the highly anthropomorphized animal characters that populate animal fables such as we find in the Pāli *jātakas* are fundamentally different from the more naturalistic animals we looked at in Chapters 1 and 2—which helps to explain, of course, why these animals so often fail to conform to the standard doctrinal view of the animal realm. It is for this reason that I believe these animals are worthy of separate treatment.

Here, however, another question arises: If these animals are really allegorical human beings rather than animals, then why should we look at them at all?

The Continuing Significance of Animality

Ultimately, I believe that viewing the animals within animal fables as allegorical human beings—as useful as it may be—is nonetheless insufficient, and fails to do justice to the complexity of the tales. The *animality* of these animals continues to matter; in fact, such tales rely for their effectiveness upon a constant tension—or, perhaps, a constant alternation—between seeing the animal characters as stand-ins for human beings and seeing the animal characters as animals. This has been demonstrated in many different contexts.

In his analysis of ancient Greek animal fables, for example, Edward Clayton cites the many animal tales (such as that involving the wolf and the lamb) that seem to convey the simple lesson that "might makes right, the weak suffer at the whim of the stronger, and rebellion by the weak is futile."[15] Such tales have generally been interpreted as "cautionary tales, warning of the dangers of being the weaker party, and providing advice on how to behave if one is in a position of weakness."[16] Although this is undoubtedly true, to read the fables in this way is to interpret the animal characters as straightforward stand-ins for human beings. A very different message can be found "if we read the fables with an eye not only to how animals and people are similar but also to how they are different."[17] In the ancient Greek view, according to Clayton, human beings are different from animals through their possession of reason and their ability to adopt the principles of justice, democracy, and a well-ordered political life. And this allows us to derive an alternative message from such tales—the message that "it is *not* all right for human beings to treat each other in this way . . . and it is the responsibility of those with power to make sure that justice guides human political relationships."[18] And yet, this alternative message does not obviate the validity of the first message (that of "might makes right"). The ability to see the animal characters as either human beings or as animals thus lends more complexity and multivocality to the tale's significance.

Complexity of a different type is elucidated in Gillian Rudd's analysis of Robert Henryson's late-fifteenth-century version of Aesop's "The Town Mouse and the Country Mouse." Rudd argues that all animal fables require us "to move with ease between the human and non-human worlds" and present us with "a composite space" that partakes of both worlds without privileging either one.[19] She demonstrates this fluidity through a nuanced analysis of Henryson's tale of the two sister mice. In this tale, the civilized sophistication of the urban life (as represented by the town mouse) is contrasted with the simple comforts of the rural life (as represented by the country mouse). In line with this contrast, the two mice are subjected to different degrees of anthropomorphization: "the town mouse is moved consistently towards the human realm, while the country mouse more frequently inhabits the animal world."[20] And yet this process is far from being straightforward, for every once in a while, Henryson forcefully reminds us that the town mouse is still an *animal*, while the country mouse occasionally displays *human* urbanity and wit. Ultimately, Rudd succeeds in demonstrating that Henryson's fable is full of complexity and ambiguity, constantly shifting the categories of humanity and animality (in relation to both urban and rural life) in a way that resists any single interpretation. This complexity results from the fact that, as we read the story, we are constantly "translating mice into humans and humans into mice."[21] It would be simplistic, therefore, to see the mice solely as allegorical stand-ins for human beings.

The types of complexity illustrated by Clayton and Rudd are undoubtedly true of the Pāli *jātakas* as well. My treatment of them is necessarily limited, however, and focuses on a slightly different reason why the animality of the animal characters continues to matter, which is the frequent focus of these tales on *human treatment of the animal world*. If the animal characters were merely allegorical human beings, then we would not necessarily expect the moral lessons they convey to have anything specific to do with *animals*. In fact, however, anyone who ventures to read the animal tales *en masse* must immediately be struck by their heavy preoccupation with human treatment of the nonhuman world. Speaking animals speak *about* the suffering of *animals*—and, of course, they tell us much about humanity in the process. My treatment of animals in the Pāli *jātakas* will focus primarily on this theme.

In Chapter 3, "(Human) Nature, Red in Tooth and Claw," I demonstrate that, in contrast to the doctrinal view of the animal realm as a vicious world of predator and prey, the Pāli *jātakas* suggest that it is *human beings* who are guilty of rampant cruelty, exploitation, and abuse of nonhuman animals. In Chapter 4, "Animal Saviors," I first focus on the common technique of contrasting a virtuous animal with a nonvirtuous human being, thus using animality to make a negative comment on the nature of humanity itself—particularly in regard to human treatment of the animal world. I then go on to look at several tales in which saintly animals preach the Dharma and convert human beings to virtue—but again, for the specific purpose of winning the *security of other animals* from human exploitation and abuse.

The title of this section, "When Animals Speak," is meant to suggest that when animals are given a voice—as they are in the Pāli *jātakas*—we hear a very different story than we did in Chapters 1 and 2. Their ability to speak may be what turns them into allegorical human beings—but what they have to say often comes from their status as animals.

CHAPTER THREE

(Human) Nature, Red in Tooth and Claw

Human beings say one thing with their mouths and do another thing with their bodies.

(Ruru Jātaka)[1]

In Alfred Lord Tennyson's famous poem "In Memoriam A. H. H." (a requiem dedicated to his good friend Arthur Henry Hallam and completed in 1849), the human being is spoken of as one "Who trusted God was love indeed / And love Creation's final law / Tho' Nature, red in tooth and claw / With ravine, shriek'd against his creed."[2] Tennyson thus places humankind in opposition to a violent natural world in which predatory animals' teeth and claws are perpetually stained red by the blood of their hapless prey—just as we saw Maudgalyāyana (in the *Mahāvastu*) observe of the animal realm that "they devour one another; they drink one another's blood; they kill one another; they destroy one another."[3]

In contrast, the title of this chapter—a slight alteration of Tennyson's famous phrase—is meant to suggest that when animals are given a voice (as they are in the Pāli *jātakas*), it is *human beings* who constitute "nature, red in tooth and claw." In fact, reading the animal *jātakas* as a whole, one cannot help but be struck by the constant and oppressive invocation of human cruelty, exploitation, and abuse of the nonhuman animal world. By my own (somewhat haphazard) estimate, the theme of human beings causing harm to animals is roughly twice as common as the theme of animals causing harm to one another. Moreover, while the latter theme tends to take the form of straightforward interactions between predator and prey, the former theme manifests itself in an endless variety of different methods of injury, harm, torture, and abuse. While animals in the *jātakas* merely kill and eat other animals, human beings in the *jātakas*—in addition to killing and eating the animals they encounter—also whip, beat, maim, torture, and execute them in a myriad of colorful ways, often for utterly insignificant or nonexistent reasons. Human violence toward animals is pervasive, omnipresent, and graphic in the world depicted by the Pāli *jātakas*.

Rather than attempting any comprehensive treatment of this theme, my aim in this chapter is simply to offer a few selected glimpses of some of the ways in which the theme is expressed. In focusing on this theme, moreover, I do not mean to suggest that the Buddhist voice expressed through these stories *endorses* human cruelty toward non-human animals. This is far from being the case. In fact, in line with the Buddhist moral imperative to refrain from causing harm or injury to any sentient being, the *jātakas* often depict the human beings who engage in this behavior in a thoroughly negative light, and sometimes illustrate the dire karmic consequences these characters suffer as a result. But putting aside any concern with animal ethics, what I am interested in drawing attention to here is simply the pervasiveness of the theme itself, its utterly taken-for-granted quality, and the manner in which these *jātakas* fully recognize and give voice to an animal perception of humanity as dangerous, cruel, untrustworthy, and corrupt. In the *jātakas,* it is human beings rather than animals who are frightening and morally repugnant. I find it interesting, in fact, to view the animal *jātakas* as the flip side to the doctrinal statements discussed in Chapter 1. There, we saw human beings looking warily and suspiciously at animals. Here, we see the animals looking warily and suspiciously back at us.

Humans Eat Pigs

In Chris Noonan's 1995 film *Babe* (based on Dick King-Smith's 1983 novella *The Sheep-Pig*),[4] we are plunged into a magical world of pigs, dogs, sheep, ducks, and other farm animals who speak to one another in a language that we can understand (although the human characters in the film are not privy to their conversations). The film tells the story of Babe, an adorable little piglet who is won in a carnival game at the county fair by Farmer Hoggett, who intends to fatten him up and serve him for the family's Christmas dinner. Babe saves himself, however, by learning to herd sheep (like a sheepdog) and eventually winning the local sheep-herding competition. Babe herds the sheep by befriending them and asking them politely to carry out his commands—much to the surprise of Babe's mentor, Fly, a sheepdog who thinks that all sheep are stupid and have to be frightened and bullied into compliance. At the end of the film, Babe wins the sheep-herding competition to much acclaim, the sheepdogs learn that they can be kind to the sheep in their care, and Farmer Hoggett—a man of few words—expresses his love for Babe with a simple, "That'll do, pig. That'll do."

The film is heartwarming and sweet, and the animal characters (conveyed by a combination of real and animatronic animals) are painfully cute. Nevertheless, as Erica Fudge notes in her analysis of the film,[5] the sweetness of the film is everywhere subverted by the constant invocation (from the animals' point of view) of the horrors of human consumption of animal flesh—particularly in the age of modern factory farming. Babe's first words in the opening scene of the film are "Goodbye, Mom!," spoken as his mother is taken away from him and replaced by a cold, metal udder. Babe thinks that she is journeying to a sort of Valhalla for lucky pigs, but we know that she is destined for the slaughterhouse to be turned into pork and bacon. As Fudge describes it, "The fantasy of the speaking animal begins with a recognition of the horrors of the place of the animal in a human world. . . . This is not just fantasy, it is not just farming, it is genocide."[6] Only later does Babe discover—much to his dismay—that "humans eat pigs."

The other animals on Farmer Hoggett's farm are all-too-aware of this fact and spend much of their time and energy trying to avoid becoming dinner. One of the more comic animal characters in the film is a duck named Ferdinand, who crows like a rooster every morning, thinking that animals who fulfill a useful function for human beings can avoid being slaughtered for their meat. When Farmer Hoggett's wife buys an alarm clock that threatens to make Ferdinand's crowing obsolete, the desperate duck enlists Babe's help to sneak into the farmhouse and steal the offending clock. The ensuing caper is played for laughs and full of slapstick humor, but it is also darkened by our knowledge that Ferdinand is fighting to avoid being killed and roasted. As the Christmas holiday approaches, the human characters are happy and festive, while Ferdinand can only cry out mournfully that "Christmas means carnage!" The film's skillful juxtaposition of adorable talking animals and the hard realities of human consumption of animal flesh results, as Fudge observes, in "a film that is simultaneously sweet and shocking. Anthropomorphism ceases to be sentimental ... it becomes threatening and our fantasies turn into a nightmare."[7] The speaking animals are cute and charming, yet they end up "saying something we don't want to hear."[8]

Fudge's analysis of *Babe* can open our eyes to the parallel and equally shocking horror evident in several of the Pāli *jātakas,* which also feature farm animals whose innocence is lost when they come to realize that human beings eat animals. In both the *Munika Jātaka* (No. 30)[9] and the *Sālūka Jātaka* (No. 286)[10]—which tell the same story in slightly different terms—two oxen who are brothers are owned by a farming family that clearly overworks them and gives them insufficient food to eat. This abusive situation is made even worse by the fact that a pig on the same farm is given abundant meals of rice and even allowed to sleep under the bed. Noticing the disparity in their treatment, the younger ox complains to his older brother: "Brother, we do all the work for this family, and they survive in dependence on us, and yet these people give us meager hay and straw, while they feed the pig meals of rice and let him sleep under the bed. What can he possibly do for them?"[11] His older brother (the bodhisattva) then opens the young ox's eyes to the harsh truth of human meat-eating (just as Babe's eyes similarly had to be opened):

> Cūḷalohita, my brother, don't covet his food—that pig is eating the food of death! It is because they think that upon the occasion of their daughter's wedding, there have to be delicacies for the guests who attend that

they are feeding such food to the pig. In a few days, the guests will come, and then you will see them grabbing the pig by the feet, dragging him, driving him out from underneath the bed, killing him, and turning him into curry for their guests.[12]

He continues with a canonical verse:

> Don't covet [the food] of the pig, he is eating the food of the doomed!
> Be carefree and eat your chaff—it's the sign of a long life.[13]

Sure enough, the wedding guests soon arrive, and the oxen watch in horror as the pig is slaughtered and turned into delicacies—just as, in *Babe,* Farmer Hoggett's extended family arrives for Christmas and feeds on a roasted duck named Roseanne (not Ferdinand after all), as the rest of the animals watch in horror through a window. His innocence now lost, the younger ox, Cūḷalohita, concludes, "Compared to [the pig's] food, our meager hay, straw, and chaff is a hundred—no, a thousand—times better!"[14] The Buddha himself, concluding this story, recites another verse:

> Seeing the pig cut up into pieces,
> lying [there] with his snout [looking] like a club,
> the wretched oxen thought, "Our chaff is better."[15]

In a world dominated by human beings, being an overworked draught animal is perhaps the best fate that one can hope for.

In the *Tuṇḍila Jātaka* (No. 388),[16] on the other hand, we see the pig himself come to learn of his own fate and be admonished by none other than the bodhisattva that he must resign himself to it. In this story, an old woman raises two piglet brothers from birth (the older of whom is the bodhisattva) and treats them lovingly as her own children. But even this offers no protection, for when a gang of rogues comes along, hungry for pork, and the woman refuses to sell them one of her pigs, the rogues simply get her drunk and pressure her until she finally relents and agrees to sell them the younger pig, Cūḷatuṇḍila. She fills a trough with delicious food to get the young pig to approach, while the rogues stand nearby with nooses in their hands. Cūḷatuṇḍila is rightly suspicious: "Today," he says to his older brother, "something new and mysterious is being offered; the trough is full, and our mistress is standing [nearby]. There are many people with nooses in their hands—I don't think I should eat."[17] His brother's response is notable, especially coming from the bodhisattva himself:

> The Great Being said, "Cūḷatuṇḍila, my brother, the very purpose for which our mother raises pigs in the first place has today reached its fulfillment, so don't fret about it." And preaching the Dharma in a sweet voice and with the grace of a Buddha, he recited two verses:
>
> "You tremble and shake and seek your salvation,
> but it's hopeless—where will you go?
> Be carefree and eat, O Tuṇḍila!
> For we are fattened for the sake of our flesh."[18]

The inevitability of pigs being slaughtered in order to satisfy the tastes of human beings is thus described as "the Dharma" itself, and the bodhisattva states plainly that the best course for such a pig is to resign himself to this fate. Not all human beings slaughter pigs, of course—yet even a kind and compassionate human being like the old woman finally cannot be trusted: "Brother," the bodhisattva suggests, "formerly our mother was our refuge, but today, she abandons us with indifference, so now, where will you go?"[19] Human beings eat pigs—and not even a kindly human being can save the pig from this fate.

The untrustworthy nature of even the noblest of human beings is also invoked in the *Javanahaṃsa Jātaka* (No. 476),[20] where the bodhisattva appears as a goose who befriends the king of Benares. After repeatedly visiting the king and even preaching to him about the inevitable decay that afflicts all phenomena, the goose is invited to stay in the palace permanently so that the king can benefit from his wisdom. "I would stay in your home," the goose replies, "... but one day, drunk, you might say, 'Cook the goose-king for me!' "[21] The king insists that this will never occur: "Fie upon any intoxicating drink that is dearer to me than you! I will not drink any liquor as long as you live in my house."[22] But the goose-king understands all too well that human promises cannot be trusted:

> The cries of jackals and birds are easy to interpret,
> far harder, O King, are the words of human beings.
> A human may think [of someone] as a "relative,"
> "companion," or "friend,"
> but he who was formerly regarded with delight
> later turns into an enemy.[23]

Particularly interesting here is the new valance given to human language. In Chapter 1, we saw that the ability to use language allows human beings to recognize social categories such as "relative" and thus avoid the promiscuity and incest characteristic of animals. Here, however, we hear a very different story from the animals themselves: human language is suspicious and slippery, and labels such as "relative" are not to be trusted. Commenting upon the meaning of these two verses, the text explains that "the hearts of animals are straightforward"—as reflected in their animal cries—while "the hearts of human beings are difficult to understand."[24] The animals of the *jātakas* may be able to speak—but only so that they can tell us that human promises are empty. As the deer of the *Ruru Jātaka* (No. 482)[25] puts it, "Human beings say one thing with their mouths and do another thing with their bodies."[26]

"Full of Tricks and Clever in Stratagems": Hunting as a Contest of Wits

The eating of animals is only the end-stage of a much longer process that involves trapping them, shooting them, killing them, and cooking them. The animals of the *jātakas* are fully aware that human beings are very good at these things and have devised elaborate means for carrying them out. As a goose observes in the *Mahāhaṃsa Jātaka* (No. 534),[27] "Human beings are cruel, full of tricks, and clever in stratagems."[28] The *jātakas* paint a vivid portrait of the many ways in which human beings trap and kill animals, or otherwise submit them to human control.

Deer are the quintessential wild animal in India—as suggested by the Pāli term *miga,* which means both "deer" and "wild animal" in general (and is opposed to *pasu* or "domesticated animal")—and thus the quintessential object of hunting in Indian literature, especially hunting by kings.[29] We should not be surprised, therefore, to find that multiple *jātakas* focus on the various methods used to trap and hunt deer.[30] Hunting them is easier, of course, if they are first confined to groves set aside for this purpose. Thus, in the *Nigrodhamiga Jātaka* (No. 12),[31] the king's men, upon locating a herd of deer, "beat the trees, bushes, and ground with their clubs, and drove the deer out from their lair. Carrying knives, daggers, bows, and all sorts of weapons, and making a great noise, they drove the herd of deer into the [hunting-]grove and shut the gate."[32] Once confined to such a grove, the deer are easy targets and suffer accordingly: "As soon as the deer saw the bow, they would flee, terrified by the fear of death. But after being struck two or three times, they would grow weary, be weakened, and die."[33] Alternatively, deer can also be killed by trapping them in a snare, which causes them excruciating pain. In the *Suvaṇṇamiga Jātaka* (No. 359),[34] the bodhisattva is a deer who gets his foot trapped in such a snare:

> Thinking that he would cut himself free, he pulled, and his skin was cut. He pulled again, and his flesh was cut. He pulled a third time, and his tendon was cut, until the snare penetrated through to the bone. Unable to free himself from the snare, he was terrified with the fear of death and let out the cry of those who are bound.[35]

Such snares and traps come in multiple forms. In the *Lakkhaṇa Jātaka* (No. 11),[36] in order to kill the many deer who are eating their crops, "men here and there dug pitfalls, they erected stakes, they set

FIGURE 3.1.
Violence against deer: depiction of the *Lakkhaṇa Jātaka* (*Jātakaṭṭhavaṇṇanā* No. 11), from a 19th c. Burmese illustrated manuscript. © The British Library Board, Burmese 202, f. 11r.

traps made out of rocks, they lay all kinds of traps and snares, so that many deer fell into ruin" (see Figure 3.1).[37] Moreover, "men know the route [the deer] take; they know when the deer climb up into the hills and when they descend again. Thus, lying in wait here and there in various hiding-places, they shoot and kill many deer."[38] Whereas in Chapter 1 we saw that a monkey did not even possess the *paññā* that would allow him to construct a shelter from the storm, here we see that human beings, taking advantage of their native intelligence, can build all sorts of traps and devices against which animals are helpless—in fact, they can even study the animals' patterns of migration in order to make their hunting more timely and efficient. Fully endowed with the higher mental faculties, human beings, as the goose observes, are indeed "full of tricks and clever in stratagems" (P. *bahumāyā upāyakusalā*).

And yet the *jātakas* are unique in depicting a world in which animals *speak*—and therefore, think, plan, anticipate, and reason. Thus, in many of the *jātakas*, it seems that animals, too, are "full of tricks and clever in stratagems"—skillfully avoiding capture, freeing themselves once they are caught, or otherwise outwitting the human beings who seek to kill them. In the *jātakas*, the animal's supposed lack of intelligence that we saw in Chapter 1 is everywhere subverted and belied: Hunting becomes a contest of wits between human beings and animals, and animals are sometimes depicted as possessing a *tradition* or *culture* of useful skills that they can pass down to future generations.

Once again, this is particularly clear in the case of deer, as the archetypal targets of the hunt. In the *Sarabhamiga Jātaka* (No. 483),[39] we learn that deer are quite good at not being shot:

> Now, deer are very good at avoiding arrows. If arrows come toward them, they avoid their force by standing still. If they come from behind them, they quickly outrun them. If they come from above them, they bend their backs. If they come from the side, they swerve a bit. If they come toward their bellies, they fall down and turn over, and when the arrows have passed by, they run away as quickly as a cloud broken up by the wind.[40]

While such maneuvers could arguably be considered as nothing more than instinctual in nature, other *jātakas* depict more elaborate methods of escape and deception that need to be learned and passed down. In the *Tipallatthamiga Jātaka* (No. 16),[41] the bodhisattva is a deer-king who instructs his nephew in the "ruses of deer" (P. *miga-māyā*). When the nephew is later caught in a hunter's snare, the bodhisattva assures the young deer's mother that her son will surely escape, since "he has learned the ruses of deer very well"—in particular, the "six tricks" (P. *chahi kalāhi*) by means of which a deer caught in a snare can deceive the hunter into thinking that he is dead and then flee once the hunter has freed him from the snare.[42] The word commentary on the phrase "six tricks"—using a fully commentarial style—offers three different interpretations of what these "six tricks" are, including such complex maneuvers as "blocking the air coming into one's upper nostril and . . . breathing only with one's lower nostril while keeping it pressed against the earth."[43] The text's three alternative ways of counting up the "six tricks" immediately call to mind the multiple interpretations so often found within commentarial explanations of the many numbered lists of Buddhist doctrine (such as the twelvefold chain of dependent origination or the seven factors of awakening)—almost suggesting the image of different lineages of deer who pass down different textual traditions of what the "six tricks" are. This image stands in marked contrast, of course, to the idea that all animals are lacking in *paññā*.

Regardless of how we interpret the exact contents of the "six tricks," it is clear that the young deer of the *Tipallatthamiga Jātaka* has learned them very well, for we are then given a full description of the many ruses he makes use of to play dead and deceive the hunter:

> And the young deer did not struggle when he was trapped in the snare. He lay down heavily on one side on the ground, with his legs stretched out; he used his hooves to strike the ground near his legs to uproot the dirt and the grass; he released his feces and urine; he let his head fall down; he lolled out his tongue; he made his body wet with saliva; he made his belly bloated by sucking in the air; he let his eyes roll back [into his head]; he breathed through his lower nostril only, while blocking the air from his upper nostril; he made his entire body stiff—and he played dead. Even the black flies began to circle him, and crows settled on the ground here and there.[44]

Sure enough, the hunter is fooled by this clever display, and the young deer flees to safety once the hunter has cut him free from the snare. The fact that "playing dead" successfully requires a formal education is made clear, moreover, by the *Kharādiya Jātaka* (No. 15),[45] which tells an identical story, except that the nephew in question (a previous birth of Devadatta) fails to show up for his "lessons" for seven days in a row. Without any formal schooling in the "ruses of deer," he soon falls prey to the hunter's snare.

Animals, too, are thus "full of tricks and clever in stratagems," constantly using their powers of reasoning to outwit and outsmart the human beings around them. This is demonstrated over and over again. In the *Kuruṅga Jātaka* (No. 21),[46] for example, an antelope concludes that there must be a hunter perched in a tree ready to kill him from the fact that the fruit of the tree is thrown toward him, rather than falling straight downward through the force of gravity. In the *Sammodamāna Jātaka* (No. 33),[47] a large flock of quails who are repeatedly caught in a fowler's net figure out that if they each stick their head through a hole in the net and fly upward simultaneously, they can all escape—and by alighting on a tree simultaneously, they can then free themselves from the net. In the *Vaṭṭaka Jātaka* (No. 118),[48] another quail understands that quails are sold for their fattened flesh, so he saves his own life by starving himself until nobody has any desire to buy him. In the *Tiṇḍuka Jātaka* (No. 177),[49] a monkey understands the usefulness of creating a distraction, setting fire to a human village and thus distracting the villagers who are about to kill the monkey's relatives, stuck up in a tree. In the *Mahākapi Jātaka* (No. 407), another monkey constructs a bridge from one tree to another to allow his troop to escape from some hunters (alas, his math is a bit off, forcing him to use his own body as part of the bridge).[50]

In some of these stories, moreover, different species of animals work effectively together. In the *Kuruṅgamiga Jātaka* (No. 206),[51] when an antelope is caught in a hunter's snare, a tortoise chews through the snare to set the antelope free, while a woodpecker distracts the hunter—and when the tortoise is then caught by the hunter, he is likewise freed by the antelope. And in the *Mahāukkusa Jātaka* (No. 486),[52] an osprey, a tortoise, and a lion all work together to save some baby hawks from the hungry humans who want to eat them. We could, of course, treat all of these animals as allegorical human beings, and the stories themselves as offering human lessons of practical wisdom. The sheer number of such stories militates against this, however, and the stories instead accumulate into a vivid portrait of the oppressiveness of human domination of the animal world, the enormous suffering it causes; the constant burden borne by animals to *elude, evade*, and *escape*; and the considerable natural intelligence they bring to bear upon this task.

Once an animal *has* escaped, it is important that he not be flattered and cajoled right back into captivity—and here, we return again to the theme of human language being suspicious, deceptive, and untrustworthy. Both the *Sālaka Jātaka* (No. 249)[53] and the *Ahiguṇḍika Jātaka* (No. 365)[54] involve a snake charmer who cruelly abuses his pet monkey by beating him with a bamboo staff. When the monkey succeeds in escaping by climbing into a mango tree, the snake-charmer attempts to lure him back through flattery and empty promises. In the *Sālaka Jātaka*, he pleads with the monkey:

> You'll be my only little son,
> you'll be the master of our family.
> Come down from the tree, my brother,
> come now, and we'll go home.[55]

But the monkey reminds us again that human labels like "son" or "friend" are never to be trusted:

> You think of me as a "friend,"
> and yet you beat me with a bamboo staff?
> I'll enjoy myself in this grove of ripe mangoes.
> You can go home, if you wish.[56]

In the *Ahiguṇḍika Jātaka*, the snake charmer attempts to flatter the monkey by calling him "good-looking" (P. *sumukha*). But again, the monkey is clever enough not to be fooled by such flattery:

> What a lie! My friend, you flatter me untruthfully,
> where have you ever heard or seen that a monkey is "good-looking"?
> Even today, Snake-Charmer, I still remember what you did to me:
> Entering the grain-shop drunk, you beat me when I was hungry.
> Remembering that bed of pain,
> even if I were to be the king,
> I'd give you nothing for which you begged,
> so terrified with fear [did you make me].[57]

Like an elephant who never forgets, the monkey may have succeeded in escaping from captivity, but the memory of his bondage still lingers.

The constant presence of *fear* and *terror*—even before an animal has been caught or after it has escaped—is perhaps the greatest cost borne by the animals of the *jātakas*, and the phrase "terrified by the fear of death" (P. *maraṇa-bhaya-tajjita*) becomes a constant refrain, appearing in one story after another. In the *Kāka Jātaka* (No. 140),[58] we learn that the reason that crows have no fat on their bodies is because they are "constantly anxious in heart"[59]—due to the threat posed by human beings. Fear of humanity likewise afflicts the elephant of the *Dubbalakaṭṭha Jātaka* (No. 105)[60] after he has been trained to serve as a war-elephant for the king. Although the *jātaka* itself does not tell us much about this kind of training, the *Dantabhūmi Sutta* of the *Majjhima Nikāya* (No. 125)[61] contains a long and evocative description: First, the elephant tamer "buries a large pillar into the ground and binds the forest elephant to it by his neck in order to suppress his forest habits, suppress his forest memories and intentions, suppress his anxiety, fatigue, and distress relating to the forest, get him to take pleasure in the village, and instruct him in habits pleasing to human beings." In order to train the elephant in the "skill of imperturbability" (P. *āneñjaṃ kāraṇaṃ*), the elephant tamer "ties a large plank to his trunk"; then, "a man holding a lance sits upon his neck; men holding lances stand surrounding him on all sides; and the elephant tamer, holding a long lance pole, stands in front of him," such that the elephant "cannot move his front feet or his back feet, he cannot move his fore-body or his hind-body, he cannot move his head, ears, tusk, tail, or trunk." And once he is trained in this task, the elephant "becomes hardened to blows from knives, blows from swords, blows from arrows, blows from other weapons, and the sounds issuing forth from kettledrums, drums, small drums, and conch-shell trumpets." Only then is he "worthy of the king."[62]

The elephant of the *Dubbalakaṭṭha Jātaka* may, at first, seem lucky—for being "unable to endure the sensations as he was being trained in that skill, he broke free from the stake, put the men to flight, and retreated to the Himalayas."[63] Nevertheless, the damage has already been done: An elephant never forgets, and this elephant remains deeply haunted by his experience at humanity's hands:

> There [in the forest], the elephant was still terrified of dying. Hearing the sound of the wind, he would tremble, and terrified by the fear of death (P. *maraṇa-bhaya-tajjito*), he would run away at full speed, with his trunk shaking. For him, it was as if he were still tied to that stake and still being trained in the skill of imperturbability. He wandered about trembling, experiencing no enjoyment of body or mind.[64]

The bodhisattva in this story is a tree-spirit who warns the elephant that the sound of the wind is so omnipresent that "if you're afraid of that, you will constantly be terrified; your flesh and blood will wither away, and you'll waste away into nothing"[65]—just as crows are unable to hold onto any fat, so overcome are they by fear. In Chapter 2, we saw a venomous snake and a fierce buffalo willfully starving themselves to death in a symbolic negation of animality itself. Here, we see that even when free from human control, an overbearing *fear* of humanity remains, and may have something of the same effect.

Animal Sacrifice

One of the most defining markers of the various non-Brahmanical *śramaṇa* movements from which Buddhism first arose was not only their denial of the divine authority of the Vedic revelation, but also their utter repudiation of the practice of animal sacrifice prescribed and required by Vedic texts. The Buddha's rejection of animal sacrifice is well known from the discourses of the Pāli *suttas*. In the *Kūṭadanta Sutta* of the *Dīgha Nikāya*,[66] for example, the Buddha, in conversation with the brahmin Kūṭadanta, criticizes the practice of animal sacrifice (as well as its negative effects upon human beings and the larger environment) by describing an ideal sacrifice undertaken long ago by King

Mahāvijita (under the guidance of his brahmin chaplain, who was the Buddha himself in a previous life):

> Indeed, in that sacrifice, Brahmin, no bulls were killed, no goats or sheep were killed, no chickens or pigs were killed, nor did various living beings meet with slaughter. No trees were cut down to make sacrificial posts, no grass was cut to make sacrificial grass, and none of those who are called "slaves," "servants," or "workers" were made to work, terrified of the staff and terrified with fear, crying, and with their faces full of tears. Rather, those who wanted to work worked, and those who did not want to work did not work—and they did what they wanted to do, not what they did not want to do. And the sacrifice was carried out with ghee, oil, butter, yogurt, honey, and sugarcane alone.[67]

The Buddha then goes on to describe several other types of "sacrifice" that are even better than King Mahāvijita's vegetarian offerings: supporting the Sangha, going for refuge to the three jewels, taking the five moral precepts—and, best of all, going forth from home into homelessness to follow the Buddha's teaching and attain nirvana. "Brahmin," the Buddha concludes, "this sacrifice is less work, less effort, greater in fruit, and greater in profit than any of the former sacrifices. Compared to the benefits of this sacrifice, Brahmin, the benefits of no other sacrifice are better or greater."[68] This redefinition of Vedic sacrifice in terms of Buddhist asceticism and spiritual cultivation became a common trope in Buddhist discourse.

The Buddha further condemns animal sacrifice in a passage from the *Aṅguttara Nikāya*, in which he notes that "one who prepares the sacrificial fire and raises up the sacrificial post, even before the sacrifice itself, is raising up three swords that are unwholesome and will result and ripen into suffering." These are "the sword of the body, the sword of speech, and the sword of the mind." For the "sword of the mind," the Buddha notes that "even before the sacrifice itself, one gives rise to such a thought as this: 'Let so many bulls be slaughtered for the sacrifice! Let so many male calves . . . so many female calves . . . so many goats . . . so many sheep be slaughtered for the sacrifice!' " Likewise, the "sword of speech" occurs when he actually says these things aloud, and the "sword of the body" occurs when he prepares to do these things. All three of these swords are "unwholesome and will result and ripen into suffering," and the man who raises these swords is deluded, for "he thinks he is making merit, but he is making demerit. He thinks he is doing something wholesome, but he is doing something unwholesome. He thinks he is seeking the path to a fortunate destiny, but he is seeking the path to an unfortunate destiny."[69]

In these and other such passages from the *suttas*, animal sacrifice is clearly condemned, yet the focus is upon its ineffectiveness—the fact that it *doesn't work*—and its negative consequences *for the sacrificer* in the form of karmic retribution. No attention is paid to the pain, suffering, or voice of the sacrificial animal itself.[70] This is precisely the perspective that is added, however, when we turn to the Pāli *jātakas*. With their animal-centric focus, the *jātakas* dealing with animal sacrifice shift our perspective from the sacrificer to the sacrificial animal to give the animal a voice and reveal the animal's pain and suffering. In the process, these *jātakas* also succeed in blurring the distinction between *sacrificer* and *sacrificed*, thus enabling a sense of communion, kinship, and empathy between human beings and animals.

Thus, in the *Matakabhatta Jātaka* (No. 18),[71] a brahmin is preparing a goat for a public sacrifice before a great crowd of people when he hears the animal first laugh and then weep. Right away, we are struck by the fact that the sacrificial animal is given a *voice*, and the sacrifice is thereby interrupted. This being a *jātaka,* moreover, the animal is also endowed with the human power of speech. Thus, when the brahmin asks the goat why he first laughed and then wept, the goat is able to respond:

> Brahmin, at one time, I was a brahmin well-versed in the Vedic scriptures just like you. Thinking that I would make an offering for my ancestors, I killed a goat and made the offering. And because I killed that single goat, I have had my own head cut off in 499 existences. This is the 500th and final existence [in which I will suffer this punishment]. Realizing that today I would become free of such suffering, I was full of joy, and this is

> why I laughed. But then I thought to myself, "Just as I have endured the suffering of having my head cut off in 500 existences because I killed a single goat . . . this brahmin, having killed me, will likewise endure the [same] suffering. . . ." And feeling pity for you, I cried.[72]

Rather than the Buddha stating abstractly that animal sacrifices result in negative karmic consequences, here we are given the violent image of a goat having its head cut off in 500 successive rebirths—and we are told of this truth from the mouth of the goat himself. We also see here the direct reciprocity between *sacrificer* and *sacrificed*: he who was once the human *sacrificer* will soon become the animal *sacrificed.* The distinction between sacrificer and sacrificed is blurred, and the communion between them is furthered by their shared ability to laugh, weep, and speak. The brahmin, as we might expect, immediately puts a stop to the sacrifice.

The bodhisattva in this story is neither the brahmin nor the goat, but rather a nearby tree-deity, who now thinks to himself, "If these beings were to know the fruit of such evil deeds, perhaps they would not take life." Seating himself cross-legged in midair, he recites a canonical verse for the benefit of the assembled crowd: "If living beings knew that this is the cause of a birth into suffering, then no living being would kill another living being—for one who takes a life soon regrets it."[73] This abstract statement of karmic consequences comes from the mouth of the bodhisattva—a mere bystander—but it originates from the voice and concrete circumstances of the sacrificial animal itself. The power implicit in this origin has its desired effect—for the story concludes with the statement that from then on, everyone in the crowd refrained from taking life. The voice and emotions of the goat here strike us as more powerful motivators than the abstract pronouncements of the future Buddha.

The communion between human beings and animals is realized in a different but equally powerful manner in the *Lomasakassapa Jātaka* (No. 433).[74] Here, a saintly ascetic named Kassapa is offered the king's daughter in marriage if he will only agree to perform a violent animal sacrifice. Overtaken by lust and passion for the beautiful princess, he falls away from his state of virtue and agrees to do the sacrifice. But just as he is raising his sword to bring it down upon the neck of an elephant,

> the elephant, seeing this, was terrified by the fear of death (P. *maraṇa-bhaya-tajjita*) and let out a great cry. And hearing this cry, the rest of the elephants, horses, bulls, and other animals, terrified by the fear of death, also cried out in fear. And the great crowd of people likewise cried out in fear.[75]

Here, it is not human language that bridges the gap between human beings and animals, but rather the equal tendency of both humans and animals to cry out when overcome by fear (in fact, verb forms related to the root *rav*, "to cry out," are used for both the humans and the animals). Hearing this cacophony of nonlinguistic cries, Kassapa is "shaken to the bone" (P. *saṃvega-ppatto*):

> Then he looked down [at himself] and realized that he, too, had matted hair, a beard, and body hair like grass. Full of remorse, he thought to himself, "Alas! I am doing an evil and unworthy deed!"[76]

In this case, it is the realization that both human beings and animals have bodies that are covered with hair—and both erupt into guttural noises when shaken by the fear of imminent death—that bridges the gap between sacrificer and sacrificed and puts an immediate end to the slaughter. This realization is brought about by the fearful cries of the animals, which then spread among the humans in attendance as well. The animals here may not *speak*, but—as is usual in the *jātakas*—they are still given a *voice*. The Buddhist critique of animal sacrifice seems to gain in power and poignancy when it comes from the mouths of the animals themselves.

Crime, Punishment, and Execution

The turn of the twentieth century in the United States saw the rise of a remarkable and odd phenomenon, in which dozens of captive elephants (belonging to circuses, zoos, or parks) who had killed or injured human beings or otherwise become dangerous were put to death—executed, in fact—often before large crowds of cheering spectators. There was Albert in 1885, executed by firing squad before a crowd of two thousand spectators in Keene, New Hampshire. There was Tip in 1894, strangled by a noose in Bridgeport, Connecticut, after an earlier dose of cyanide failed to do the trick. There was Mary in 1916, hung from a railroad crane in Erwin, Tennessee, her hanging corpse immortalized in a widely distributed photograph.[77] And, most famous of all, there was Topsy, electrocuted by 6,600 volts of electricity before a large crowd at Coney Island—an execution filmed by the Edison Film Company and still available for gruesome viewing on YouTube.[78]

While putting dangerous animals to death was nothing new, "what is fascinating"—as Amy Louise Wood observes in her analysis of this phenomenon—"is that the killings of these animals were not infrequently staged as public executions, with the elephant playing the role of the menacing criminal facing his just rewards before a crowd of eager witnesses," and with news reports portraying them as "stories of murder, remorse, and retribution."[79] Thus, newspapers described Topsy's death as an "execution" and said that she had "paid the death penalty" for the three "murders" she had committed. As Topsy was led to the execution ground, people in the crowd looked for signifiers of remorse and repentance, and the elephant complied by revealing "grave apprehension as to what the occasion meant" and showing signs that she recognized "the solemnity of the situation."[80] The elephant Tip was likewise described as having been "tried and convicted"; officials read out the "indictment" for his crimes, and he was strangled "like a murderer on the scaffold."[81] Rather than attributing the elephants' violence to instinct or the conditions of captivity, moreover, people searched for "rational, human-like explanations ... such as jealousy, frustration, or anger."[82] The violence committed by an elephant named Black Diamond, for example, was attributed to his "love-crazed" nature and the fact that he was overcome with jealousy because his former keeper had become enamored of a certain woman.[83] Thus, in stark contrast to the idea that animals are lacking in moral agency, these elephants were attributed with an independent will and viewed as being morally culpable for their deeds. (As one local man observed after the execution of Mary, "She paid for her crimes as anyone else would.")[84] Some elephants were even executed in the presence of other elephants, so that their deaths would serve as a deterrence. In 1899 an elephant named Nick was strangled with a noose "in view of all the other elephants, possibly as a sort of warning to them of the result of disobedience."[85]

Far from being reduced to irrational and unthinking brutes, these executed elephants were profoundly *humanized* so they could be subject to the language of moral guilt, criminal punishment, and execution. While Wood's analysis attributes this phenomenon to certain features characteristic of turn-of-the-century America—such as the disappearance of public executions (for human criminals) and a growing fascination with modern technology such as electricity—the human desire to hold animals morally and legally accountable for the harms they cause to human beings, even when it conflicts with dominant understandings of animal intelligence, is perhaps more universal in nature. As Wood herself notes, it was relatively common in medieval Europe, for example, to prosecute domestic animals in legal courts and execute them publicly for the injuries they had caused to human beings.[86] In modern-day America, the growing criminalization of pit bulls perhaps bears something of the same significance.[87] The human desire for vengeance and restorative justice is thereby played upon and satisfied through the helpless bodies of animals—even as human beings denigrate their moral and cognitive worth. Animals who are otherwise believed to act solely out of instinct are suddenly attributed with an independent will that *chooses* to behave immorally and to violate the law. Just as we love some animals and dine on others, this is yet another manifestation of humanity's contradictory treatment of the animal world.

In ancient India, it was the king who had the authority to administer legal punishments and order executions (the branch of knowledge known in Sanskrit as *daṇḍa-nīti*), and several *jātakas* feature kings who order the execution of animals. One particularly interesting example is the *Kukkura Jātaka* (No. 22),[88] in which a king discovers that the leather fixings of his chariot have been chewed upon and ruined by dogs. He quickly issues an order—"Kill dogs wherever you see them!"—which results in "a great slaughter of dogs."[89] The fact that a crime has been committed, that property has been destroyed, and that the king is sitting in his "Hall of Judgment" (P. *vinicchaya*) when the execution order is given clearly suggests that this is a legal issue of crime and punishment: Despite their supposed lack of moral agency, dogs are found guilty of a crime against the king; therefore, they should be punished by execution, which the king alone has the legal authority to demand. The bodhisattva in this story is the leader of a pack of several hundred stray dogs who eke out a living in a cemetery. As the execution gets underway, these dogs (who are innocent of the crime in question) become terrified and quickly resort to the bodhisattva for help. Just as we saw in the case of the executed elephants, human convenience here demands that irrational animals be suddenly transformed into criminals who have violated the law of the king.

Unlike Albert, Tip, Mary, and Topsy, however, the bodhisattva belongs to the magical world of the *jātakas*—a world in which animals *speak* and can thereby engage human beings in a contest of wits, which in this case consists of taking the human notions of crime and punishment unfairly projected onto them and turning them back upon the humans themselves. Making his way to the palace and gaining an audience with the king through his powers of benevolence (P. *mettā*), the bodhisattva engages the king in a sophisticated discussion of crime, punishment, and human notions of justice:

> "Lord, is it you who are having the dogs killed?"
>
> "Yes, it is I."
>
> "Lord of Men, what is their offense?"
>
> "They have chewed up the straps and leather attached to my chariot."
>
> "Do you know [exactly] *who* has done the chewing?"
>
> "No, I don't know."
>
> "Lord, without knowing exactly which ones have stolen and chewed up the leather, it isn't right to have all dogs killed wherever they are seen."

"Because it was dogs who chewed up the leather of my chariot, I have ordered dogs to be executed, commanding that *all* of them are to be killed, wherever they are seen."

"But are your men killing *all* of them, or are there some who are not being killed?"

"There are some: the purebred dogs in my household are not being killed."

"Great King, just now you said that because it was dogs who chewed up the leather of your chariot, you have ordered dogs to be executed, commanding that *all* of them are to be killed, wherever they are seen—and yet now, you are saying that the purebred dogs in your household are not being killed. This being the case, you are following the [four] evil courses of passion, [hatred, delusion, and fear][90]—and these evil courses are not right, they are not the Dhamma of kings! A king, when deciding on a punishment, should be [as impartial] as a scale. But in this case, purebred dogs are not being killed, and only weak dogs are being killed; therefore, this is not the execution of all dogs—it is the murder of weak dogs!"

. . . And teaching the Dhamma to the king, he spoke this verse:

"The dogs who have grown up within the royal household,
the purebred dogs endowed with beauty and strength—
They are not being executed; only we are being executed.
This is not true execution; this is the murder of the weak!"[91]

Once again, we find in the *jātakas* not only the human oppression of animals, but also animals' ability, through the powers of speech and reasoning, to turn this oppression into a contest of wits: "If you're going to turn *us* into quasi-human beings endowed with moral agency," the bodhisattva seems to suggest, "then you yourself must adhere to the moral conduct—the Dhamma—involved in administering crime and punishment." By ordering the execution of *all* dogs when only *some* dogs have committed the crime—and by exonerating the palace dogs (who are later proven to be the culprits)—the king himself becomes guilty of a crime. Far from exercising his authority to administer legal punishments, he is, in fact, committing "murder."

The bodhisattva's clever words also illustrate another faulty feature of the king's reasoning: his failure to distinguish between the *individual* and the *species*. If animals are endowed with moral agency and can be judged to be "guilty" of committing a particular "crime," then they must be judged as *individuals*, not as an entire species. The king treats the dogs as individualized legal persons when he subjects them to the legal punishment of execution, but he reverts to treating them as a species when he orders the execution of *all* dogs, rather than finding out which specific dogs are guilty. (This would be equivalent to ordering the execution of all human beings whenever a single human being commits a crime.) An element of social class also enters the mix: only the "weak" stray dogs who have no owner are being killed, while the pampered dogs of the palace escape from any punishment. We might even compare this to the current controversies surrounding pit bull ownership in the United States: Just as breed-specific legislation (BSL) unfairly discriminates against entire breeds of dogs (often in a highly racialized manner) rather than focusing on dangerous dogs individually (or, better yet, their often irresponsible human owners), the king of the *Kukkura Jātaka* is guilty of the same injustice. ("Punish the deed, not the breed"—as those who are opposed to BSL are fond of saying.) In a world of speaking animals, however, it is the dogs themselves who are able to make this clear. Through the powers of speech, rational argument, and legal reasoning, even a lowly stray dog who lives in a cemetery can condemn the king himself.

Translating Animals

Cooking, eating, hunting, sacrificing, and executing do not exhaust the range of harms inflicted upon animals in the *jātakas*. So many other examples could be cited—work animals who are overworked and abused;[92] elephants who are mutilated for monetary gain;[93] a swan who is stoned through both eyes, just for kicks;[94] a crow whose feathers are plucked out in revenge;[95] and baby birds who are squeezed to death by careless children.[96] In lieu of exploring any further themes, however, I will conclude with one final *jātaka* that might be seen as offering a representative snapshot of "(human) nature, red in tooth and claw," as well as returning us once again to the theme of animal sounds, human language, and the difficulties of translation.

In the *Aṭṭhasadda Jātaka* (No. 418),[97] the king of Benares is sitting on his bed in the middle of the night when he hears eight ominous sounds that fill him with fear; these sounds are made by a crane, a female crow, an insect, a cuckoo, a deer, a monkey, a *kinnara*, and a *paccekabuddha* (S. *pratyekabuddha*). Terrified, the king consults his brahmin ministers, and the brahmins—greedy for gain—tell the king that these sounds portend great danger for the kingdom, which can only be averted by sacrificing hundreds of living animals. As preparations for the massive animal sacrifice get underway, a young brahmin pupil begins to object, but the other brahmins silence him: "What do you know, Son? Even if nothing else comes of it, at least we'll get a lot of fish and meat to eat!"[98] The young brahmin sets out to find a truly pious ascetic who might be able to interpret the sounds correctly and thus avert the impending slaughter of animals.

Sure enough, in the king's garden, he finds an ascetic—the bodhisattva—who correctly interprets the sounds (only the first six of which will concern us here): The first sound was made by a crane (P. *baka*) living in the king's pleasure-park, who wished to convey that she is now starving to death because the king's men no longer stock the park's pond (which is the crane's "ancestral home")[99] with fresh water and fish. The second sound was made by a female crow (P. *kākī*) living in the doorway of the king's elephant stables, who cried "out of grief for her son"—because whenever the cruel elephant-keeper passes through the doorway, "he strikes the crow and her babies with his elephant hook and destroys their nest."[100] The third sound was made, out of hunger, by a wood-eating insect (P. *ghuṇapāṇaka*) trapped in the roof-peak of the palace. Having eaten all of the soft wood and unable to chew through the hard, he is devoid of any food source, yet unable to escape. The fourth sound was made by a cuckoo (P. *kokilā*) kept in a cage by the king: "Suddenly remembering and longing for the dense jungle where she used to live—wondering, 'Oh when will I be released from this cage and go to the delightful jungle?' "[101]—she cried out of longing for her former home. The fifth sound was made by a deer (P. *miga*) kept captive in the palace, who cried out of longing for his former life as the leader of a herd in the forest. And the sixth sound was made by a monkey (P. *makkaṭa*) kept captive in the palace, as he remembered his former life in the Himalayas, when he "wandered around, mad with passion for the female monkeys."[102] In truth, the king has nothing at all to fear from these sounds—they do not portend any danger to him. Instead, they are expressions of animal suffering at the hands of human beings, which the king himself has the power to ameliorate. In response to the bodhisattva's explanation, the king calls off the animal sacrifice, takes the necessary action to eliminate each animal's suffering, and grants security to all animals within his kingdom.[103]

Unlike the majority of the animal *jātakas,* which feature animals who speak, in this case, each animal has uttered an ordinary animal sound, and it is the bodhisattva who must "translate" each sound into human language that the king can understand (with each "translation" becoming a canonical verse). In the case of the cuckoo, for example, the cuckoo's plaintive call is "translated" to mean: "Oh, when will I leave from here, released from the king's palace? When will I enjoy myself, living in the branch of a tree?"[104] Only when he is provided with the correct "translation" is the king able to respond with generosity and compassion, releasing his captive animals and taking care of those who remain.

In this way, the *Aṭṭhasadda Jātaka* effectively suggests that when animals cry out in their ordinary animal sounds, these sounds are self-servingly misinterpreted by greedy human beings (like the ministers), who respond to them with wholesale acts of abuse and exploitation, such as the animal sacrifice the king is about to carry out. If we only had the wisdom to "translate" such sounds correctly, however, they would tell us a very different tale—a tale of rampant human cruelty toward animals and a longing, on the part of animals, to simply be *left alone*. The animal *jātakas* are unique among Buddhist literature in their ability to grant us such a translation. Moreover, the fact that it is the bodhisattva himself who serves here as the consummate translator suggests that there *is* a Buddhist voice speaking up in defense of animals—and standing in marked contrast to the lowly depiction of animals we saw in Chapter 1.

CHAPTER FOUR

Animal Saviors

Human beings are stupid
and do not see the noble Dhamma.

(Garahita Jātaka)[1]

As we have seen, the *jātakas* featured in Chapter Three condemn humanity for its oppression and abuse of the animal world, as well as portraying an alternative world in which thinking and speaking animals have the ability to contest this abuse through a closely matched contest of wits. Other *jātakas* in the Pāli collection go significantly further than this, however, by depicting animals who are not only clever, but also *virtuous*—and whose virtue is intentionally contrasted with a lack of virtue in the human beings around them. This contrast between *virtuous animals* and *nonvirtuous human beings* is a common trope that uses the exaggerated virtue of a supposedly inferior animal to make a biting comment about the shortcomings of humankind. The bite is intensified, in many cases, by depicting an animal who compassionately saves the life of a human being—only to be met by human ingratitude and wickedness. Since *gratitude* (S. *kṛtajña*) was sometimes cited as one of the qualities that distinguishes human beings from animals—the *Dazhidulun* or *Mahāprajñāpāramitā Śāstra* attributed to Nāgārjuna, for example, states that "those who do not know gratitude are beasts"—the contrast between a compassionate animal and an ungrateful man becomes a potent way of highlighting human beings' inhumanity.[2]

In the *Sīlavanāga Jātaka* (No. 72),[3] a magnificent white elephant "adorned with the ten perfections" is contrasted with a "wicked" (P. *pāpa*) and "backstabbing" (P. *mitta-dubbhin*) man. When the man gets lost in the wilderness and cannot find his way home, the elephant, out of compassion, saves his life by bringing him back to the "haunts of men" (P. *manussa-patha*). Far from being grateful, however, the greedy man goes straight to the ivory-workers' quarters and asks them how much they will pay for the tusks of a living elephant. He then returns to the elephant three times in a row—first sawing off the elephant's tusks, then removing the stumps of the tusks, then gouging into the flesh itself to retrieve every last ounce of ivory, with each gift being freely offered up by the compassionate elephant.[4] A nearby tree-spirit, observing this scene, utters the canonical verse: "An ungrateful man always sees what he lacks. Even if you gave him the whole world, he still wouldn't be satisfied."[5] As we might expect, the elephant is a previous birth of the Buddha, while the wicked man is a previous birth of Devadatta. Just as Devadatta was ungrateful and backstabbing to the Buddha in the present lifetime, he also was in the past. Above and beyond these identifications, however, the animal status of the kind and compassionate elephant serves as an effective foil for the wickedness of the man. If even an *animal* can be so compassionate, the story asks, how can a *human being* possibly be so wicked?

The animal-human contrast is invoked more explicitly in another tale of human ingratitude, the *Ruru Jātaka* (No. 482).[6] Here, a magnificent golden deer saves a man from drowning and shows him the way back to human civilization. Again, the man proves to be ungrateful, for he immediately goes to the king and offers to lead him to where a golden deer might be shot. The king is just about to shoot the golden deer, when the deer utters an enigmatic verse of censure against the man who has betrayed him. The king then asks him, "O Deer, who among the wild animals, birds, or human beings do you blame? Great fear takes hold of me when I hear you speak like a human." "Great King," the deer responds,

> I do not blame a wild animal or a bird—I blame a human being!
> . . . The very one whom I rescued as he was being swept along
> by a great torrent of swift, rushing water—

because of *him* has danger come upon me.
Indeed, King, association with the lowly leads to suffering.[7]

Overturning our assumptions about what kind of being is "lowly" (P. *asabbhin*), the deer uses the power of human speech to make it clear that neither animals nor birds have put him in this predicament, but human beings alone.[8]

The themes of rescue and ingratitude are similarly present in the *Saccaṃkira Jātaka* (No. 73),[9] a story that adheres to the common cross-cultural tale type involving "grateful animals and ungrateful man" (Aarne-Thompson-Uther Tale Type 160).[10] Here, a wicked man (his name is even Prince Wicked), a snake, a rat, and a parrot are all clinging for dear life to a log being swept down a river during a terrible storm. All four beings are saved by a kindly ascetic who wades into the raging river to rescue them and bring them to his hermitage. When the ascetic first offers food to the three animals—since "they are weaker"—and only afterwards offers it to Prince Wicked, the prince thinks to himself in anger, "This fake ascetic pays honor to mere animals, without regarding the fact that I am a royal prince!"[11] Offended by the ascetic's failure to recognize his superior human status, Prince Wicked remains ungrateful for his rescue, while the animals are full of thanks. The snake, rat, and parrot all offer the ascetic abundant gifts of thanks, whereas the prince (upon their next meeting) tells his minions to "grab [the ascetic], tie his arms behind his back, beat him at every intersection, drive him out of the city, cut his head off at the execution ground, and impale his body on a stake!"[12] The ungratefulness of the human prince is thus effectively contrasted with the gratefulness of the animals[13]—especially since snakes, rats, and birds are relatively lowly animal forms, while a prince is a high-status human being—and this contrast is heightened by the prince's own remark, which conveys a sense of human precedence and entitlement.

The ironic contrast between virtuous animals and a wicked human being is extended even further in the canonical verse uttered by the saintly ascetic (as he is being led to his execution): "People in the world have surely spoken truly when they said: 'A log thrown into the water is better than some men.'"[14] Thus, not only are *animals* capable of better behavior than wicked human beings, but even an *inanimate object* like a *log* can be judged superior—for, as the word commentary explains, such a log can at least be used for cooking or to warm oneself up (not to mention saving oneself from drowning). The ordinary hierarchy of inanimate objects → animals → human beings (a hierarchy of intelligence and mental faculties) is thus subverted in order to emphasize the depths of moral wickedness to which humanity may fall.

We find a similar invocation of the greater virtue of inanimate objects in comparison to the wicked human being in the *Nandiyamiga Jātaka* (No. 385),[15] yet another story involving the theme of kings hunting for deer. Here, a king traps a herd of deer in a hunting-grove for the sole purpose of shooting one deer every day. In spite of this cruel treatment, a deer named Nandiya feels *grateful* to the king for providing the grove with regular food and water. When his turn comes to be shot, therefore, he willingly stands immobile and turns his massive flank directly toward the king's arrows. Overcome by this magnificent display of virtue, the king finds that he is physically unable to shoot the arrow: "Even this unthinking arrow of wood," he declares to the deer, "immediately recognizes your virtue, while I fail to recognize your virtue, even though I am a human being endowed with the power of thought. Forgive me, Deer-King, I grant you security."[16] In this way, human thought—the very quality that defines the human being as morally superior, according to Buddhist doctrine—is shown to be weaker in responding to virtue than an "unthinking" arrow of wood.

One final effective use of the contrast between virtuous animals and nonvirtuous human beings can be found in the *Mahākapi Jātaka* (No. 516).[17] Here, a man gets lost in the wilderness and wanders without food for seven days, then falls into a deep abyss and languishes there for another ten days. A compassionate monkey rescues the man by physically carrying him out of the abyss (first practicing with a large stone to make sure that he can bear the man's weight). This effort leaves the monkey exhausted, so he asks the man to watch over him while he rests, since "lions, tigers, panthers, bears, wolves, and hyenas—they could kill me while I am not on guard. If you see them, you must stop them."[18] The monkey himself thus confirms our easy assumption that it is dangerous *animals* we need to be worried about, while the human being can be trusted to guard and protect. This assumption is immediately overturned, however, when the man, standing over the peacefully sleeping monkey, thinks to himself, "This [monkey], like other wild animals in the forest, is food for men. Since I am hungry, why don't I kill and eat this monkey?"[19] He picks up a rock and bashes the monkey in the head—but the monkey is alert enough to escape into a tree. "Smeared with blood" and "crying, with his eyes full of tears," the monkey cries out to the man in shocked disbelief:

> Alas, you wretched man who has committed such an evil deed!—
> and after I pulled you out of such a dangerous and difficult abyss!
> Brought back from the other world, you only thought of injuring me.
> And through that evil thought, you conceived of an evil deed.[20]

How wicked can a human being possibly be?, the monkey seems to be asking. And yet he is still compassionate, viewing the man "as if he were his own beloved son" and worrying about his karmic future: "Evil-Doer," he says to the man, "may terrible sufferings not afflict you! May your evil deed not kill you, as its fruit kills the bamboo tree!"[21] Repaying cruelty with kindness, the monkey is still willing to lead the man safely out of the forest and back to the haunts of humankind (see Figure 4.1).

His last remark to the man, however, is bitingly sarcastic:

> You've escaped from the claws of predatory animals,
> you've reached the human world.
> This is the path, Evil-Doer. Take it as you please.[22]

In this way, the story subtly asks the question, Who are the *real* predatory animals here? And as the man leaves the forest, *who* is escaping from *whom*?

In many *jātakas* of this type, the virtuous animal in question is a previous birth of the Buddha and displays the same kinds of virtues we would ordinarily expect (generosity, compassion, and self-sacrifice)

FIGURE 4.1.
Depiction of the *Mahākapi Jātaka* (*Jātakaṭṭhavaṇṇanā* No. 516). On the right: The ungrateful man raises a rock to smash the monkey's head. On the left: The monkey admonishes the ungrateful man. Cave 17, Ajaṇṭā. © Benoy K. Behl.

from any being traveling on the bodhisattva path, whether animal, human, or god. I am less interested in the use of animality in connection with the bodhisattva (or with specifically Buddhist values), however, than in the use of animality as an ironic comment on the moral depths to which humanity may fall. The animals of the *jātakas* use the human power of speech to speak about their own capacity for virtue, condemn the wickedness of the human beings around them, and thus blur the moral distinction between animals and human beings—suggesting once again that human moral superiority is not everything it's cracked up to be.

Animal Liberation?

A final step in what we might call the Pāli *jātakas*' "rehabilitation" of the animal occurs in those stories in which animals act as true *saviors*, converting the wicked human beings around them to goodness and virtue—and often saving the lives of animals in the process. This pattern is perhaps most clearly exemplified by the *Nigrodhamiga Jātaka* (No. 12).[23]

In this story, two herds of deer have been trapped in a hunting-grove by the king, and whenever the king and his men go hunting, many deer are injured in the ensuing chaos. The leaders of the two herds of deer thus agree with each other that they will minimize the violence by voluntarily offering up one deer every day, drawing lots and taking turns between the two herds. One day, the lot falls upon a pregnant doe. She begs the leader of her herd—a previous birth of Devadatta—to skip her turn until after she has given birth, but he refuses. She then resorts to the leader of the other herd—a previous birth of the Buddha—and he immediately agrees to take her place, willingly lying down with his own neck upon the chopping block. The man who comes to retrieve the daily offering of deer, surprised to see the magnificent golden deer-king himself upon the chopping block, goes and reports this to the king, whereupon the king comes and asks the deer-king why he is lying there. When he learns of the deer-king's compassionate self-sacrifice on behalf of a lowly doe, he is astounded that such virtue could be displayed by an animal. "Lord Deer-King of Golden Hue," he says, "I have never before seen anyone endowed with such forbearance, benevolence, and compassion—even among human beings! Therefore, I am pleased with you. Get up! I grant security to both you and the pregnant doe."[24] The deer-king then uses this momentary advantage to gradually win the security of all living beings:

> "Lord of Men, though the two of us have been granted security, what will the rest [of the deer in the park] do?"
>
> "I grant security to the rest, too, Lord."
>
> "Great King, though the deer in your pleasure-park have thus been granted security, what will all other deer do?"
>
> "I grant security to them, too, Lord."
>
> "Great King, now that deer have been granted security, what will other four-footed creatures do?"

"I grant security to them, too, Lord."

"Great King, now that four-footed creatures have been granted security, what will flocks of birds do?"

"I grant security to them, too, Lord."

"Great King, now that flocks of birds have been granted security, what will fish living in the water do?"

"I grant security to them, too, Lord."

Having thus entreated the king for the security of all living beings, the Great Being got up [from the chopping block], established the king in the five moral precepts, and said, "Great King, behave righteously toward mothers and fathers, sons and daughters, brahmins and householders, townsfolk and countryfolk. Behaving righteously and with impartiality, upon the breaking up of the body after death, you will go to a good destiny, the heavenly world." And having preached the Dhamma to the king with the grace of a buddha, he stayed in the pleasure-park for a few days, gave further instruction to the king, and then returned to the forest, surrounded by the herd of deer.[25]

Having pushed himself into the king's circle of moral concern through a display of more-than-human-like virtue, the deer-king then gradually extends this circle outward, beyond himself as an individual, until it encompasses the other deer in the pleasure-park, then deer in general, then four-footed creatures, then birds, and then fish—thus winning the "security of all living beings." His subsequent words to the king also go on to suggest that one's treatment of animals reverberates back up the same hierarchical ladder and has a salutary effect upon one's treatment of "mothers and fathers, sons and daughters, brahmins and householders, townsfolk and countryfolk"—in other words, human beings as well.

In this passage, we find what might be described as an inverted version of the "argument from marginal cases" frequently used in animal rights theory. The "argument from marginal cases" is perhaps most well-known from Peter Singer's classic 1975 work *Animal Liberation*.[26] In arguing for the basic moral principle of giving equal consideration to the interests[27] of all sentient beings, Singer makes use of "marginal" human beings to illustrate the illogicality of our current treatment of animals: If we justify our abuse and injury of other animals (through meat-eating, scientific experimentation, and other means) by recourse to their lower intelligence, lack of self-awareness, inability to use language, or any other such features, then we must be prepared to admit that the same treatment should be justified when enacted upon very young infants, the old and senile, or those with severe mental retardation—human beings whose measures, in all of these respects, are well below those of the higher animals. The fact that we shrink in horror from treating *any* human being—even the most "marginal"—in this way demonstrates that our justifications for the abuse of nonhuman animals are nothing but "pure speciesism" and "exactly the kind of arbitrary difference that the most crude and overt kind of racist uses in attempting to justify racial discrimination."[28] Singer's animal ethics are ultimately derived from the utilitarian moral philosophy of Jeremy Bentham, who himself made use of the argument from marginal cases. Writing in the late eighteenth century, Bentham stated,

> The French have already discovered that the blackness of the skin is no reason why a human being should be abandoned without redress to the caprice of a tormentor. It may one day come to be recognized that the number of the legs, the villosity of the skin, or the termination of the *os sacrum* are reasons equally insufficient for abandoning a sensitive being to the same fate. What else is it that should trace the insuperable line? Is it the faculty of reason, or perhaps the faculty of discourse? But a full-grown horse or dog is beyond comparison a more rational, as well as a more conversable animal, than an infant of a day or a week or even a month, old. But suppose they were otherwise, what would it avail? The question is not, Can they *reason*? nor Can they *talk*? but, Can they *suffer*?[29]

By invoking marginal cases such as the young infant or the severely retarded, these arguments effectively complicate the distinction between animals and human beings and demonstrate the illogicality of drawing any arbitrary, purely speciesist boundary between them.

The deer-king's strategy in the *Nigrodhamiga Jātaka* might be seen as the flip side of the arguments of Singer and Bentham, for rather than invoking the most *animal-like human being* one can imagine (an infant or a severely handicapped person), the story invokes the most *human-like animal* one can imagine—the bodhisattva himself, appearing in the form of a magnificent golden deer and displaying the virtues of generosity, compassion, and self-sacrifice. This strategy is also employed in the animal rights movement. One might compare it, for example, to the Great Ape Project founded by Peter Singer and others in 1993, which advocates for a United Nations Declaration of the Rights of Great Apes (including chimpanzees, bonobos, gorillas, and orangutans), based on their possession of rationality, self-consciousness, and other qualities characteristic of personhood.[30] But whether we invoke an animal-like human or a human-like animal, the effect is the same in both cases: The line between human beings and animals is complicated and blurred, and we are led to conclude that the only relevant criterion that should govern our moral treatment of others is each being's capacity to *suffer* (especially crucial, of course, in a Buddhist worldview): "The question is not, Can they *reason*? nor Can they *talk*? but, Can they *suffer*?"

Nor is the *Nigrodhamiga Jātaka* unique in making such an argument, for several other *jātakas* also involve a savior animal who converts the king through his exaggerated virtue and then uses this leverage to win the safety of all other animals—including the deer of the *Nandiyamiga Jātaka* (No. 385),[31] the deer of the *Ruru Jātaka* (No. 482),[32] the crow of the *Supatta Jātaka* (No. 292),[33] the crow of the *Kāka Jātaka* (No. 140), [34] and the dog of the *Kukkara Jātaka* (No. 22).[35] The fact that the human being who is converted is a *king* in all of these cases further heightens the contrast between virtuous animals and nonvirtuous human beings, suggesting that even a lowly and despised animal like a crow can teach and edify the most powerful human being—the king. The last two of these tales also employ an additional trope shared in common with several other *jātakas* involving virtuous animals who preach to kings: This is the suggestion that a king who has been converted to the side of virtue by an animal can then "purify" or cleanse his kingship and free it from its prior moral taint by having it *pass through* the hands of the virtuous animal. In the *Kāka Jātaka* (No. 140), after a crow has demonstrated to a king that it was wrong and immoral of him to order the summary execution of all crows, the king offers his very kingship to the crow, whereupon the crow immediately offers it back to the king. It is at this point that the king undertakes the five moral precepts and grants security to all living beings. We find a similar scenario in the *Kukkura Jātaka* (No. 22, discussed in Chapter 3), in which a king unfairly orders the execution of all dogs. After being censured by a dog for this unjust behavior, the king hands his white umbrella—an insignia of kingship—over to the dog. Holding the umbrella, the dog recites ten verses on righteous conduct to the king, admonishes him to be diligent, establishes him in the five moral precepts, and then returns the white umbrella to him—whereupon the king grants security to all living beings. In both stories, the suggestion is thus made that before the king can widen the circle of his moral concern to encompass animals as well as humans, the human institution of kingship itself—tainted by previous immoral conduct—must first be purified by being symbolically passed through the hands of the virtuous animal. The animals here do not literally *become* kings, but rather seem to serve as powerful devices through which the institution of kingship can be ritually purified.[36] Particularly effective in this regard is the *Sarabhamiga Jātaka* (No. 483),[37] for it begins with a king who is so good at hunting that "he did not even regard other men as worthy of being called 'Man' " (P. *manussa*).[38] But after his own life is saved when he is rescued from a deep pit by the very deer he was trying to shoot and kill, the king is deeply humbled and offers his kingship to the deer. "Great King," the deer responds, "I am an animal, what use do I have for kingship? If you have affection for me, observe the moral precepts that I have given you, and make the inhabitants of your kingdom observe them, too."[39] The mere *offer* of kingship to the animal is here sufficient, and the king succeeds in learning what *true* "Man"-liness (or, perhaps, true "Human"-ity, *manussa*) entails. And he learns this from an animal, who has no need for institutions such as kingship.

Since the king in ancient India was responsible for the administration of law and justice, we find here the remarkable suggestion that the human institutions of kingship, law, and justice might be purified when they have gone astray by refinding their moral compass in the more uncomplicated virtue of the animal. It is striking to note, in fact, that this constitutes an exact reversal of traditional Indian ideas regarding the origins of kingship. According to Kauṭilya's *Arthaśāstra,* for example, human beings invented kingship precisely in order to avoid being governed by the "law of the fish" (S. *matsya-nyāya*), which classical Indian thought posits as being *the* defining characteristic of the animal world—a cruel law of predation by which little fish are eaten by bigger fish, bigger fish are eaten by still bigger fish, and so on (what we would call the "law of the jungle"). "Oppressed by the law of the fish," Kauṭilya tells us, "people made Manu, the son of Vivasvat, king. They allocated to him as his share one-sixth of the grain and one-tenth of the merchandise, as also money. Subsisting on that, kings provide security to the subjects."[40] Elsewhere, he further observes that "when [the king] fails to dispense [punishment] ... it gives rise to the law of the fish—for in the absence of the dispenser of punishment, a weak man is devoured by a stronger man, and, protected by him, he prevails."[41] Thus, for the political philosopher Kauṭilya, the institution of kingship allows human beings to escape from their own beastly natures and rise above the cruel law of predator-and-prey. For these *jātakas,* in contrast, it is the virtue of the *animal* that is capable of purifying the tainted institution of kingship, ensuring that the king's punishment is administered with impartiality, and extending the king's protection and security beyond the kingdom's human subjects to encompass its animals as well.

In all of these stories, the virtuous animal who acts as a savior is always the bodhisattva, displaying the typical bodhisattva virtues of wisdom, compassion, and generosity. But rather than emphasizing the remarkable fact that the *bodhisattva* appears as an *animal*, I have attempted to shift our perspective on these stories by emphasizing the equally remarkable fact that the *animal* appears as the *bodhisattva*. In other words, my emphasis is upon the animal appearing as a thinking, speaking, and rational being who is able to condemn the wickedness of the human beings around him, convert them to the side of virtue, awaken them to the reality of animal suffering, purify their human institutions, and, in the process, often save the lives of other animals. We might even describe some of these tales as containing an incipient Buddhist theory of animal rights—one, moreover, that seems to violate some of the doctrinal assumptions concerning animals that we saw in Chapter 1. The animality of these animals is thus crucial, for far from serving merely as allegorical human beings within simple didactic tales teaching lessons of practical wisdom, the speaking animals of the Pāli *jātakas* speak *about* the suffering of animals and call upon their Buddhist readers to respond.

Do these animals speak in the voice of "Buddhism" or do they merely echo a sort of perennial "folk" wisdom deriving from the pre-Buddhist animal folklore of India? As I noted before, I do not subscribe to the view that the ultimate *origin* of a story is paramount, or that a pre-Buddhist origin in folklore or oral tradition is enough to designate a particular story "non-Buddhist" or "not really Buddhist." It is obvious, moreover, that the sentiments expressed by these animal saviors are intimately tied to the first of the five moral precepts, which prohibits the killing or injuring of any sentient being, and which is the very heart of Buddhist ethics—and there is ample evidence that the ethical lessons conveyed by these *jātakas* had a discernible effect. On the elite level, we can do no better than to point to King Aśoka (r. 269–232 BCE), who, under the influence of Buddhism, listed "abstention from killing living creatures" as one of four meritorious practices incumbent upon his subjects (in Rock Edict III); forbade the slaughter of a long list of different animals, including "all quadrupeds which are not useful or edible" (in Pillar Edict V); and even altered the dietary regimen within his own palace to lessen the consumption of meat (noting, in Rock Edict I, that "only three living creatures are killed daily [for the royal kitchens], two peacocks and a deer," and promising to eliminate even these in the future).[42] On the popular level, as well, multiple anthropological studies have confirmed that village Buddhists take the ethical lessons of these *jātakas* to heart.[43] To cite just one example, in his study of village Buddhism in 1970s Sri Lanka, Martin Southwold notes the following:

> In the early days of my fieldwork, before I had much idea of villagers and their Buddhism, I had asked a number of people what, as a Buddhist, is it that one has to do? Vividly I recall the answer I had got from several seemingly unsophisticated rustics: 'Well, sir, not to kill animals.' . . . How preposterous, I thought, that a philosophy so noble, rich and subtle as Buddhism is reduced by these clods to the level of a childish, ludicrous taboo![44]

It is only after several years of fieldwork and extensive reflections on the nature of "religion" itself that Southwold comes to conclude that this answer is "not half as daft as it had seemed"—and, in fact, might be seen as expressing "virtually the whole basis of Buddhism" with "exquisite economy."[45] The animals of the Pāli *jātakas* also speak with "exquisite economy"—speaking truth to power and avoiding the glib and slippery nature of human discourse and its attendant institutions.

Hear No Evil, Speak No Evil

I conclude this chapter (and Part II of this book) with the *Garahita Jātaka* (No. 219),[46] a story in which animals speak among themselves about the horrors of the human world. According to the "Story of the Present," this tale was related by the Buddha for the benefit of a monk who could not focus on anything because he was afflicted with passion and mired in discontent. "Monk," the Buddha says to him with some exasperation, "this passion has been censured in the past even by animals. Having gone forth in such a teaching, how can you be dissatisfied because of a passion that even animals have censured?"[47]

The Buddha then relates that long ago ("when Brahmadatta was reigning in Benares"), he was born as a monkey who was captured in the forest, brought to the king, and turned into a pet. He lived for many years within the king's palace, where he "came to learn a great deal about the ways of the human world." The king, being pleased by the monkey's faithful service, eventually releases him back into the forest. The other monkeys in the forest are deeply curious about the bodhisattva's life among the humans. They gather around him eagerly upon a rock-face, and the following conversation takes place:

> Then the monkeys said to him, "You must know about the ways of the human world. Tell us about them, we want to hear!"
>
> "Don't ask me about the ways of human beings."
>
> "No, please tell us, we want to hear!"
>
> The Bodhisattva said, "Human beings—even brahmins and khattiyas—[constantly] cry out, 'Mine! Mine!' They do not realize that because of impermanence, everything that exists will disappear. Listen, now, to the ways of those blind fools ...
>
> 'The gold is mine, the gold is mine!'—
> This is all they talk about, day and night.
> Human beings are stupid
> and do not see the noble Dhamma."[48]

Here, in an exact reversal of the sentiments we saw in Chapter 1, it is human beings rather than animals who lack the higher mental faculties and are thus incapable of realizing the truth of impermanence or other Buddhist teachings. It is human beings who fail to see the Dhamma. Instead, they spend their entire lives turning everything around them into "Mine! Mine!"—not only gold, as the word commentary clarifies, but also "every jewel of the ten varieties, the seven kinds of grain, the seven kinds of vegetables, everything in field and farm, and *both two-footed and four-footed creatures*."[49] Human dominance over both other human beings and nonhuman animals is thus revealed to be just one symptom of a pervasive human self-centeredness. Moreover, human abuse of animals is here linked directly with their inability to comprehend the Dhamma.

From the animal's point of view, human social institutions such as marriage also take on a bizarre and frightening cast. As the other monkeys listen raptly, the bodhisattva explains:

> There are two householders in each house.
> One of them has no beard, breasts that hang down,
> braided hair, and pierced ears,
> and she is bought for a high price.
> The other one beats the people [of the household].[50]

As the word commentary on this verse explains, the female in each household is "bought from her mother and father with a lot of money; then she is dressed up and adorned, placed into a vehicle, and brought to the house with a great retinue." As for the male in each household: "From the moment they arrive in his house, the householder strikes people such as slaves, servants, and so forth, with verbal daggers: 'Hey, you wicked male slave or female slave, don't do that!' Acting as if he owns them, he orders many people around." The commentary concludes: "Thus does the bodhisattva censure the human world, saying that there is much in the human world that is not right."[51]

By making its readers privy to a private conversation among the monkeys, the *Garahita Jātaka* thus succeeds in opening our eyes to the strange and frightening nature of human social institutions that lead inevitably to the power structures of gender, class, and caste—which are perceived with far more terror than the natural laws of predator and prey. The monkeys, in fact, react with horror to the bodhisattva's words:

> Hearing this, all of the monkeys cried out: "Stop talking! Stop talking! We have heard things that are not fitting to hear!" And they covered their ears tightly with both hands. And because they had heard something terrible in that place, they came to despise that place and went elsewhere. And that rock-face became known as the Rock-Face of Blame.[52]

Faced with the horrors of human domination over both animals and other human beings, the monkeys have heard enough. They clasp their hands over their ears and beg the bodhisattva to *stop talking*. The animals of the Pāli *jātakas* thus use the power of human speech to condemn the human world and its treatment of nonhuman animals. But ultimately, the horrific nature of what they speak about makes their speech lapse back into silence.

PART III

Animal Doubles of The Buddha

Introduction To Part III

I turn now to examine three animal characters that I refer to as "animal doubles of the Buddha." Unlike the speaking animals explored throughout Part II, these animals do not express themselves by means of human language, and are thus significantly less anthropomorphized than the chatty animals of the Pāli *jātakas*. Likewise, these animals do not function as saviors, nor do they preach the Dharma, nor do they display a degree of virtue that is superior to that of the human beings around them. In all of these ways, they are different from the highly anthropomorphized, speaking animals that I have focused on in Chapters 3 and 4.

Instead, these animals are closer in nature to the animals of the *Divyāvadāna* and *Avadānaśataka* (explored in Chapter 2), with whom they bear a number of similarities: First, they are *mute* and lack the power of human speech. Second, they seem to act primarily *as animals* rather than as allegorical human beings who speak, reason, and plan. And third, they all have transformative encounters with the Buddha that lead to their spiritual betterment. At first glance, it thus seems to make sense to place these animals within the same general category as the animals of Chapter 2—animals who improve their positions within the karmic hierarchy while still adhering to the constraints of an animal rebirth.

Nevertheless, these animals are distinct from the animals of Chapter 2 in two major ways. The first is that each one of them is a *named* and *individualized* being rather than a generic representative of its species. Unlike the "black snake," "parrot," "buffalo," and "geese" that we encountered in the *Avadānaśataka*, it is a specific horse named Kanthaka that will be featured in Chapter 5, and two specific elephants, named Pārileyyaka and Nāḷāgiri, that will be featured in Chapters 6 and 7, respectively. The significance of *naming* an individual animal is easy to see when we consider the difference, say, between a pet dog and a lab rat. I see my pet dog Dusty as a wholly unique individual rather than a generic representative of her species, and would therefore be upset if I came home one day to find that she had been replaced by some other dog. Her unique personality, her individual subjectivity, my relationship with *her* specifically, and her total non-interchangeability with any other dog are all embodied by the fact that she bears a *name.* In contrast, while a lab rat may be assigned a specific number (in order to keep track of the results of any experiments done upon it), it is generally not given a name. This is because the lab rat is not seen as an individual; instead, it is seen as a generic representative of its species, fully replaceable by other, similar lab rats. This deindividualization—which also creates the emotional distance that makes scientific experimentation upon animals easier—is indicated by the lab rat's lack of a name. The same thing goes, of course, for the chicken wrapped in plastic that we buy at the supermarket. If the chicken wore a tag that said "Dusty," it is likely that more of us would be vegetarians.

A similar contrast can be drawn between the generic animals of Chapter 2 and the named animals I will focus on in Chapters 5, 6, and 7. While the "black snake" of the *Avadānaśataka* could well be replaced by any other black snake, Kanthaka the horse could never be replaced by any other horse. He has his own unique personality and characteristics that distinguish him from all other horses, and his individuality is fully recognized by the human beings who interact with him—in particular, by the Buddha himself. In fact, the same is true of each of the three animals in this section: Each one is described at some length, and this stands in contrast to the minimal descriptions given for the animals of Chapter 2.

The second feature that distinguishes these animals (which is directly related to the first) is the significant role each one of them plays within the life-story of the Buddha—a role that is unique to that specific animal alone. Once again, we can draw a similar contrast as that given above: While the Buddha's encounter with the "black snake" in the *Avadānaśataka* takes place at some generic point in time and might well have taken place in a very similar manner with other animals at other times, the same is not true of his encounter, say, with the elephant Nāḷāgiri. That encounter was wholly unique in nature, taking place at a specific point in time, and not replaceable by any other, similar encounters—it has its own individual "personality," as it were. And the same goes for Kanthaka and Pārileyyaka. Thus, Kanthaka, Pārileyyaka, and Nāḷāgiri all distinguish themselves as *named* and *individualized* animal characters who interact with the Buddha in wholly unique ways.

Each one of these animals, I will further argue, can be seen as an "animal double of the Buddha"—in other words, a figure who illuminates the Buddha's character through identification, contrast, or parallelism with an animal "other." My interpretation of these animals as "doubles" or shadows of the Buddha is supported by the fact that in each case (as we will see), there is a clear attempt to *identify* the Buddha with the animal in question, while also highlighting the *differences* between them. Through this interplay of similarities and differences, the Buddha's own character is further illuminated.

As one illustrative example (drawn from the Hindu tradition) of the use of such animal "doubles" and how much they can contribute to the depiction of a character, I would point to Vālmīki's Sanskrit epic the *Rāmāyaṇa*, and its masterful depiction of the race of monkeys who aid the hero-god Rāma. Technically speaking, these are not ordinary monkeys, but rather *vānaras*—monkey-like supernatural creatures created by the gods themselves and possessing many divine and human qualities. Nevertheless, they do appear in the form of monkeys and are often spoken of as animals. Throughout the epic, as many scholars have noted, these monkey characters often seem to constitute "doubles" of the human heroes, simultaneously paralleling and contrasting their actions and decisions. The human/divine hero Rāma, for example, finds his "double" in the exiled monkey-king Sugrīva, for both characters have experienced the usurpation of their thrones by a brother and the forcible taking of their wives. Thus, when Rāma agrees to assassinate Sugrīva's brother Vālin in order to regain the throne of the monkey kingdom for Sugrīva—an act that has traditionally been considered one of the most morally problematic events in the epic—we see the extent to which Rāma *identifies* with Sugrīva and *uses* Sugrīva (his monkey "double") to act out his own repressed feelings of rage. Through the medium of the monkeys, as Wendy Doniger notes, "Rāma's unconscious mind is set free to take the revenge that his conscious mind does not allow him in the world of humans."[1] One of the consistent messages running throughout the *Rāmāyaṇa* epic, in fact, is that human beings are defined by their ability to repress and control feelings of both sexuality and aggression.[2] And this message is illuminated, over and over again, by the similar-yet-contrasting examples offered by the monkeys (as well as by the demons, or *rākṣasas*, who function similarly to the animal characters).[3] Animal characters thus allow the epic story to "try out alternative plots and personalities"—they provide "a kind of narrative thought experiment" and present us with "possibilities that no mere doubling by means of another human subplot could."[4]

While the use of animal "doubles" is a frequent strategy of narrative literature, the type of function such a "double" might fulfill can vary widely from one instance to another. Whereas the monkey Sugrīva can be seen as representing Rāma's unconscious impulses—or, perhaps, his *id*—it is equally easy to imagine a different animal character who might fulfill a very different kind of doubling. And the same goes for the Buddha: Kanthaka, Pārileyyaka, and Nāḷāgiri can all be seen as "doubles" of the Buddha, but as doubles, they function in very different ways. In the chapters that follow, I will use the concrete images of the *scapegoat*, the *mirror*, and the *billboard* to capture these different types of doubling—arguing that the horse Kanthaka serves as a *scapegoat* for the Buddha, the elephant Pārileyyaka serves as a *mirror* for the Buddha, and the elephant Nāḷāgiri serves as a *billboard* for the Buddha's powers and charisma. Finally, I will also point to some of the ways in which each animal's *animality* is crucial to his functioning as a "double." It is important, in other words, that these doubles are *animals*.

CHAPTER FIVE

Scapegoat for the Buddha

The Horse Kanthaka

Don't cry, Kanthaka, you've shown what a good horse you are!
Be patient, and this exertion of yours will quickly bear fruit.
(*Buddhacarita*)[1]

The magnificent horse Kanthaka, "eighteen hands in length ... and thoroughly white, like a bleached-out shell,"[2] plays a crucial role within the Buddha's life-story, for he is born at exactly the same moment as the bodhisattva, serves him throughout his youth, and then helps him to renounce the world in pursuit of the ultimate goal of buddhahood. Carrying the prince upon his back and allowing him to escape from the kingdom in the middle of the night, he is later dismissed by the prince on the banks of the Anomā River (along with the charioteer Chandaka). Depending upon the source, he either dies of heartbreak on the spot, or returns in grief to the city of Kapilavastu, where he becomes a convenient target for the prince's loved ones and their turbulent emotions regarding the prince's departure, dying soon thereafter. As the karmic reward for his assistance to the bodhisattva, Kanthaka is reborn as a deity in the Trāyastriṃśa heaven, where he lives in luxurious splendor and later recounts the tale of his exploits to the visiting monk Maudgalyāyana. The role played by Kanthaka in the bodhisattva's Great Departure is treated at length in most Buddha-biographies, including the *Nidānakathā, Buddhacarita, Lalitavistara, Mahāvastu, Saṅghabhedavastu* (of the *Mūlasarvāstivāda Vinaya*), and *Abhiniṣkramaṇa Sūtra* (T. 190), and his life as a deity is chronicled in both the *Mahāvastu* and the (Pāli) *Vimānavatthu*. My discussion draws freely upon all of these sources.

In thinking about the character of Kanthaka[3] and how he functions within the Buddha's biography, I have found it useful to interpret him as a "double" of the Buddha—an animal character who is closely identified with the Buddha (or, more accurately, the bodhisattva, the "buddha-to-be") and serves particular functions within the life-story. As mentioned in the Introduction, I will be arguing, moreover, that while Kanthaka, Pārileyyaka, and Nāḷāgiri all serve as "doubles" of the Buddha, they do so in slightly different ways, as *scapegoat, mirror*, and *billboard*. Kanthaka's *scapegoating* function is intimately related to his death, either at the moment when the bodhisattva dismisses him or slightly later, after he returns to Kapilavastu. My discussion in this chapter thus aims to answer the following questions: How and why is Kanthaka identified with the bodhisattva before and during the prince's Great Departure? What does the bodhisattva's relationship with his horse add to the Buddha's life-story? What function is served by Kanthaka's animality? What is the significance of his death, and how does he serve as the bodhisattva's scapegoat?

KANTHAKA IN THE GREAT DEPARTURE

Kanthaka is closely identified with the bodhisattva from the very moment of his birth through the tradition of the seven "co-natals" (S. *sahaja, sahajāta*)—seven people, animals, or objects that came into existence at exactly the same moment the bodhisattva was born, most of which were destined to play an important role within his life. Kanthaka is always included in this list, in addition to other crucial figures such as the "Mother of Rāhula" (who would become the bodhisattva's wife), Chandaka (his charioteer), and the Bodhi Tree (under which he would become a buddha).[4] While most likely intended to provide the bodhisattva with a complement to the famous "seven treasures" of a cakravartin monarch, the seven co-natals also have the effect of suggesting that the bodhisattva's future destiny is assured from the very moment of his birth, and that other living beings—including Kanthaka—must live parallel lives in order to play their necessary roles in the unfolding of this destiny. Kanthaka's status as a co-natal immediately elevates him above all other horses, as well as individualizing him such that he is no longer just a generic embodiment of the "horse" species. Kanthaka's uniqueness is further reinforced through the fact that he has a *name*, and through his elaborate physical description, which makes him worthy of being associated with the bodhisattva. Kanthaka is "an excellent horse, endowed with strength, spirit, speed, and good lineage" (*Buddhacarita*),[5] "white as a blooming white water-lily or bunch of jasmine, and beautiful as the full moon" (*Mahāvastu*).[6] His "limbs have the finest features," and he is "ready, swift-footed, and moves with the foremost grace" (*Mahāvastu*)[7]; in fact, he is "capable of traversing the entire universe from end to end . . . yet still make it back before breakfast-time to forage and eat his meal" (*Nidānakathā*).[8] Clearly not your ordinary horse!

Kanthaka features most centrally, of course, in the episode known as the bodhisattva's Great Departure (S. *mahābhiniṣkramaṇa*). The basic story is the same in all sources: Determined to "go forth from home into homelessness," Prince Siddhārtha (P. Siddhattha), in the middle of the night, wakes up his charioteer Chandaka (P. Channa) and asks him to prepare the horse Kanthaka. Overcoming various obstacles, and benefitting from the help of the gods, who have caused everyone in the palace to sink into a heavy slumber, the three of them succeed in passing through the locked gates of the city and escaping from the kingdom (see Figure 5.1). They travel through three territories in a single night, and arrive upon the banks of the Anomā River at sunrise, whereupon Siddhārtha dismisses Chandaka and Kanthaka to continue on his journey alone. As mentioned previously, Kanthaka either dies of grief on the spot, or returns with Chandaka to Kapilavastu, where he dies of grief shortly thereafter.[9]

The first thing we should notice is that throughout this sequence of events, Kanthaka is not merely an animal upon which the bodhisattva happens to ride, but is instead depicted as an active, conscious, and willing participant—one who is keenly aware of the bodhisattva's

FIGURE 5.1.
The Great Departure of Prince Siddhārtha, riding upon the horse Kanthaka. Railing pillar from Amarāvatī, 3rd c. CE. © The Trustees of the British Museum.

quest and closely identified with it. In the *Nidānakathā*, for example, as soon as Channa begins to saddle him, Kanthaka immediately understands: "This saddling is very tight; it is not like the saddling of other days, such as when we go to amuse ourselves in a pleasure-park. It must be that my master wishes to go forth on the Great Departure this very day!"[10] In response, he neighs loudly out of joy, and "the sound of it would have spread throughout the entire city, but the gods silenced it, so that nobody could hear it."[11] Once the bodhisattva has mounted Kanthaka, and Channa has grabbed onto his tail, they approach the city gate, which has been locked and bolted by King Suddhodhana in order to prevent the bodhisattva's departure. At this point, all three of them—the bodhisattva, Channa, and Kanthaka—formulate exactly parallel plans to leap over the wall if they have to, with Kanthaka thinking to himself, "If that gate does not open [by itself], I will leap up, with my master still sitting on my back, just as he is, and with Channa still grasping my tail, and jump over the city-ramparts!"[12] In the *Lalitavistara*, at the urging of the gods, Kanthaka tells himself, "There will be no danger, misfortune, or calamity for me, when I am carrying the World-Protector! Each and every deity celebrates [me], for I am the vehicle for the Guide of the World!"[13] In the *Vimānavatthu*, Kanthaka—now reborn as a deity and recounting this episode to the monk Maudgalyāyana (P. Moggallāna)—makes it clear what a willing participant he was, stating that upon hearing of the bodhisattva's determination to attain awakening, "I gave rise to abundant joy. I was happy and elated, and I fervently wished for [his words to come true]!"[14]—which the commentary glosses as, "I wished for it, I desired it, I agreed with it."[15] Throughout this sequence, then, there seems to be a concerted effort to fuse Kanthaka's will and motivation with those of the bodhisattva himself.

We should note, however, that in several other sources, Kanthaka actively tries to *prevent* the bodhisattva's departure. The disagreement between our sources on this matter seems to revolve around the proper interpretation of Kanthaka's *neighing*. In the *Nidānakathā*, as we have seen, Kanthaka neighs out of joy at the bodhisattva's renunciation, and the gods have to muffle the sound; the same is true in the *Abhiniṣkramaṇa*

Sūtra.[16] In the *Buddhacarita*, Kanthaka is again supportive of the bodhisattva's departure, but for this very reason he goes "without making any sound that would cause fear in the night or awaken the attendants . . . without neighing."[17] In the *Lalitavistara*, however, we are given a wholly different picture, for here, Chandaka instructs Kanthaka to neigh loudly in order to *prevent* the bodhisattva's departure; Kanthaka does so, but nobody wakes up because of the deep sleep they have been put into by the gods. In the *Mahāvastu*, this seems to be Kanthaka's own idea, for we are told that Kanthaka "neighed loudly, thinking that the sound of his neighing would wake up King Śuddhodhana and all of the people"[18]—but once again, people fail to wake up. The ambiguity of Kanthaka's neighing—a type of willful animal speech that human beings are unable to understand—perhaps results in some uncertainty regarding Kanthaka's attitude toward the prince's renunciation: Did he encourage it or oppose it? Why did he neigh, and what did this neighing mean? As we will see below, Kanthaka's neighing becomes a focus of anxious concern later on in the story as well. Regardless of how it is interpreted, Kanthaka's neighing again demonstrates his active involvement in the bodhisattva's Great Departure and his conscious awareness of the role he is being asked to play.

The bodhisattva himself also seems to recognize the importance of Kanthaka's assistance, for in several sources he speaks directly to the horse, asking Kanthaka to help him with his renunciation and giving him credit for the part he will play in bringing about the bodhisattva's buddhahood. In the *Buddhacarita*, the bodhisattva addresses Kanthaka at some length and explicitly states that those who contribute to an accomplishment must inevitably share in its fruits:

> So many times has the king mounted you to destroy his enemies in battle! O Best of Horses, act such that I, too, may attain the deathless state! . . . Those who are one's companions here in this world, whether in impure deeds or commitment to dharma—they, too, are surely entitled to a share of the fruits. . . . Therefore, Excellent Horse, realizing that my departure from here is in accordance with dharma and for the benefit of the world, exert yourself with speed and valor, both for your own welfare and that of the world![19]

In the *Saṅghabhedavastu*, the bodhisattva similarly acknowledges the role Kanthaka plays, telling him that "when I have awoken to perfect full awakening, I will be grateful to you."[20] In such passages, Kanthaka appears not as an ordinary beast of burden who cannot help but respond to the master's whip, but rather as a fully autonomous actor who has the *choice* to participate in the bodhisattva's quest—and to share in its ultimate reward. Though animals, as we saw in Chapter 1, are generally devoid of such moral agency, Kanthaka's agency in this episode is a reflection of the bodhisattva's own. Attributing such agency to the horse furthers the close identification this episode seeks to establish between Kanthaka and the bodhisattva's impulse to renounce.

Perhaps most striking of all, in terms of this identification, are those passages in which Kanthaka's physical "carrying" of the bodhisattva upon his back is explicitly compared to the future buddha's spiritual "carrying" of the world from this shore of samsara to the farther shore of nirvana. This parallelism is developed in several sources. In the *Nidānakathā*, the bodhisattva says directly to Kanthaka, "Tonight, dear Kanthaka, carry me across (P. *tāraya*) in a single night, and through you, I will become a buddha and carry across (P. *tāressāmī*) the world, together with its gods!"[21] Thus, the bodhisattva acknowledges that he will become a buddha *through* Kanthaka's assistance, and the horse's physical "carrying across" is directly parallel to the Buddha's spiritual "carrying across" of living beings from this shore of samsara to the farther shore of nirvana—a parallelism that is concretized later on in the same text, when Kanthaka leaps over the Anomā River in a single jump to land "on the farther shore" (P. *pārima-tīre*).[22] In the *Vimānavatthu*, as well, the bodhisattva slaps Kanthaka's thighs and says to him, "Carry me across (P. *vaha*), my friend, and when I have attained the highest awakening, I will carry the world across (P. *tārayissaṃ*)!"[23] Although this passage uses two different Pāli verbs for the phrase "carry across," the commentary makes it clear that a direct parallel is being drawn between the two "carryings":

> "*Carry me across, my friend*"—i.e., "Kanthaka, my friend, carry me across (P. *vaha*) today, in a single night; be a worthy vehicle for me!"

> Moreover, speaking of the purpose of this carrying across (P. *vahane*) ... he says, *"And when I have attained the highest awakening, I will carry the world across!"*—i.e., "And when I have reached and attained the highest, unexcelled, perfect awakening, I will carry (P. *tārayissāmi*) the world, together with its gods, across the great flood of samsara! Therefore you shouldn't think that this carrying (P. *gamanaṃ*) is insignificant." In this way, he explains the extreme importance of the purpose of this carrying (P. *gamane*).[24]

In fact, even in a context that has nothing to do with the Great Departure, the same parallel between the two "carryings" is still drawn. In a verse from the *Buddhavaṃsa,* the bodhisattva is described as one who will "awaken to the deathless state and carry [the world] with its gods across."[25] The *Buddhavaṃsa Commentary* then glosses the verb "carry across" (P. *tārayati*) in several different ways, one of which directly invokes Kanthaka:

> "Carry across" also means: ... [The bodhisattva] mounted Kanthaka and departed, along with his companion Channa; he was carried across (P. *atikkamitvā*) three kingdoms, and went forth on the bank of the Anomā River.[26]

The consistent parallel drawn between Kanthaka's "carrying across" and the Buddha's "carrying across" further solidifies the identification between them: Kanthaka's movements as a horse are like a physical embodiment of the Buddha's saving work as a buddha.

Our sources thus make it very clear that Kanthaka is not just an ordinary, generic horse who happens to be ridden by the bodhisattva on this particular evening. Instead, Kanthaka is a *named, individualized*, completely unique being, born at the same moment as the bodhisattva, destined from the moment of his birth to play a role in the bodhisattva's Great Departure, fully conscious of the role that he plays, and closely associated with the bodhisattva's impulse to renounce the world (whether or not he is depicted as being in favor of it). In all of these senses, Kanthaka can be described as a "double" of the bodhisattva, an animal "other" who silently reflects and reinforces the will, motivations, and actions of the bodhisattva himself.[27]

What kind of functions might such an animal "double" fulfill within the Buddha's life-story? Hopefully, these will become apparent as we continue Kanthaka's story from here—remembering, however, that there are two different outcomes to deal with, depending upon the source: one in which Kanthaka dies as soon as the bodhisattva dismisses him, and one in which Kanthaka returns to Kapilavastu to bear the consequences of the bodhisattva's departure.

Kanthaka's Dismissal, Death, and Rebirth in Heaven

At daybreak, on the banks of the Anomā River, the bodhisattva engages in a number of actions that clearly indicate, as John Strong has noted, that he is "making himself into a monk, a *bhikṣu*"[28]—actions, in fact, that would later come to be ritually reenacted by candidates for monastic ordination in many Buddhist cultures. These actions vary slightly from one source to another, but generally include cutting off his hair with a sword, throwing his topknot into the air (where it is caught by the deities and enshrined within a *stūpa* in heaven), removing his royal garments and jewelry, and receiving monastic robes and other requisites from a deity (or from a passing hunter, who may be a deity in disguise). The final act within this sequence is the dismissal of Chandaka and Kanthaka: "Channa, my friend," he says in the *Nidānakathā*, "take my ornaments and Kanthaka and go. I will go forth!"[29] In the *Buddhacarita,* he also speaks directly to Kanthaka, telling him, "Your task is accomplished" (but literally, "you have crossed over" [S. *nistīrṇam*]).[30]

As Strong notes, "the dismissal of Chandaka and Kaṇṭhaka is important because they represent the bodhisattva's last tie binding him to his home."[31] Indeed, from this point onward, the bodhisattva is completely alone (until he meets his first two teachers), and the gods, who had played such a major role in the Great Departure, now seem to retreat from the scene. In fact, I would argue that the dismissal of Chandaka and Kanthaka represents a crucial turning point within the Buddha's life-story—the exact moment when the bodhisattva makes a decisive break with his former life as a prince; the hyper-liminal moment when Prince Siddhārtha definitively *dies* and the imminent "buddha-to-be" begins to gestate. The great significance of this moment—indeed, the need to *mark* this moment in some manner—is suggested in several sources. In the *Lalitavistara*, the location of the dismissal is commemorated by a shrine called the *Chandaka-nivartana* (The Turning Back of Chandaka),[32] while in the *Nidānakathā*, there is some suggestion that the shrine may have been named after Kanthaka instead (as the *kaṇḍaka-nivattana*, or Turning Back of Kanthaka).[33] In the *Abhiniṣkramaṇa Sūtra*, the spot is marked in a slightly different way, for as soon as the bodhisattva dismounts from his horse, he states, "This is the last time I will ever dismount from my steed; and this is the spot where for the last time I have alighted."[34] The *Mahāvastu* tells us explicitly *why* the moment is so significant, for with the dismissal of Chandaka and Kanthaka, the bodhisattva "cut the bonds that tied him to his home, threw all of this away, and departed with indifference."[35]

It is in this context that the bodhisattva's final interactions with Chandaka and Kanthaka become significant. In several sources, Chandaka either argues against the bodhisattva's decision to renounce the world or expresses the wish to join him in his renunciation. These discussions are sometimes quite lengthy; in the *Buddhacarita*, for example, the back-and-forth dialogue between the bodhisattva and Chandaka goes on for almost fifty verses, and functions as an extensive discourse on the possible arguments one might make both for and against the practice of world-renunciation (a discourse that was well developed in premodern India). The bodhisattva's final interaction with Kanthaka, on the other hand, is dealt with more briefly—but packs a greater emotional punch:

> The excellent horse Kanthaka licked the bodhisattva's feet and shed warm tears. The prince stroked the horse with his hand . . . and spoke to him like a friend: "Don't cry, Kanthaka, you've shown what a good horse you are! Be patient, and this exertion of yours will quickly bear fruit."[36]

While Kanthaka does not die at this point in the *Buddhacarita*, in other sources, Kanthaka's licking of the bodhisattva's feet and shedding of tears are immediately followed by his death and rebirth in heaven (see Figure 5.2). In the *Vimānavatthu*, for example, Kanthaka (now reborn as a deity) remembers: "I licked his copper-nailed feet all over, and wept as I watched the Great Hero leaving. Because I could no longer see that glorious Son of the Sākyas, I became gravely ill and quickly met my death."[37] Expanding upon these verses, the *Vimānavatthu Commentary* explains:

> With a heart full of love, Kanthaka licked the Great Man's feet with his tongue and opened his eyes, which were soft with devotion. He kept looking at the bodhisattva for as long as he remained within sight, but once

FIGURE 5.2.

Kanthaka licks the bodhisattva's feet before taking leave of him. The figure holding the parasol and raising his right hand is likely Chandaka. Gray schist panel (Peshawar, Pakistan), Gandhāra school, Kushan period, 2nd–3rd c. CE. British Museum. (Photo © Marie Lan-Nguyen, licensed under CC BY 2.5.)

> the World Protector had passed beyond his range of vision, Kanthaka's heart became full of faith (P. *pasanna-mānas*), and he thought to himself, "I carried the Great Man, who is such an excellent Leader of the World—this body of mine has indeed borne fruit!" Unable to endure the grief of separation, due to the influence of long-standing love between them ... he died and was reborn in the Tāvatiṃsa heaven.[38]

The idea that Kanthaka survives only as long as the bodhisattva remains within his line of sight is also found in the *Nidānakathā*:

> Kanthaka ... unable to endure his grief at the thought that *he would never be able to see his master again, departed from his view* and died of a broken heart, whereupon he was reborn in the Tāvatiṃsa heaven as a deity named Kanthaka.[39]

With Kanthaka's death, all ties to worldly life have been severed, and the bodhisattva continues onward alone.

If we consider the contrast between the bodhisattva's final interaction with Chandaka and his final interaction with Kanthaka, we can see that the two characters are performing different functions, brought about by their human versus animal status. The human character of Chandaka allows for a conversation to take place. The bodhisattva can explain his motivations in renouncing the world, and Chandaka can argue against him or express a wish to join him. Rational arguments both for and against the practice of world-renunciation can be expressed in order to justify the bodhisattva's departure. With Kanthaka, however, such rational discourse is not possible—for Kanthaka, as an animal, is unable to express himself through human speech, nor is he capable of understanding complex arguments concerning renuncation. Thus, in lieu of words and arguments, we instead get a focus upon the physical manifestations of Kanthaka's enormous grief: He *licks* the bodhisattva's feet, he *weeps*, he *looks at* the bodhisattva for as long as he can, and as soon as their eye contact comes to an end, he *dies*.

Though Kanthaka follows the same basic pattern as the animals we looked at in Chapter 2—*seeing* the Buddha, giving rise to *faith*

(P. *pasanna-mānaso*), and then *dying*—the sequence here carries a greater significance. The emotional poignancy of this scene, the collective grief brought about by the prince's rejection of worldly life, the cruelty of the prince's severance of all emotional ties—all of these elements of Buddhism's founding story (and, I might note, the "founding story" for every monk and nun) are far better captured by the mute animal Kanthaka than by the talkative human Chandaka. It is precisely because Kanthaka is an animal, I would argue, that he becomes the bearer of all of the emotional consequences of that original act of severance—from family, community, and kingdom—that gave birth to the Buddhist path. An animal, after all, does not care about your rational justifications, logical reasons, or ultimate spiritual goals. An animal—as any pet owner can attest—just licks your feet mutely with affection. Displaying an animal's response to the bodhisattva's departure thus allows these emotions to find powerful, yet also silent, expression. One sense in which Kanthaka serves as a *scapegoat*, then, is by acting as a kind of container for all of the highly fraught emotions surrounding the bodhisattva's departure—a container that is definitively separated from the bodhisattva upon the riverbank, so that the bodhisattva can continue on "with indifference."

Moreover, if we see Kanthaka as a "double" of the bodhisattva—an identification, as we have seen, that has been repeatedly reinforced throughout the earlier part of the story—then the *death* of Kanthaka at this point can be interpreted in several ways. Perhaps the bodhisattva's own emotions and emotional ties to others—as embodied in his "double," Kanthaka—must literally *die* at this point, so that he can become a dispassionate buddha. The prince who loves his subjects, the husband who loves his wife, the son who loves his father, and the father who loves his son—perhaps, as embodied by Kanthaka, all of them are allowed to have one final lick and cry before permanently exiting the scene. Kanthaka seems to mourn the prince's loss of worldly life on behalf of the prince himself—and because Kanthaka is an animal, this moment of poignant mourning is allowed to remain unopposed by any rational justifications or opposing reasons. Finally, beyond these emotional functions, Kanthaka, in a larger sense, is an apt representative of the bodhisattva's entire worldly life as Prince Siddhārtha—a life that must definitively *die away* before buddhahood can be attained. Since Kanthaka appears to have also been King Śuddhodhana's horse, he is equally identified with both father and son; thus, his death represents the permanent severance of the prince's royal lineage, in favor of the lineage of the buddhas. The death of Kanthaka thus represents the final death of "Prince Siddhārtha" and everything that figure stood for.

Kanthaka's Return to the Palace and Its Aftermath

In other sources, however, we find an alternative plot line, according to which Kanthaka does *not* die at this point, but returns to Kapilavastu along with Chandaka. Whether or not he was in favor of the bodhisattva's departure—a point that is in dispute, as noted above—various sources make it clear that now that he has been separated from the bodhisattva, he is full of grief, a mere shell of the magnificent horse he once was. The *Buddhacarita* states:

> The powerful horse Kanthaka walked onward, soberly and exhausted in spirit. Though he was still adorned with ornaments, now that the bodhisattva had abandoned him, he seemed bereft of majesty. Turning back in the direction of the ascetic grove, he neighed loudly and pitifully again and again. Even though he was hungry, he did not welcome or consume the grass and water along the road, as before.[40]

In the *Abhiniṣkramaṇa Sūtra*, Kanthaka is so weakened by grief that it takes him eight days to get back to the city, even though the journey out had taken only a single night.[41]

It is within the context of this scenario that an even stronger sense of Kanthaka's functioning as a *scapegoat* comes into play. For as soon as he returns to Kapilavastu, Kanthaka seems to become a convenient target for the loved ones the prince has left behind—an object of longing, blame, and censure who, as an animal, is powerless to defend himself or respond. The bodhisattva, in a sense, is spared from bearing the brunt of these emotional reactions because Kanthaka—his animal scapegoat—bears them for him.

In several sources, this sequence begins with a rather heartbreaking episode in which the ambiguity of Kanthaka's *neighing* once again comes into play. The *Buddhacarita* describes it this way:

> Entering the king's residence, Kanthaka looked around with eyes full of tears and let out a loud neigh, as if announcing his grief to the people. Then the birds living within the king's residence and the favored horses tied up nearby, assuming that the prince had returned, echoed that horse's cry. And the people standing near the king's harem apartments, deceived into an abundance of joy, thought to themselves, "Since the horse Kanthaka is neighing, surely the prince has arrived!"[42]

Kanthaka neighs out of *grief*—yet his animal cry is ambiguous and is misinterpreted even by the other animals, resulting in an animal cacophony that deceives the palace folk into thinking that the prince has returned. This is followed by a long and pathetic description of the women of the palace rushing "hopefully" (S. *āśayā*)[43] toward Chandaka and Kanthaka, only to discover that the bodhisattva is *not* with them, whereupon they weep, wail, faint, swoon, and beat their breasts in a great paroxysm of grief. Similarly, in the *Abhiniṣkramaṇa Sūtra*, upon entering the palace complex, Kanthaka neighs "in recognition of his home"—whereupon people come rushing to their windows, crying out, "[T]he Prince has come back! [T]he Prince has returned!" Upon seeing that they have been deceived, however, "they left their places of observation in sorrow and retired within the precincts, weeping and with great lamentation."[44] In the *Saṅghabhedavastu*, meanwhile, Kanthaka is forced to enter the city alone because Chandaka is so overcome with grief that he cannot hold himself together. Again, the horse neighs, and "upon hearing that sound, the people of the king's harem and many other people quickly came out. When they did not see the bodhisattva, they clasped Kanthaka around the neck and began to cry."[45] Thus, just as the ambiguity of Kanthaka's neighing causes doubt and suspicion about his attitude toward the prince's renunciation, it also causes a cruel deception of the loved ones the prince has left behind. This episode seems to set up Kanthaka as an object of blame and censure—which then comes to fruition in the responses of the bodhisattva's wife, Yaśodharā, and his father, King Śuddhodhana.

The wife responds to the horse with a poignant mixture of both longing and anger. In the *Lalitavistara* (where the wife is Gopā rather than Yaśodharā), it is the emotions of grief and longing that seem to predominate: Upon seeing Kanthaka, she faints and falls to the ground, and her attendants worry out loud that she may even lose her life. She throws her arms around Kanthaka's neck and "babbles and laments incoherently": "Alas, Kanthaka, noble [horse], my husband's companion, where did you take him?"[46] In the *Mahāvastu,* however, grief and longing quickly morph into accusation and blame:

> Yaśodharā, weeping, threw her arms around Kanthaka's neck and said, "Where have you taken the prince, Kanthaka? How have I offended against you and Chandaka such that you would take the prince and leave while I was happily sleeping? Now I and the sixty thousand women of the harem have been made into widows!"[47]

In the *Buddhacarita*, finally, her words are full of anger and vitriol, and it is once again the frustrating unreliability of the horse's neighing that comes to the fore:

> This horse Kanthaka must surely wish me misfortune in every way, since he took away from here my everything, at night, while people were sleeping, like a jewel-thief! . . . Today, he neighs loudly, as if he were filling up the king's abode. But when he was carrying away my beloved, this vile horse fond of ignoble deeds remained mute. For if he had neighed, waking up the people . . . then I wouldn't be experiencing such grief.[48]

Despite the seeming contrast Yaśodharā draws between her husband—"my everything"—and Kanthaka—"this vile horse fond of ignoble deeds"—it is clear that Kanthaka can be seen here as a *substitute* for the bodhisattva, a *scapegoat* for the bodhisattva, and a convenient target for all of the turbulent emotions Yaśodharā feels toward her absent husband. The bodhisattva is spared from suffering the full onslaught of these emotions because his horse is there to do it for him. (In many Buddha-biographies, it is exactly these same emotions, in fact, that Yaśodharā will later display toward the Buddha himself, when he visits Kapilavastu shortly following his attainment of buddhahood.)

The bodhisattva's father, King Śuddhodhana, also takes this opportunity to vent his feelings upon the animal scapegoat. In the *Buddhacarita*, "lying on the ground and looking up at the horse with eyes full of tears,"[49] he wails,

> O Kanthaka, after doing so many favors for me in battle, today you have done me a great disfavor!—for you have carried off into the forest my beloved, the lover of virtue, as if you were an enemy, even though you are a friend. So take me to him today, or go there quickly and bring him back!—for I cannot live without him, just as one whose disease is advanced cannot survive without the right medicine.[50]

King Śuddhodana not only castigates the horse as an "enemy," but also seems to place his very life in the horse's hands, threatening to *die* if Kanthaka does not undo the enormous damage he has brought about.

In arguing that Kanthaka here fulfills the classic functions of a scapegoat, it is important to point out that Chandaka, too, plays this role to some extent; in fact, in several sources, the accusations Yaśodharā levels against Chandaka—*how could you let him leave? why didn't you wake anyone up?*—are even more extensive than the accusations she levels against Kanthaka. Nevertheless, there are several important differences between Chandaka and Kanthaka, differences that are the direct result of Kanthaka's *animality*. One difference is that Kanthaka, as an animal, is able to serve as a *physical* object of Yaśodharā's longing. Given the cultural context, it would be inappropriate for her to throw her arms around Chandaka, but she *can* throw her arms around Kanthaka the horse—for the horse is a highly favored animal in India, replete with royal and aristocratic associations.[51] In just the same way,

King Śuddhodhana can lie on the ground and look *up* at the horse—a highly inappropriate posture if the object of his gaze were a human being subservient to the king. Kanthaka's animality thus allows for raw expressions of intimacy that are unencumbered by the norms of behavior operative among humans.

A second and more important difference between Chandaka and Kanthaka is that Kanthaka—as an animal—*cannot defend himself or respond*. Lacking the ability to express himself through human language, he can only mutely absorb (and thus nullify?) the anger and blame being cast his way. In fact, it is striking to note, in one source after another, that Chandaka feels compelled to speak on Kanthaka's behalf and defend the noble horse against these accusations. In the *Buddhacarita*, for example, he pleads with Yaśodharā: "Please do not blame Kanthaka, my queen, nor should you be angry with me! Know that we are completely guiltless."[52] After explaining to Yaśodharā that the gods themselves seemed to compel them to act as they did, he concludes, "Therefore, Queen of Men, you shouldn't blame the two of us for his departure; neither I nor this horse acted of our own free will, for he departed with the help of the gods!"[53] In the *Mahāvastu*, he likewise protests: "What wrong have I committed? For I cried out in a loud voice—and Kanthaka, too, as he was taking the prince away, neighed loudly, yet none of you woke up!"[54] Finally, in the *Abhiniṣkramaṇa Sūtra*, Chandaka feels compelled to defend Kanthaka even though Yaśodharā, in this text, has not even blamed him: "Your slave, oh Yaśodharā! deserves not to be reproached; for he has committed no fault indeed, neither has Kanthaka, the noble steed, done wrong."[55] The very fact that Chandaka feels compelled to provide a defense for the defenseless horse further highlights the animal's complete inability to speak up on its own behalf. The muteness of the animal and its inability to communicate thus make it a more effective scapegoat.

A final feature that distinguishes Chandaka from Kanthaka is the fact that Kanthaka *dies*. Whereas Chandaka survives the attacks upon his character and later becomes a monk—though he, too, seems to suffer significantly throughout his later career[56]—Kanthaka does not. In the *Abhiniṣkramaṇa Sūtra*, Kanthaka's death is a direct result of the accusations made against him by the bodhisattva's father: "The horse Kanthaka having heard the reproachful words of the King in his affliction, unable to bear the sorrow that afflicted him, lay down and died."[57] In other sources, it is more generally the result of his continuing grief at being separated from the bodhisattva. Especially poignant is a long passage from the *Mahāvastu* in which Kanthaka starves himself to death out of grief, despite the desperate measures people take to save his life—a passage that again reflects the physical intimacy the women can share with the horse:

> Sweetmeats coated in honey were placed before him, and other foods and sweetmeats, fit for a king, were piled up before him—yet Kanthaka did not eat. Constantly remembering the bodhisattva, he wept. Some women of the harem used their regal and costly garments of cotton, silk, and wool to wipe away Kanthaka's tears. Others stroked his head, others his neck, others his back ... flanks ... forelegs ... joints ... tail ... and hooves. Others held morsels of food coated in honey up to his mouth; others held delicacies of various types; others held sweetmeats and confections.... Yet Kanthaka would not take food. Unable to see the bodhisattva, starving himself out of grief for the bodhisattva, Kanthaka died.[58]

We might say that Kanthaka here commits suicide. However, the suicide of Kanthaka is distinct from the suicides of the black snake and the fierce buffalo of the *Avadānaśataka* (discussed in Chapter 2), for here the animal commits suicide out of grief rather than to rid himself of animality. Moreover, Kanthaka's death immediately after bearing the brunt of the anger, blame, and other negative emotions vented by the bodhisattva's loved ones is in line with his function as a *scapegoat*: First, he is closely identified with the bodhisattva and the bodhisattva's impulse to renounce the world. Then, the two of them are wrenched apart, and it is Kanthaka alone, as the bodhisattva's substitute, who returns to bear the consequences of the prince's departure. After mutely absorbing blame and sin on behalf of the absent bodhisattva, Kanthaka dies, thus nullifying and taking these negative emotions away. Though Chandaka, too, fulfills some of these functions,

Kanthaka's animality, muteness, and death make him a more effective scapegoating vehicle.

The final step in this scapegoating process, I suggest, is to *reward* or *compensate* the scapegoat in some way—and this is brought about by Kanthaka's immediate rebirth as a deity in heaven. "As soon as he died," the *Mahāvastu* informs us,

> he was reborn among the Trāyastriṃśa gods. . . . He was a god of great supernatural power and enormous authority, and he surpassed the thousands of other gods who had been reborn there before him in the ten divine qualities—that is, divine lifespan, divine appearance, divine happiness, divine sovereignty, divine retinue, and divine forms, sounds, smells, tastes, and touches.[59]

Thus, Kanthaka is assaulted with blame and criticism and suffers death as a result, yet he is also amply rewarded by an immediate rebirth in heaven. Though Kanthaka follows the same basic pattern as the animals we looked at earlier from the *Divyāvadāna* and the *Avadānaśataka*—that is, an association with the Buddha and a heart full of faith, followed shortly by the animal's death and rebirth in heaven—I believe the pattern here bears a different significance, with Kanthaka's splendor in heaven serving to *compensate* him for his contribution to the bodhisattva's departure and the suffering he thereby endured. One argument in favor of this interpretation is the fact that the textual tradition itself seems determined to allow the deity Kanthaka to finally speak for himself—and to assure us of his more-than-adequate compensation.

Maudgalyāyana's Visit to Kanthaka in Heaven

Both the *Mahāvastu* and the (Pāli) *Vimānavatthu* contain narrative accounts in which the monk Maudgalyāyana (P. Moggallāna)—well-known for his superior psychic powers—visits the Trāyastriṃśa (P. Tāvatiṃsa) heaven and encounters Kanthaka, who has been reborn there as a deity (also named Kanthaka). In both accounts, there is an obvious impulse to allow Kanthaka to speak for himself and tell us—this time, through intelligible human speech—of his willing role in the Great Departure. Coupled with this is a corresponding desire to emphasize as much as possible the enormous *reward* Kanthaka now enjoys as a direct result of his fulfilling of the scapegoating function.

In the *Mahāvastu* account, Maudgalyāyana, upon encountering Kanthaka in heaven, first launches into an elaborate description of Kanthaka's divine abode: It is filled with light and full of precious jewels, lotus-pools, trees, birds, celestial nymphs, and heavenly maidens, and Kanthaka reclines there in regal splendor on a beautiful couch. When asking Kanthaka what deed he performed in the past to attain such a glorious station, Maudgalyāyana repeats the question in so many ways that the direct connection between the original deed and its resultant fruit cannot possibly be left in doubt:

> What deed did you previously perform in other lives? By what root of merit were you reborn in the Trāyastriṃśa heaven? . . . How did you obtain this mastery over lifespan? How did you come to enjoy this vigor, supernatural power, and celestial retinue? What auspicious deed did you perform in other lives? By what auspicious action have you experienced this fruit? By what religious observance? What restraint? What self-control? By what auspicious action do you rejoice among the multitudes of heaven? How did you attain such blazing power and beauty? By what auspicious action do you illuminate all directions? I've asked you, Deity, so tell me about the action of which this is the fruit![60]

Following this interrogative overkill, Kanthaka responds with a first-person account of his role in the bodhisattva's Great Departure—making it clear that he was a willing and joyful participant—and then concludes by again repeatedly emphasizing the connection between the deed and its fruit:

> *This* is how I have attained this lifespan, this beauty, this fame, and this power; this is why I enjoy supernatural power and a celestial retinue. It is by this religious observance, this restraint, and this self-control that

> I have won such unlimited and divine supernatural power. I performed this auspicious deed; I engaged in it, and I stored it up. Because of that auspicious deed, I am now enjoying this fruit. . . . See how this pure deed succeeded for one who was only a horse![61]

Why such repetitive overkill in both question and answer (whereas the narrative of the events themselves is quite brief)? I would argue that now that the horse's scapegoating function has been fulfilled, the audience demands some reassurance that the animal was, indeed, a willing victim after all, and enjoyed a more-than-compensatory reward. Thus, the horse's unintelligible neighing—formerly a cause of anxiety and suspicion—is now replaced by a clear and upbeat first-person account, while the horse's muteness—so useful when it was serving as an object of people's blame—must now give way to a rational justification of the horse's role.

The *Vimānavatthu*'s version of this episode is significantly less repetitive, but again makes it clear that Kanthaka was a willing participant in the bodhisattva's Great Departure. Here, Kanthaka relates:

> When I heard [the bodhisattva's intention to go forth], I gave rise to abundant joy. I was happy and elated, and I fervently wished for [his words to come true]! And when I knew that the very famous Son of the Sākyas had mounted me, I was elated and full of joy, knowing that I would carry that excellent man.[62]

Equally clear is the connection between the deed and its fruit: "Through the power of that deed alone, I dwell in the city of the gods, in this divine residence furnished with all sensual pleasures."[63] The *Vimānavatthu* is unsatisfied, however, with merely a reward in heaven; instead, it feels compelled to hint at Kanthaka's ultimate destiny as well, for it has Kanthaka himself make a prediction: "And since I gave rise to joy upon hearing talk of awakening, by that wholesome root alone, I will [someday] attain the destruction of the fetters."[64] The *Vimānavatthu Commentary* then clarifies this verse by explaining that Kanthaka was, in fact, *the very first being in the universe* to hear of the bodhisattva's intention to attain awakening—and by this root of merit, he is destined to attain nirvana in the future.[65] Even more, the *Vimānavatthu Commentary* seems determined to let us *see* an actual reunion between Kanthaka and the Buddha, telling us that Kanthaka, the deity, went to see the Buddha, "grateful and mindful of all that had been done for him"—whereupon "his Dhamma-Eye was purified." [66]

In these narratives involving Maudgalyāyana's encounter with Kanthaka as a deity, we see how determined the tradition is to compensate the animal scapegoat. The same animal whose neighing was confusing or deceptive, who was blamed as a "vile" and "ignoble" beast, and who suffered starvation and death as a result, now appears in a form that can confidently reassure us that he was perfectly willing to perform this role, enjoyed a more-than-adequate divine reward, and even attained the spiritual goal of stream-entry—with an unbreakable promise of nirvana in the future. Human language replaces muteness, and divine rewards make up for the abuse and mistreatment suffered earlier.

Perhaps the *Saṅghabhedavastu*'s version of the story goes the furthest of all—skipping heaven altogether and proceeding directly to nirvana. For in contrast to the tradition that Kanthaka was reborn as a deity in heaven, it tells us that when the horse died, he was reborn as a brahmin—and when the bodhisattva became a buddha and established the Dharma, this brahmin was "liberated through a discourse on unruly horses, escaped from the hardships of samsara, and was established in the everlasting spiritual success of nirvana."[67] Kanthaka thus moves from serving as an animal scapegoat to attaining the ultimate reward of nirvana—all within the lifetime of the Buddha. Here, the scapegoating process has come full circle and reached its satisfying resolution.

Kanthaka as Sacrificial Animal

Two scenarios have been outlined above. In the first, Kanthaka dies as soon as the bodhisattva dismisses him, and this death represents the final death of Prince Siddhārtha, which is necessary before the fully enlightened Buddha can emerge. In the second, Kanthaka returns to

Kapilavastu to absorb blame and censure on the bodhisattva's behalf, sparing the bodhisattva himself of the negative forces unleashed by his departure, and nullifying these forces through his death—thus fulfilling the classic functions of a scapegoat. In both scenarios, there is a sacrificial logic at work, and Kanthaka can be likened to a *sacrificial animal*—one who is closely identified with the sacrificer and loses his life on the sacrificer's behalf, allowing the sacrificer to undergo a profound transformation and often serving as a scapegoat for the sacrificer's sins. This analogy with animal sacrifice is intended to be loose and suggestive only, for there is no explicit invocation of sacrifice within our sources. Nevertheless, in spite of Buddhism's thoroughgoing condemnation of the Vedic tradition of animal sacrifice, it has been shown, time and again, that Buddhist discourse in India remained deeply indebted to the logic, imagery, and themes of Vedic sacrifice.[68]

Kimberly Patton has enumerated four cross-cultural features of the animals used in animal sacrifice, and it is striking to note the extent to which these four features, taken together, constitute an almost perfect reflection of the concerns driving the depiction of Kanthaka. First, she notes, animals offered for sacrifice "must be 'perfect' according to certain ideologically determined categories: male, unblemished, and whole; they must be in the prime of life"[69]—which is reminiscent of Kanthaka's physical description as a magnificent and powerful white stallion. "Further gilding the lily," she adds, "sacrificial victims were and are often elaborately adorned"[70]—just as the bodhisattva (in the *Lalitavistara*) requires Kanthaka to be "beautifully decorated,"[71] and Chandaka (in the *Abhiniṣkramaṇa Sūtra*) complies with this request by preparing Kanthaka with a "beautifully adorned bit" and a "beautifully soft and pliable saddle-cloth, adorned with gold and gems of every description."[72] Second, Patton notes, the animal victim must be depicted as a willing participant in the sacrifice and as assenting to its own demise; it must be "an active, even self-conscious ritual participant" and "never divested of agency and free will"[73]—just as we have seen to be the case for Kanthaka's willing and conscious participation in the Great Departure. Thirdly, the sacrificial animal is characterized by extreme *individualization* and *elevation* above all others of its type; by being chosen for sacrifice, it is uniquely removed from "a life among countless other domesticated animals" to become "a player in a sacred drama," one who bears "a kind of charged individuality"[74]—features, as we have seen, similarly brought about by Kanthaka's personal name and his status as a co-natal of the bodhisattva. And fourth, far from suffering a cruel and ignoble death, the sacrificial animal's already semi-divine state "is often rendered permanent, and its eschatological future assured in a kind of glistening light."[75] Here, Patton cites the Vedic horse sacrifice, or *aśvamedha*, as her primary example, noting that according to Brahmanical texts, "the horse will dwell among the gods" and undergo a "spectacular apotheosis" by means of its sacrifice.[76] Thus, a hymn from the *Ṛg Veda* directly addresses the sacrificial horse and asserts, "You do not really die through this, nor are you harmed. You go to the gods on paths pleasant to go on"[77]—just as, in the *Lalitavistara*, the gods urge Kanthaka onward by saying, "Look, Kanthaka, at this charming and lovely path laid out in the sky, beautifully adorned with jeweled benches and scented by perfumes made of the most excellent divine nectars!"[78] The path Kanthaka follows during the Great Departure is thus a path that leads directly to heaven—as confirmed within our sources by Kanthaka's immediate rebirth, upon dying, in the Trāyastriṃśa abode.

All four features of the sacrificial animal enumerated by Patton, then, apply equally to the horse Kanthaka—and this is the case, I would argue, because a similar sacrificial logic is operative in both cases. Just as the animal in a Vedic sacrifice is closely identified with the sacrificer (since the sacrificer is, in truth, sacrificing something of himself),[79] so the same is true of Kanthaka's close identification with the bodhisattva, who is sacrificing his former identity as a prince. Just as the animal in a Vedic sacrifice is elevated, individualized, consecrated, and made sacred prior to its death, with its death resulting in a powerful release of vital energy that either transforms the sacrificer or removes his sin (or both)—so the same might be said of Kanthaka, whose death simultaneously allows the bodhisattva to annihilate his identity as Prince Siddhārtha, turn himself into a fully enlightened buddha, and expiate the sin and blame he might otherwise incur by abandoning his worldly duties. The *practice* of sacrifice may be absent from our story, but the same basic logic is at work: Kanthaka is sacrificed upon the altar of the Buddha's quest for buddhahood.

The Indian Horse

Finally, we might ask: Why is the *horse* a particularly suitable animal to serve the various functions here fulfilled by Kanthaka? As Wendy Doniger has noted, horses are not native to India, but have generally arrived through foreigners and conquerors, beginning with the Indo-Aryans themselves. Moreover, horses do not thrive in the Indian environment but generally have to be imported, making them highly valuable and expensive animals. Throughout Indian history, horses have thus been seen as "prized animals, used only in elite royal or military circles"—and, first and foremost, as symbols of "the power and aristocracy of the Kshatriyas, the royal warrior class."[80] The horse is thus a fitting symbol of the worldly ambitions of kingship—as confirmed by the enormous prestige of the Vedic *aśvamedha* or royal horse sacrifice, which involved letting a royal stallion roam freely for a year and claiming for the king any lands that it crossed (after which the horse was returned to the kingdom and sacrificed). Thus, if Kanthaka represents the worldly life and ambitions of "Prince Siddhārtha"—that which must *die* or *be dismissed*—then it is quite fitting for him to be a *horse*.

At the same time, however, there must remain *some* connection between "Prince Siddhārtha" and the fully enlightened Buddha—since the former turns into the latter—and once again, the horse is a useful animal for this purpose. For "once domestication [of the horse] took place, the primary relationship between horse and humans became that of *taming*, and it is this metaphor that dominates the mythology of the horse in the historical period."[81] Thus, horses in Indian tradition are also common metaphors "for the senses that must be harnessed, yoked through some sort of spiritual and physical discipline such as yoga (a word whose basic meaning is 'to yoke,' as in 'to yoke horses to a chariot')."[82] Several discourses in the *Majjhima Nikāya*, in fact, compare the gradual training of a horse (through wearing a bit, wearing a harness, keeping in step, etc.) to the gradual training of a monk through spiritual discipline (through right view, right intention, right speech, etc.).[83] The horse can thus simultaneously symbolize the worldly ambitions of kingship that the bodhisattva must renounce *and* the potential of this same bodhisattva to engage in spiritual discipline that will transform him into a buddha. Finally, the horse is not a passive animal in its relationship with humans, for its taming requires the active participation of the horse itself—which furthers the tradition's ability to depict Kanthaka as an active and willing participant in the bodhisattva's story. In a particularly intriguing passage, Doniger not only makes this observation about the horse-human relationship but explicitly describes it as a kind of *sacrificial logic* that can be connected to the Vedic *aśvamedha*:

> In the taming of a horse, force is used, but so is persuasion. At a certain moment, force becomes useless; there are some things that no one can make a horse do unless he wants to, unless he understands what is wanted of him and is willing to give up his freedom in exchange for something that he derives from his contact with humans. One might, perhaps, think of this in sacrificial terms, as a sacrificial exchange: the horse sacrifice is not merely a sacrifice *of* a horse, but a sacrifice *by* a horse. And it is this exchange that is mythologized in the narratives of people who have horses, narratives about horses ... that love their masters and willingly sacrifice their lives for them.[84]

Everything Doniger says in this statement applies equally to the horse Kanthaka and the role he plays within the bodhisattva's life.

Horses in Indian tradition thus have particular associations that make it suitable for the role played by Kanthaka to be fulfilled by a horse. Putting such associations aside, however, we should also give due credit to the raw appeal and power exerted by the very animal itself—its mute and impenetrable *animality*. For it isn't Kanthaka the talkative *deity* who finally moves us. It is Kanthaka the *horse*—weeping, grief-stricken, refusing oats and honey, and mutely licking the bodhisattva's feet with affection.

CHAPTER SIX

Mirror for the Buddha

The Elephant Pārileyyaka

Living in solitude is better,
for there is no companionship with a fool.
Let one wander alone, not doing evil, living at ease,
like an elephant [wandering] in an elephant-forest.
(Dhammapada)[1]

Just as the horse Kanthaka serves as a *scapegoat* for the world-weary bodhisattva, so, at a later point in time, does the elephant Pārileyyaka serve as a *mirror* for the fully enlightened Buddha. This episode occurs in the tenth year after the Buddha's awakening (according to the *Buddhavaṃsa Commentary*),[2] when the Buddhist Sangha is represented as having spread throughout much of North India. At the time in question, the monks residing in the city of Kosambī are embroiled in a rancorous dispute, fighting and quarreling with each other and ignoring the Buddha's reprimands. Frustrated and annoyed, the Buddha retreats in a state of disgust to the Pārileyyaka Forest, where he lives in isolation and quietude, attended only by a magnificent elephant, also known as Pārileyyaka. Only after spending an entire three-month rainy-season retreat in the company of this elephant does the Buddha feel ready to return to human society and finish dealing with his quarreling monks. This intriguing episode involving the Buddha's companionship with an elephant, which seems to have attracted little scholarly attention, exists in three major versions in Pāli canonical and commentarial literature: one from the *Vinaya Piṭaka* (Chapter 10 of the *Mahāvagga*), one from the *Udāna* (a discourse called the *Nāga Sutta*), and one from the *Dhammapada Commentary* (the commentary on verse 6 of the *Dhammapada*).[3] In the summary and analysis that follow, I weave all three versions together, while treating the *Vinaya* version as primary.

The Buddha in Pārileyyaka Forest

The story begins with a dispute over monastic discipline breaking out among the monks residing at Kosambī.[4] The two disputing factions grow larger and larger—even spreading up to heaven in one version—with the monks fighting and quarreling day and night, resisting the repeated attempts of the Buddha to bring about peace between them. The Buddha encourages the two sides to reconcile, reprimands them when they refuse to listen, warns them of the dangers of schism, relates the cautionary tale of Prince Dīghāvu, and recites several verses about the futility of wrath—yet nothing has any effect. The monks remain recalcitrant, day after day, and even tell the Buddha (in so many words) to butt out. Finally, the Buddha is fed up. In one account, he exclaims, "These foolish men are out of control, and it isn't easy to convince them!"[5] In another, he thinks to himself, "Now, I am living miserably among this crowd, and these monks do not heed my words. What if I were to live alone, secluded from the crowd?"[6] He leaves Kosambī abruptly—"without inviting any attendant or informing the Order of Monks"[7]—and, after two brief intermediate episodes,[8] comes to dwell in the tranquil Pārileyyaka Forest. Once there, he reflects upon the pleasant change in his circumstances: "Before, when I was crowded around by those monks of Kosambī, who cause quarrels, fights, arguments, disputes, and legal cases within the Sangha, I did not live at ease. But now, being alone and without anyone else, I live comfortably and at ease!"[9] The Buddha is glad to be free of his tiresome, quarreling monks.

It is at this point that we are introduced to an elephant—one whose backstory runs directly parallel to that of the Buddha, for he, too, has withdrawn from an oppressive situation:

> [Now, at that time,] a certain great elephant had been dwelling, crowded around by male elephants, female elephants, young elephants, and elephant cubs. He was forced to eat blades of grass whose tips had already been destroyed [by them], while they took and ate the branches that he had broken off [for himself]. He had to drink water that had already been muddied [by them], and whenever he descended [into the water], the female elephants would go diving down to rub up against his body. Then it occurred to that great elephant . . . "Suppose I were to live alone, secluded from the crowd?"[10]

Here, we are given a remarkable portrait of an elephant who suffers from the bondage of a life lived within society: constantly jostled by women and children, having his food and water defiled by others, and being the victim of unwanted sexual advances. Like a human householder who longs for renunciation, this elephant longs for the secluded life of the forest and gives voice to his longing in terms exactly parallel to those of the Buddha: "Suppose I were to live alone, secluded from the crowd?"

Departing from the herd, the elephant retreats into the Pārileyyaka Forest, where he encounters the Buddha and immediately begins to serve him, keeping the area free of grass and providing the Buddha with food and water. As the two of them live peaceably together, the elephant, too, reflects upon the pleasant change in his circumstances: "Formerly, being crowded around by male elephants, female elephants, young elephants, and elephant cubs, I did not live at ease. . . . But now, being alone and without anyone else, I live comfortably and at ease!"[11] The exact parallelism between the Buddha's thoughts and the elephant's thoughts is remarked upon by the Buddha himself, and further heightened when the Buddha refers to himself as an "Elephant[-Among-Men]," which is a common epithet of the Buddha:

> Then the Blessed One, being aware of his own solitude and also discerning the thoughts of the great elephant, gave rise, at that time, to this solemn utterance: "The mind of this great elephant, whose tusks are as long

as chariot poles, agrees with the mind of the Elephant[-Among-Men], since each one of us delights in being alone in the forest."[12]

The *Vinaya Commentary*, explaining this passage, emphasizes yet further the exact correspondence between their mental states:

> Because this great elephant delights in being alone and secluded in the forest—just like the Buddha-Elephant does—therefore, the mind of one elephant agrees with the mind of the other elephant. The meaning is that their minds are one and the same in terms of the delight they find in seclusion.[13]

The Buddha and the elephant, their minds perfectly in sync, thus dwell together harmoniously, with the elephant attending upon the Buddha. Once the Buddha has stayed there "for as long as he wishes" (P. *yathābhirantaṃ*)[14]—which the commentary specifies as a three-month rainy-season retreat[15]—he leaves the Pārileyyaka Forest behind and journeys to Sāvatthī, for he is ready to rejoin human society. Meanwhile, the quarreling monks of Kosambī—who have been suffering mightily in the Buddha's absence, since the laypeople of Kosambī have refused to give them any alms until the Buddha himself has forgiven them—soon arrive in Sāvatthī to seek the Buddha's guidance. There, the two factions in the dispute quickly reconcile with each other. The Buddha's strategic absence has had its intended effect: The monks are brought to their senses, and peace is quickly restored. Just as fast as it had ignited and spun out of control, the dispute among the monks of Kosambī is resolved and brought to an end.

The Buddha and the Elephant

The relationship drawn between the Buddha and the elephant is one of simultaneous identity and difference. We should begin by noticing again the basic parallelism between the Buddha and the elephant: both have been living in society with others; both are disgusted by the inappropriate behavior of those others; both have retreated into the forest to find solitude; and both now live "comfortably and at ease," free of the hassle of other beings. The Buddha explicitly reflects upon this similarity (even calling himself an "elephant" in the process) and recites a "solemn utterance" (P. *udāna*) that emphasizes it. The elephant here serves as a double of the Buddha—or, going further, a *mirror* for the Buddha, a reflective surface that projects his own image back to him and allows for recognition and affirmation.

Yet in spite of the obvious identity drawn between the Buddha and the elephant, the story must also discount this identity in favor of human superiority to the animal world. This is often how animal doubles function in relation to human characters: they allow for simultaneous identification and distance—mirroring our own selves back to us at one moment, yet submitting themselves to human domination at the next. The Buddha is identified with the elephant—yet this identification is only rendered safe by a simultaneous assertion of the *hierarchy* between man and animal.

In the story, I would argue, this hierarchy is achieved by having the elephant *serve* the Buddha submissively and with great devotion. While the *Vinaya* account describes this service only briefly, the *Udāna Commentary* gives us a long and rich description of the profound effect the Buddha has on the elephant and the many services the elephant performs on the Buddha's behalf:

> When [the elephant] saw the Blessed One there, he became quenched (P. *nibbuto*), like a fire that has been extinguished by a thousand pitchers [of water], and he stood in the presence of the Blessed One with a heart full of faith (P. *pasanna-citto*). From then on, making this his foremost duty, he would keep the area . . . free of grass by sweeping it with bunches of twigs. He would give the Blessed One water for rinsing his mouth, bring him water for bathing, and give him his toothbrush. He would gather sweet fruits from the forest and bring them to the Teacher, and the Teacher would eat them. . . . He would gather pieces of wood with his trunk, rub them against each other, start a fire, and get the fire going; then he would heat up rocks in the fire, moving them around with a stick, and throw them into a tank [of water]. When he knew that the

> water was hot, he would approach the Blessed One and stand there. The Blessed One would think, "The great elephant wants me to bathe," and go there and do his bathing duties. This same method was also used in regard to the drinking water, except that he would approach the Blessed One once the water had become cool.[16]

So solicitous is the elephant that he even heats up the Buddha's bath water! The *Dhammapada Commentary* further adds:

> He would perform [various other] duties [for the Teacher], and fan the Teacher with a branch. At nighttime, in order to ward off the danger posed by beasts of prey, the elephant would roam throughout the forest tract until sunrise, carrying a large club in his trunk, with the intention of protecting the Teacher.... At sunrise, the elephant would give the Teacher water for rinsing his mouth, and so on. And in this way, he would perform all of the customary services.[17]

The elephant thus has a dual nature: In relation to the other elephants, he is a powerful and superior leader who has retreated from the rabble in search of noble solitude. But in relation to the human Buddha, he is a devoted and submissive servant, looking after the Buddha's needs and attending to him with great devotion. This dual nature allows the Buddha to identify with the elephant, yet also maintain his human superiority. The Buddha, too, thus shares with the rest of humanity a contradictory desire to both dominate and find oneself reflected in the animal "other."

What purposes might such an animal "other" fulfill in terms of clarifying the Buddha's character? In order to elucidate these purposes, let us consider more closely now the fact that he is an *elephant.*

Elephas Maximus Indica

Why does the *elephant* constitute an especially resonant choice to serve as a mirror for the Buddha? As Daston and Mitman have noted, in order to convey any symbolic meaning, "an animal must [first] be singled out as a promising prospect for anthropomorphism. We do not choose to think with any and all animals."[18] Although the features that mark a particular species as a promising candidate may vary from one case to another (and from one culture to another), Paul Waldau points to the particular suitability of those species characterized by "large brains, communications between individuals, prolonged periods of development in complex familial and social envelopes, and levels of both social integration and individuality that humans can recognize"—all of which contribute to the existence of "unique individuals with distinctive personalities, histories, and community membership."[19] Elephants, along with great apes and cetaceans, are placed by Waldau within this group of species particularly prone to anthropomorphic imaginings.

In regard to the Indian context, we might further note that the Indian elephant (*Elephas maximus indica*) is native to the subcontinent and has been a persistent and pervasive feature of life there since the time of the Indus Valley Civilization. Buddhist texts thus display "a high degree of familiarity with these animals' natural history" in the wild, as well as their taming by human beings.[20] Frequently associated with royalty (since it was kings who most often owned elephants) and with military power (the elephant corps being one of the four divisions in the standard "four-fold" Indian army),[21] elephants in India generally have positive, powerful, and auspicious connotations. One of the standard Sanskrit words for "elephant" is *hastin*, meaning "one who possesses a hand" (that is, in the form of its trunk), and this feature, too, elevates the elephant into the same esteemed category as human beings and apes. Elephants have been a valuable commodity (particularly for kings and armies) throughout South Asian history and are consistently celebrated in Sanskrit literature for their power, grace, and intelligence, as well as having a long-standing association with the rains and agricultural fertility.[22]

Buddhism shares with the larger South Asian context a particular appreciation for the elephant. Thus, the Buddha and the arhats are often referred to as "elephants";[23] the Buddha's birth is heralded by his mother's dream of an auspicious white elephant; the bodhisattva of the Pāli *jātakas* is born as an elephant on seven different occasions (and always depicted in a positive light); and the "elephant-treasure" is one of the seven treasures that mark the reign of an idealized cakravartin monarch. It is Buddhism, in fact, that provides the earliest indication in India of the elephant coming to bear a sacred status (long before Hinduism's development of the elephant-headed god Ganesha). The elephant is thus a natural choice to serve as a mirror for the Buddha.[24]

There are other aspects of elephant behavior and imagery, moreover, that are particularly pertinent to the specific religious themes explored by the Pārileyyaka story. In the wild, she-elephants and elephant calves always live within matriarchal family groupings, whereas mature bull elephants live either with other males or completely on their own. This seems to make the wild bull elephant a particularly apt image for the male monastic—who either lives in a community with other male monks or dwells in the forest alone. As Florin Deleanu notes, "this latter case"—of the lone wild bull elephant—"seems to have offered the Buddhist authors a model of majestic solitude"[25] and an appropriate image for the solitary, forest-dwelling monk. Such an elephant is often idealized in Buddhist ascetic literature: "Living in solitude is better," as the *Dhammapada* says, "for there is no companionship with a fool. Let one wander alone, not doing evil, living at ease, like an elephant [wandering] in an elephant-forest."[26] Likewise, in the *Theragāthā*, the monk who "lives in the forest, gathering alms, delighting in whatever gleanings come into his bowl" is encouraged to "destroy the army of death, as an elephant destroys a house of reeds!"[27] The image of an elephant destroying a house of reeds pays tribute to the wild elephant's instinct to escape from the haunts of men and return to a peaceful life in the wild—much as the Buddha does within our story. Thus, when the elephant Pārileyyaka withdraws from the herd and retreats into the wilderness alone, he becomes a natural symbol for the solitary, forest-dwelling monk—and thus an effective mirror for the Buddha. The Buddha, after all, is the original model for the ideal of the solitary, forest-dwelling monk—one who rejects worldly life and retreats into the forest alone in order to attain the goal of buddhahood, and one whose power is still regularly replenished by the periods of meditation and solitude he spends within the wilderness. Affirming this aspect of the Buddha's character seems especially important in the present context, when his monks have descended into a petty squabble and his own powers as a teacher have so far failed to bring about peace between them. The mirroring of the Buddha in the form of a magnificent wild elephant reminds us of his status as the consummate Renouncer—untainted by any worldly strife.

At the same time, however, the elephant imagery employed within Buddhist discourse is inherently unstable, for in other cases it is the *tamed* elephant, rather than the *wild* elephant, that is idealized. As Rajmohan Ramanathapillai notes,

> Monks . . . observed that these massive animals can be extremely treacherous when they lose their temper but by using proper methods these intelligent animals could be trained and tamed. Once this precious insight was gained, monks began to compare the control of a wild elephant with controlling the human mind. Taming elephants becomes a central Buddhist analogy for taming passions.[28]

In traditional India, the process of taming an elephant was often cruel and violent, requiring the mahout to beat the animal into submission until it became pliant and docile[29]—a highly effective image for the rigorous spiritual discipline of a meditating monk.[30] "Formerly," the *Dhammapada* states, "this mind wandered about as it wished, wherever it liked, however it wanted. But now, I will thoroughly restrain it, just as [a mahout] uses his goad [to restrain] a maddened elephant!"[31] Likewise, the monk Tāḷapuṭa, in the *Theragāthā*, says to his own mind, "I will bind you by force to the object of meditation, just as an elephant is bound to a post with strong rope!"[32] Here, we should note that the Buddha is not only the original tamed elephant—having permanently tamed his own mind—but in addition, the *elephant tamer* who now tames the minds of others. Thus, the Buddha is sometimes likened to a skillful mahout who firmly wields the goad of meditation in order to tame the wild elephant of the unruly human mind. The tamed elephant here is not the Buddha himself, but the Buddha's *disciple*, who submits himself to the Buddha's "taming" and thus reflects the Buddha's status as consummate Teacher rather than as consummate Renouncer.

The elephant Pārileyyaka equally partakes in this image of the idealized elephant as one who is *tamed*. For as soon as he encounters the Buddha, he stops his aimless wandering, his heart becomes "quenched" (P. *nibbuto*), he gives rise to faith (P. *pasanna-citto*), and he settles down in one place to serve the Buddha with great devotion. Acting as the Buddha's gentle and tame companion, he is like a monk whose mind is well-controlled and who submits himself to the Buddha's authority—thus reminding us of the Buddha's status as consummate Teacher (in spite of his failure with the monks of Kosambī). The elephant thus simultaneously reflects the Buddha as consummate Renouncer and the Buddha as consummate Teacher (which is appropriate, we might note, to this time-period of the Buddha's life, ten years after his attainment of buddhahood). Through the double functioning of the elephant, we are assured both that the Buddha remains untainted by the petty quarreling of his monks *and* that, despite appearances, he has the power to bring this quarreling to an end. As we have seen, this dual perspective on who the elephant is allows for both identification and distance: The Buddha identifies with the elephant, yet he also maintains his human dominance over the animal world. Moreover, the elephant fulfills these various functions *silently*.[33] He exerts his effects in a way that requires no conscious acknowledgment—either from the audience of the story, or from the Buddha himself. This is often how animal characters function: Hoyt Long notes that "as the animal 'other' has not the means to voice any objection, at least linguistically, it has proved all the more useful for the acquisition and reinforcement of stable notions of the human 'self.' "[34]

Humanity and Animality

Beyond the relationship I have posited between the Buddha and the elephant, I also think that if we reconsider the larger context of the story as a whole, we can see that the story itself is engaged in a complex manipulation of the categories of humanity and animality. The quarreling monks of Kosambī are human beings, but through their stubborn fighting, they behave as if they were animals (an impression that is perhaps furthered by the fact that their dispute first arises over matters of bathroom etiquette). The elephant, on the other hand, is an animal, but through his devoted religious behavior, he behaves like a human being. Likewise, Kosambī is technically a human city, but in moral terms it has become a wilderness full of mindless animals—whereas the Pārileyyaka Forest, though technically a wilderness, is the only realm in which civilized human behavior seems to prevail. The story thus conveys the message that outward appearances may be deceptive: what makes one truly human has nothing to do with biological species or habitat.

This interpretation of the larger story can be further supported by taking a closer look at the cautionary tale of Prince Dīghāvu, which the Buddha relates to the monks of Kosambī in an effort to convince them to give up their fighting. In this tale,[35] Prince Dīghāvu sees his family's kingdom conquered by a rival king, King Brahmadatta, and watches helplessly as his own parents are cruelly executed. His father, just before dying, manages to recite a verse to him (a variation on verse 5 of the *Dhammapada*), warning him of the futility of seeking vengeance in the future: "Wrath (P. *vera*), dear Dīghāvu, is not appeased by wrath; wrath, dear Dīghāvu, is appeased by non-wrath."[36] Several years later, when Prince Dīghāvu has a perfect opportunity to exact his revenge against King Brahmadatta, he stops himself at the last minute by remembering his father's verse. The two men make peace and grant each other security, and Prince Dīghāvu then explains to King Brahmadatta the meaning of his father's verse:

> King, my mother and father were killed by you. But if *I* were to deprive *you* of life, then those who are desirous of *your* welfare would deprive *me* of life—and then those who are desirous of *my* welfare would deprive *them* of life. In this way, wrath would not be appeased by wrath. But now, the King has granted me life, and I have granted the King life. Thus, wrath has been appeased by non-wrath. This is why, King, my father said

> to me as he was dying, "Wrath, dear Dīghāvu, is not appeased by wrath; wrath, dear Dīghāvu, is appeased by non-wrath."[37]

Here, it is striking to note that the endless cycle of violence invoked by Prince Dīghāvu bears a stark resemblance to the "law of the fish" (S. *matsya-nyāya*) mentioned earlier (in Chapter 4)—the cruel law of predator-and-prey that governs the animal world in the absence of civilized human institutions such as kingship.[38] By exercising restraint and giving up his desire for revenge, Prince Dīghāvu has rejected the "law of the fish"—choosing to behave like a civilized human being rather than like an animal. Thus, when the Buddha relates this cautionary tale to the monks of Kosambī, he is telling them, in effect, to *stop behaving like animals and start behaving like human beings*. It is only when they refuse to heed his advice that the Buddha is forced to withdraw into the forest and dwell harmoniously with a truly "human" companion—who happens, of course, to be an elephant. The humans have turned into animals, while the animal has become human.[39]

And yet, as we saw before, the categorical distinction between human and animal must occasionally be reasserted. In the *Dhammapada Commentary*'s version, this is accomplished not only by having the elephant submissively serve the Buddha, but also by a particularly striking passage dealing with the Buddha's alms-gathering. Here, we are told that while the Buddha was dwelling in the Pārileyyaka Forest, he would go to a nearby village for alms, and the elephant would accompany him and carry his bowl and robe. However,

> once the Teacher reached the outskirts of the village, he would say to the elephant, "Pārileyyaka, you cannot go any farther than this! Give me my bowl and robe." And having retrieved his bowl and robe, he would enter the village for alms. And until the Teacher came back out, the elephant would stand right there, and when he came out, the elephant would go forth to meet him.[40]

The humanity attributed to the elephant thus seems to have certain spatial limits: Ultimately, the village is a *human* realm, and the elephant—as an *animal*—is barred from entering. The categorical distinction between animal and human is embodied by the physical border of the village and the Buddha's explicit command that the elephant is *not permitted to cross*. He can "go forth to meet" the Buddha, but he cannot cross the line. In this way, human superiority to the animal world is once again upheld. As we will see, this is only the first of several examples of the salience of physical borders and border-crossings in the *Dhammapada Commentary*'s version of this tale.

The Monkey's Gift of Honey

Among the three versions of the Pārileyyaka story, the *Dhammapada Commentary* version is unique in including an additional animal character—a monkey who observes the elephant's actions and is inspired to behave in similar ways. Here, too, we see the same tension between fellowship and otherness, between human identification with the animal and an assertion of human dominance. The monkey is humanized and ennobled—but ultimately, the story tells us, he is only a monkey.

The passage begins as follows:

> Now, at that time, a certain monkey, having observed the elephant getting up and exerting himself, day after day, to perform minor duties for the Tathāgata, thought to himself, "I will do something, too." One day, as he was roaming around, he saw a beehive that was free of flies. He broke off the beehive, brought the beehive together with its honeycomb to the Teacher, pulled a leaf off a plantain tree, deposited [the honeycomb] there, and gave it [to the Teacher]. The Teacher accepted it. Looking to see whether or not the Teacher would eat [the honey], the monkey saw the Teacher sit down holding [the honeycomb, but without eating any honey]. Wondering why, the monkey used the tip of a stick to turn the honeycomb over and examine it. Seeing some tiny eggs there, he gently removed them and again offered [the honeycomb to the Teacher]. The Teacher ate the honey.[41]

Here, we see that just as the elephant is moved by the presence of the Buddha to engage in human devotional behavior, so the monkey is similarly influenced by his observation of the elephant. Due to this salutary influence, the monkey leaves behind his animalistic ways and behaves like a human devotee (see Figure 6.1). The movement from *elephant* to *monkey* represents a considerable rise in the stakes, for while the elephant, as we have seen, is one of the favored animals of Buddhist literature—a noble animal often associated with royalty and frequently used to symbolize the Buddha himself—the monkey in Indian literature is the quintessential wild animal (P. *miga*), often referred to as the "*miga* of the trees" (P. *sākhāmiga*), and famous, as Wendy Doniger notes, for its "ingenious (and sometimes sinister) mischievousness"

FIGURE 6.1.

As far as I know, there are no depictions from India of the *Dhammapadaṭṭhakathā*'s version of the Pārileyyaka story, involving both the elephant and the monkey. Such depictions do appear to be common, however, in Thailand. This outdoor tableau at Wat Thep Phitak Punnaram in Pak Chong District, Nakhon Ratchasima Province, Thailand, depicts both the elephant Pārileyyaka's service to the Buddha and the monkey's gift of honey on a beehive. (Photo courtesy of Patrick Lepetit.)

as it leaps mindlessly from branch to branch.[42] Paul Waldau likewise observes that "the overall view of these animals is quite negative," and in much of Buddhist literature, "they are stupid and malicious" and "have a nature that precludes them from making anything constructive."[43] In some Buddhist texts, the monkey becomes an image for the agitated human mind: "The mind is agitated, like a monkey," the Buddha says in the *Theragāthā*[44]—while in the *Saṃyutta Nikāya*, the agitated human mind that flits about aimlessly from one idea to the next is compared to "a monkey roaming in a forest or woodland who grabs a branch, releases it and grabs another, then releases that and grabs yet another."[45] It is precisely such capricious "wildness" that the human mind should strive to overcome through spiritual discipline—causing the monk Valliya, for example, to admonish his own mind, "Stay still, Monkey, do not run!"[46]

In line with the greater degree of "wildness" characteristic of the monkey, the Buddha does not simply accept the monkey's service, as he willingly accepted the elephant's service. Instead, he *tests* the monkey's humanity by refusing to partake of any honey until the monkey has removed the eggs from the honeycomb and thus prevented tiny creatures from being killed. In this way, the monkey proves—much as Prince Dīghāvu did—that he has rejected the animalistic "law of the fish" and left animality behind. It is only at this point that the Buddha accepts the monkey's offering, for the monkey has earned his membership in this odd "human" community of the forest. The monkey is thus humanized, and his devoted religious behavior again serves to reflect the Buddha's status as consummate Teacher—one who exerts a calming and civilizing influence that spreads from the already-wild elephant to the even-wilder monkey.

The end of this episode, however, is perhaps equally instructive, for here we learn that the monkey is, after all, just a monkey—and human dominance over the animal world is thus reestablished:

> Being pleased in mind [*i.e., because the Buddha had eaten the honey*], the monkey leapt from one branch to another as if he were dancing. Then, the branch he had grabbed and the branch he had stepped on both

broke, and the monkey fell down onto the tip of a certain stake and was impaled.[47]

The monkey, it seems, has *not* totally eradicated his animalistic instincts after all, for now he jumps around carelessly—like a monkey—and this results in his sudden and painful death. Once the monkey has fulfilled his mirroring function, we might say, he is forcefully returned to animal status.[48]

When I first read this passage, I found it to be strangely reminiscent of a famous episode from Vālmīki's Sanskrit *Rāmāyaṇa*, involving the monkeys who serve as allies of the hero-god Rāma.[49] In this episode, the monkey troops led by Hanumān, having just discovered the location of the kidnapped princess Sītā, are hurrying back to bring this urgent news to Rāma when they unexpectedly stop at a pleasure-grove. There, they get intoxicated on honey-wine and engage in a "Rabelaisian orgy of drunkenness and destruction,"[50] leaping around violently and causing utter mayhem. For the reader of the epic, this odd and unanticipated episode seems to come out of nowhere, and it has the effect of suddenly pulling us back from the heroic nature of the monkeys and forcefully reminding us that they are *animals*. Likewise, in our story, the same monkey who, a moment earlier, had carefully plucked each tiny egg off a honeycomb out of respect for living beings, now leaps around with wild abandon, breaking branches left and right and managing to impale himself in the process. The monkey's humanity has been abruptly negated.

The monkey can thus be seen as a shadow of the elephant. Both the elephant and the monkey move back and forth between the categories of humanity and animality—the border between them sometimes collapsing, only later to be forcefully reinscribed. In this way, the image of the Buddha is refracted through a double set of mirrors that seem to vanish once their function has been fulfilled. In the process, his status as the consummate Teacher and Tamer—and his ultimate victory over the quarreling monks of Kosambī—are quietly reaffirmed.

More Borders, Border Crossings, and Tests

The *Dhammapada Commentary* version now continues the story with further playful manipulations of humanity, animality, borders, border crossings, and tests. As the Buddha dwells contentedly in the Pārileyyaka Forest, attended upon by the elephant, five hundred monks in the city of Sāvatthī, having learned of his location and growing increasingly anxious to see him, send Ānanda into the forest to retrieve him. Upon Ānanda's approach, the elephant Pārileyyaka—perhaps experiencing a momentary relapse into pure animality—rushes forth to attack him, but is forcibly stopped by the Buddha, who informs him, "This is the Buddha's personal attendant!"[51] Brought to his senses, the elephant immediately ceases his attack and resumes his civilized human demeanor—so much so, in fact, that he now enacts a sort of "test" of Ānanda before welcoming him into their midst:

> The elephant thought to himself, "If he is observant, he will not put his own requisites on the slab of stone where the Teacher sits," [and, sure enough,] the elder Ānanda put his bowl and robe on the ground. For those who are observant do not place their requisites on the beds or seats of venerable Teachers.[52]

Here, we have yet another moral "test": just as the Buddha tested the monkey for civilized human behavior, which consisted of rejecting the "law of the fish," so the elephant now tests Ānanda for civilized human behavior, which consists of being "observant" of the forms of monastic etiquette. In the first case, a human being tests an animal, while in the second case, an animal tests a human being. Once again, we are made to understand that true "humanity" is defined not by one's outward form or species, but rather by one's conscious exercise of moral decorum and restraint. The monkey passes this test by showing respect for other beings' lives, and Ānanda passes this test by showing respect for the exalted status of the Buddha. In this way, both prove themselves to be "human" and earn their proper place in the civilized realm of Pārileyyaka.

Let us pass quickly now to the end of the story, where there are several further invocations of borders and border crossings. Eventually, the Buddha summons the five hundred monks into the Pārileyyaka Forest, recites some verses to them about the benefits of dwelling alone or with virtuous companions (from the *Nāgavagga*, or "Elephant Chapter," of the *Dhammapada*),[53] and agrees to return with them to Sāvatthī. As they begin to depart, however, the elephant blocks the Buddha's path to prevent him from leaving the forest. This is met by a rather stern rebuke on the part of the Buddha—a rebuke that explicitly invokes the inferiority of the animal state and the spiritual uniqueness of human beings:

> Then the Teacher said to the elephant, "Pārileyyaka, I am not turning back! In your present state of existence, you cannot attain the transic states, nor insight, nor the fruits of the path. You must stay here!" Hearing these words, the elephant placed his trunk into his mouth, and slowly retreated, weeping.[54]

In other words, now that the peaceful interlude in the forest is over, and the elephant has finished serving his mirroring function, we are plunged right back into the world depicted in Chapter 1—the world of the animal rebirth as an "unfortunate destiny" (P. *duggati*), a realm lacking in wisdom, insight, moral agency, or any potential for spiritual progress. Likewise, we are back in the world depicted in Chapter 2, in which animals can do nothing but weep when reminded of their animal status. The forest, too, has been suddenly transformed. Now that the episode is coming to an end, the forest is no longer the truly civilized "human" realm, but has reverted to its natural condition as the proper habitat for birds and beasts. Human dominance once again reigns supreme.

This is followed, however, by one last border (and prevented border crossing)—one that seems to introduce a final element of ambiguity into the story:

> When the Teacher reached the entrance to the village, he said to the elephant, "Pārileyyaka, you must not go beyond this point, for the

> habitations of men are full of danger. Stay here!" Weeping, the elephant stayed right there, and when the Teacher had gone beyond his range of vision, he died of a broken heart.[55]

Once again, the Buddha prevents the animal from entering the human village—but this time he does so because "the habitations of men are full of danger." In saying this, the Buddha seems to suggest that it is the elephant who constitutes the civilized being, whereas the village is full of animalistic humans who—following the "law of the fish"—might cause harm to the noble elephant. Here, we are reminded of the Pāli *jātakas'* world of "(human) nature, red in tooth and claw," and the humanity of the elephant thus receives one final (if subtle) acknowledgment. Ultimately, however, much like the black snake and fierce buffalo of the *Avadānaśataka,* the elephant can only respond to this acknowledgment by weeping and losing his life.[56] His function as the Buddha's double is over.

* * *

I hope I have succeeded in demonstrating that the story of the Buddha's sojourn in the Pārileyyaka Forest is far more than just a charming fable about Buddha-elephant companionship (though it is surely that, as well). Instead, the story is a complex construction that cleverly manipulates human and animal characters, human and animal habitats, and the abstract categories of humanity and animality themselves—sometimes reversing these categories with each other, and sometimes using physical and spatial borders to once again pry them apart. Central to this overall process is the elephant's role as a *mirror* for the figure of the Buddha—underlining his glorified status as both Tamer and one who is Tamed.

CHAPTER SEVEN

Billboard for the Buddha

The Elephant Nāḷāgiri

Nāḷāgiri, you are an Animal-Elephant,
but I am the Buddha-Elephant!

(*Cullahaṃsa Jātaka*)[1]

Another elephant who constitutes a "double" of the Buddha—though in a very different manner than Pārileyyaka—is the cruel and fierce elephant Nāḷāgiri, sent forth on a rampage in order to kill the Buddha, yet instantaneously tamed and made docile by the enormous power of his presence. In the following, I will argue that Nāḷāgiri serves as a *billboard* for the Buddha's power and charisma. The Buddha's effortless and instantaneous taming of the maddened elephant Nāḷāgiri dramatically demonstrates his absolute mastery over the forces of nature, animality, and passion, as well as his superior masculinity in comparison to the many male disciples who surround him. This mastery, moreover, is outwardly displayed within a grand public spectacle that converts millions of living beings to Buddhism, with hardly a drop of the Dharma or Buddhist teaching—thereby highlighting what might be referred to as the Buddha's "grace." Throughout the episode, Nāḷāgiri's status as an animal is crucial to the way in which he functions. Yet here again, we will see the same dynamic at play as we saw in the case of Pārileyyaka: on the one hand, a *parallelism* between Buddha and Elephant, and on the other hand, a *hierarchy* by means of which human domination over the animal world is celebrated and affirmed.

The Devadatta Cycle of Stories

The episode involving Nāḷāgiri takes place within a larger cycle of stories involving the Buddha's cousin and archenemy, Devadatta. Though I am not concerned here with analyzing the figure of Devadatta or the significance of his involvement in the Buddha's life, a basic familiarity with this cycle of stories is essential to placing the Nāḷāgiri episode within its proper context.[2]

According to various Pāli sources, Devadatta was the Buddha's cousin and joined the Sangha during the Buddha's visit home to Kapilavastu shortly after his attainment of buddhahood. His early career as a monk seems to have been exemplary; as Reginald Ray has pointed out, various Buddhist sources depict Devadatta as "an impeccable saint whose sanctity is acknowledged by other Buddhist saints"—such as when Sāriputta praises his "great psychic power" and "great majesty," or when the Buddha includes him in a list of eleven mindful and awakened disciples, or when the *Saddharmapuṇḍarīka Sūtra* predicts his future buddhahood and praises him for spiritually assisting the Buddha in a previous life.[3] Nevertheless, Devadatta has gone down in Buddhist history as the archenemy of the Buddha, responsible for fomenting a schism within the Sangha and trying to assassinate the Buddha on three different occasions.

According to Pāli sources, about eight years prior to the Buddha's *parinibbāna*, Devadatta begins to grow jealous of the Buddha's great fame and power. In order to compete with the Buddha, Devadatta successfully secures the patronage of Prince Ajātasattu of the kingdom of Magadha, and under the prince's patronage, he begins to enjoy great honor, gain, and fame. Emboldened by his growing notoriety, Devadatta rises one day in the assembly of monks and suggests to the Buddha that now that the Buddha is quite old, perhaps he should retire and hand leadership of the Sangha over to Devadatta. The Buddha responds with an insult and a disciplinary action against Devadatta, which further inflames the latter's jealousy and hatred. Again conspiring with Prince Ajātasattu, Devadatta formulates a plan to assassinate the Buddha and take his place.

In his first assassination attempt, he dispatches a series of men to go and kill the Buddha, but all of them are overcome by the Buddha's majesty as soon as they approach him and end up becoming devoted lay followers. In his second assassination attempt, Devadatta climbs to the top of Vulture Peak Mountain and hurls down a great stone in the Buddha's direction. At the last minute, however, two lower mountain peaks magically come together to intercept the stone, and only a fragment hits the Buddha, injuring his foot and drawing blood. Finally, in his third assassination attempt, Devadatta bribes Ajātasattu's mahouts to get the fierce war elephant Nāḷāgiri intoxicated on liquor and set him loose on the road where the Buddha is walking for alms, confident that Nāḷāgiri will attack and kill the Buddha. But this attempt, too, is foiled when the Buddha unhesitatingly approaches Nāḷāgiri, suffuses him with benevolence, and reaches out his right hand to stroke the elephant's forehead, whereupon Nāḷāgiri is immediately tamed—falling at the Buddha's feet, listening to a few words of the Dhamma preached on his behalf, and becoming docile and nonviolent forever after.

Having failed three times to kill the Buddha, Devadatta, along with four of his followers, attempts to bring about a schism in the Sangha—and although this episode involving schism may have interesting historical significance, it need not concern us here.[4] As a result of these many misdeeds, Devadatta is ultimately swallowed up into the lowest hell of Avīci, where he suffers for thousands of years. In the Pāli *jātakas*, moreover, we learn that Devadatta's hostility toward the Buddha was long-standing in nature, having been manifested repeatedly in one life after another throughout the bodhisattva's long career. Thus does Devadatta earn his status as the paradigmatic villain, archenemy, and opponent of the Buddha.[5]

The episode involving the Buddha's confrontation with the elephant Nāḷāgiri thus takes place within a larger cycle of stories, all of which allow the Buddha to demonstrate his overwhelming power and majesty. In particular, we should note the utter ease and effortlessness with which the Buddha foils the three attempts upon his life. In the first attempt, the assassins sent to kill him are immediately converted as soon as they come into the Buddha's presence; in the second attempt, the very mountains themselves move in order to prevent the Buddha's death; and in the third attempt, the elephant Nāḷāgiri is instantaneously tamed. In fact, as the Buddha himself notes, "It is impossible, Monks, it cannot come to pass that a Tathāgata would lose his life by being attacked by another. Monks, Tathāgatas do not attain *parinibbāna* by being attacked."[6] The Dhamma or Buddhist teaching is insignificant in all three cases, and what is emphasized is the power and charisma of the Buddha himself. Perhaps it is also significant that by means of these three attempts, the Buddha is shown to have mastery over *human beings,* the *world of nature,* and the *animal realm,* respectively.

Keeping this larger context in mind, I now turn to take a closer look at the Nāḷāgiri episode itself. My analysis focuses on three Pāli versions of the story: (1) the version related in the *Cullavagga* of the Pāli *Vinaya*; (2) the version related in the "Story of the Present" of the *Cullahaṃsa Jātaka* (Pāli *Jātaka* No. 533); and (3) the identical story found in the *Buddhavaṃsa Commentary* but told about the former buddha Piyadassin.[7] Regarding the last, this story is identical in all respects to the episode involving Nāḷāgiri, with the only difference being a change in the names of the characters. Rather than the monk Devadatta conspiring with the prince Ajātasattu to send the elephant Nāḷāgiri against the Buddha Gotama, we have the monk Soṇa conspiring with the prince Mahāpaduma to send the elephant Doṇamukha against the former buddha Piyadassin. Yet the story is exactly the same. In addition, I also draw upon one Sanskrit version of the story from the *Saṅghabhedavastu* of the *Mūlasarvāstivāda Vinaya*, [8] where the elephant is called Dhanapāla or Dhanapālaka rather than Nāḷāgiri (a name he also bears, but only after being tamed, in the *Cullahaṃsa Jātaka* version).[9] However, as this version of the story has several unique features that distinguish it from the Pāli accounts, it is also treated separately at the end of the chapter. Finally, for the sake of readability in the discussion that follows, I also weave all four versions together, only occasionally specifying the distinctions between them (though all such distinctions are made clear in the notes).[10]

Man versus Beast

Throughout his lifetime, the Buddha encounters a great variety of men, women, animals, deities, and supernatural beings, and these encounters take many different forms—involving teaching, worship, friendship, patronage, and hostility. Yet the Buddha's encounter with the elephant Nāḷāgiri is not an ordinary or typical encounter, by any means. Instead, it is constructed and set up as a direct confrontation between Man and Beast.

The Buddha can be seen as the quintessential Man; in fact, he is a "Great Man" (P. *mahāpurisa*), one who brings to perfect fulfillment all ideal human qualities—qualities that define what it means to be human and that distinguish human beings from the brutish animal realm. Standing opposed to the Buddha as the quintessential Man is Nāḷāgiri as the quintessential Beast. Although elephants—as we saw in Chapter 6—are often idealized in Buddhist literature and attributed with many noble and quasi-human qualities, they are also one of the paradigmatic "wild" animals, associated with the forest, the jungle, and the wilderness. Nāḷāgiri embodies these "wild" qualities to an extraordinary degree, for he is described as a "fierce, cruel, man-killing"[11] elephant, one who "approaches as if Death itself were attacking."[12] Every time he is let out of his stall, in fact, he "injures many people on the highways, streets, crossroads, and intersections"[13]—so much so that the citizens of Rājagṛha beg the king to warn them ahead of time before letting him out of his stall. During the assassination attempt itself, as he rushes toward the Buddha, he utterly destroys all signs of human civilization (such as houses, buildings, and gateways) and kills many people and other animals along the way (see Figure 7.1). His entire body is "dyed with blood," his eyes are "permeated by an inner blaze," and he "devours [the remains of his victims] like a man-eating demon."[14] Significantly, at the time when this episode takes place, Nāḷāgiri is also described as "flowing with the juice of musth in seven places."[15] Musth is a periodic condition experienced by male elephants and characterized by soaring levels of testosterone, sexual passion, extreme violence and aggression, and a telltale secretion from the elephant's temporal

FIGURE 7.1.
The elephant Nāḷāgiri goes on a rampage through the streets of Rājagṛha. White marble pillar fragment from Amarāvatī (Andhra Pradesh, India), 1st to 3rd c. CE. Government Museum, Chennai. Photo courtesy of American Institute of Indian Studies.

glands. The features of musth were well understood in the elephant lore of ancient India (known in Sanskrit as *Gaja-Śāstra*), and the elephant in musth is frequently used in Sanskrit literature as an image of uncontrollable aggression and sexuality.[16] Not content with the level of ferocity available through the condition of musth alone, however, our sources also tell us that the mahouts have fed Nāḷāgiri abundant liquor to make him intoxicated (twice his usual ration, according to one source), as well as striking him with spears and lances in order to further enrage him.

Nāḷāgiri is thus a perfect embodiment of brutish animality and passion, unchecked by any restraint and mindlessly driven forward by the natural impulses of sexuality, violence, and aggression—an extreme embodiment of the difficulty all animals experience in controlling and calming down their mental faculties. As such, he stands opposed to the Perfect Man represented by the Buddha—one who has restrained, suppressed, and finally eradicated all passions and afflictions in favor of civilized human values that need to be *cultivated*. Indeed, the Buddha stands at the very apex of the human's ability to engage in conscious mental cultivation, whereas Nāḷāgiri is motivated solely by animal instinct, uncontrolled passions, and intoxicating drink. The confrontation between them—the confrontation between Man and Beast—is thus a direct contest between brute animalistic passion and the human capacity for self-transformation.

The *animality* of Nāḷāgiri is thus central—and this is clearly recognized by the Buddha himself, who refers directly to Nāḷāgiri's unfortunate rebirth "from an inferior animal womb," as a result of which he "takes delight in killing others and destroying their lives."[17] Nāḷāgiri's animality is also central for Devadatta, for in formulating his plan, he refers explicitly to the fundamental difference between human beings and animals:

> No human being is able to approach the ascetic Gotama once they have seen his beautiful and majestic person. But the king has a fierce, cruel, man-killing elephant named Nāḷāgiri, who *knows nothing* about the virtues of the Buddha, Dhamma, and Sangha—and he will be able to kill him.[18]

Repeatedly referring to the elephant as one who "knows nothing" (P. *na jānāti*) about Buddha, Dhamma, and Sangha, the story emphasizes the lack of higher mental faculties (P. *paññā*) that most distinguishes the animal from the human, and forever condemns the animal to behavior driven primarily by passion. Human beings endowed with *paññā*, and thus capable of *knowing* the virtues of Buddha, Dhamma, and Sangha, Devadatta suggests, could never go through with actually killing the

Buddha (as he learned, no doubt, from his first assassination attempt). It is in this sense that the contest between the Buddha and Nāḷāgiri can be seen as a contest between Man and Beast.

At the same time, however, we should further understand that this confrontation between paradigmatic Man and Beast is also a contest between nirvana and samsara. Nāḷāgiri can be seen as an embodiment of the forces of samsara, whereas the Buddha embodies the ability—belonging to human beings alone—to overcome the forces of samsara and attain the goal of nirvana. In fact, it is quite clear that the confrontation between the Buddha and Nāḷāgiri is a shadow-image of the Buddha's original confrontation with Māra—or that which allowed him to attain nirvana in the first place.[19] Significantly, the figure of Māra—ruler and fundamental embodiment of the forces of samsara—is commonly depicted as riding upon an elephant in musth,[20] and he presides over troops that are characterized, first and foremost, by *animality*—described in both the *Buddhacarita* and the *Mahāvastu* as having the faces of horses, buffaloes, asses, goats, rams, camels, deer, lions, tigers, panthers, bears, dogs, hogs, cats, ravens, cocks, vultures, eagles, and fish.[21] Animality is thus used in the battle with Māra to represent the nefarious forces of samsara, which find their most potent expression in the maddened elephant in musth. In a further parallel with the Nāḷāgiri episode, the Buddha defeats Māra by extending the fingers of his right hand and touching the earth as witness (in the *bhūmisparśa-mūdra*), just as he later tames Nāḷāgiri by extending his right hand and gently stroking the elephant's forehead. And just as Nāḷāgiri responds to the Buddha's touch by falling at the Buddha's feet, so does Māra's elephant Girimekhala (in the *Nidānakathā*) "fall to the earth on his knees"[22] at the moment of the Buddha's attainment of buddhahood. The contest between the Buddha and Nāḷāgiri is thus symbolic of the larger cosmic drama pitting the freedom of nirvana against the bondage of samsara. Yet it takes the particular form of *Man* confronting *Beast*.

In this contest between Man and Beast, between animalistic passions and human self-cultivation, between the forces of samsara and the human ability to attain nirvana, it is obvious who must prevail—definitively, completely, and instantaneously. All four versions of the story make this victory clear. According to the Pāli *Vinaya*:

> Then the Blessed One suffused the elephant Nāḷāgiri with thoughts of benevolence. And the elephant Nāḷāgiri, permeated by the Blessed One's thoughts of benevolence, lowered his trunk, approached the Blessed One, and stood before him. The Blessed One stroked the elephant Nāḷāgiri's forehead with his right hand, and spoke to him in verse.... Then the elephant Nāḷāgiri took dust from the Blessed One's feet with his trunk, sprinkled it over his head, and shrank away, moving backward for as long as he could see the Blessed One. Then the elephant Nāḷāgiri went to the elephant stables and stood in his own stall. And in this way did the elephant Nāḷāgiri become tame.[23]

In the *Cullahaṃsa Jātaka*, the Buddha again suffuses Nāḷāgiri with benevolence and "summons him in a gentle voice," whereupon the elephant

> opened his eyes, and when he beheld the beauty and splendor of the Blessed One, he felt a thrill. His state of intoxication was brought to an end through the power of the Buddha, and he lowered his trunk, shook his ears, and came and fell at the Tathāgata's feet.

Again, the Buddha speaks to him briefly and strokes his forehead, "and from then on, he became extremely gentle and was hostile toward no one"—in fact, "had he not been a mere animal, he would have attained the fruit of stream-entry."[24] Similarly, in the *Buddhavaṃsa Commentary*, the Buddha (Piyadassin) suffuses the elephant (Doṇamukha) with benevolence, "with his heart calmly pervaded by compassion," and the elephant,

> the tendrils of his heart made soft by that suffusion of benevolence, became aware of the fault of anger within him. Unable to stand before the Blessed One, due to shame, he fell down with his head at the feet of the Blessed One, as if he were entering the earth.[25]

Again, the Buddha strokes his forehead with his right hand and preaches to him briefly, whereupon "that noble elephant attained discernment and became like the most well-trained disciple endowed with ethical conduct and good behavior. Thus did the Blessed One ... tame the noble elephant" (see Figure 7.2).[26]

Finally, in the *Saṅghabhedavastu*, the Buddha's taming of Nāḷāgiri takes a slightly different form (addressed further below), but it again

FIGURE 7.2.
The Buddha stretches forth his right hand to stroke the elephant Nāḷāgiri's forehead. Mathura school, 2nd c. CE. Indian Museum, Kolkata. (Photo by Anandajoti Bhikkhu, licensed under CC BY 2.0.)

results in Nāḷāgiri immediately sobering up and coming to the Buddha "with a gentle, wandering gait," after which he begins following the Buddha around like a devoted, lovesick puppy.[27]

The brute physical strength of the maddened elephant is thus no match for the Buddha's virtue of benevolence (P. *mettā*), assiduously cultivated over millions of lifetimes. The human ability to cultivate spiritual qualities such as benevolence and compassion is thus seen to prevail over the animalistic impulses of violence, sexuality, and aggression. Man overcomes Beast—and nirvana conquers samsara—in an effortless and spectacular display. Thus is human dominance over the animal world (and everything that it stands for) definitively proclaimed.[28]

Elephant versus Elephant

The dramatic opposition I have thus far drawn between paradigmatic Man and Beast is complicated, however, by the contrasting *kinship* between humans and animals—or, in this case, the fact that animals in Buddhism are not solely the embodiments of brutish instincts and uncontrollable passions, but are, in fact, capable of some limited degree of reason, rationality, moral agency, and mental control (even if they do pale in comparison to human beings in regard to these abilities). Similarly, the Buddha himself, despite being the Ultimate Human Being, is not merely a "Great Man," but is also frequently likened to powerful male animals—sometimes referred to, in fact, as a "Great Lion" (S. *mahāsiṃha*), a "Great Elephant" (S. *mahānāga*), or a "Bull of a Man" (S. *narārṣabha*).[29] In specific regard to elephants, for example, the Buddha is frequently associated with a magnificent white elephant—his conception occurring when his mother dreams of a white elephant entering her right side—and is often metaphorically described as an elephant. Elephant imagery is pervasive in Buddhist literature, and the violent and passion-ridden elephant in musth (as embodied by Nāḷāgiri) stands at one end of a continuum that includes, on its other end, the noble and compassionate white elephant sometimes associated with the Buddha. In fact, as Rajmohan Ramanathapillai has noted, the

Buddhist path of spiritual transformation can be envisioned as a sort of continuum of different kinds of elephants:

> This continuum is illustrated with Mara's musth elephant on the left (imperfection); earthly gray male elephants in the middle (potential to be tamed); and the perfect white elephant on the right. This image of a sacred white elephant embodying love and compassion illustrates the . . . perfection toward which one must strive.[30]

The suggestion being made here, of course, is that in the contest between Man and Beast, the Beast is not something wholly "other" to the Man; in fact, it is really the Beast that lies within Man himself that must be vanquished and transformed.[31] The Buddha's utter dominance over Nāḷāgiri is thus counterbalanced by a certain necessary kinship between them: both must be elephants.

This simultaneous parallelism and hierarchy come out clearly in the episode itself. Thus, in the *Buddhavaṃsa Commentary,* when the mahout releases the fierce elephant against the Buddha, this is described as one elephant being released to pursue another elephant: "Then he sent that elephant—glorious among elephants, like [Sakka's elephant] Erāvaṇa—to kill that other glorious elephant, the Elephant-Among-Sages."[32] Later on in the story, these two opponents are referred to as the "Buddha-Elephant" (P. *buddha-nāga*) and the "Elephant-Elephant" (P. *hatthi-nāga*).[33] The two figures are obviously parallel—since both are "elephants"—yet the Buddha is insistent on asserting the superiority of one elephant over another. In the Pāli *Vinaya,* he says to Nāḷāgiri, "Elephant, do not mess with the Elephant[-Among-Men], for messing with the Elephant[-Among-Men], Elephant, leads to suffering!"[34] In the *Cullahaṃsa Jātaka*, the contrast drawn is between the "Buddha-Elephant" (P. *buddha-nāga*) and the "Animal-Elephant" (P. *tiracchāna-nāga*), and the Buddha states forthrightly, "Nāḷāgiri, you are an Animal-Elephant, but I am the Buddha-Elephant!"[35]

The recognition of one "elephant's" dominance over another—and thus, of a simultaneous kinship and hierarchy in humanity's relationship to the animal—even becomes a marker for one's commitment to Buddhism. For as the Buddha and Nāḷāgiri approach each other, huge crowds of people gather to watch. According to the Pāli *Vinaya*, "those among them who were nonbelievers, had no faith, and were of weak intellect" immediately assume that the huge and powerful animal Nāḷāgiri will easily injure the weaker human being. But "those among them who were believers, who had faith, who were wise, learned, and intelligent" understand that the human "elephant" will prevail, and joyfully think to themselves, "Soon, my friends, one elephant will come into conflict with another elephant!"[36] In the *Cullahaṃsa Jātaka*, the nonbelievers again assume that since Nāḷāgiri "does not know the virtues of the Buddha, [Dhamma, and Sangha], he will destroy the golden-colored body of the ascetic Gotama and bring about his death." But those who have faith confidently declare, "Today, for sure, there will be a battle between the Buddha-Elephant and the Animal-Elephant, and we will see Nāḷāgiri be tamed through the Buddha's incomparable sport!"[37] Those who have faith in Buddhism are thus depicted as understanding both the parallelism and the hierarchy between one elephant and the other. They *know* that Man and Beast are coexistent, but they also believe in Man's ability to overcome and dominate the Beast that lies within.

The human being's impulse toward simultaneous identification and dominance in relation to the animal is not unique to Indian Buddhism, but seems to be a common dynamic in many cultural contexts. Erica Fudge has described this dynamic through the insight that "anthropocentrism creates anthropomorphism"—that is, the desire to see human beings as central leads inevitably to contrasting human beings with animals, yet this contrast is only made possible by admitting a certain likeness between them. Speaking of early modern English culture, Fudge observes that in writings dealing with the animal,

> the animal is represented as the antithesis of the human. But in presenting the animal as the thing which the human is not—begging to be eaten, for example—writers give animals a status, that of beggar, which undermines the desire to make a clear separation between the species.

> To assert human supremacy writers turn to discuss animals, but in this turning they reveal the frailty of the supremacy which is being asserted. Paradoxically humans need animals in order to be human. The human cannot be separated because in separation lies unprovability.[38]

Fudge's insight allows us to recognize the Buddha's *dependence* upon Nāḷāgiri to showcase his own humanity, and also adds a certain sense of poignancy to their encounter. The Buddha's absolute mastery over the maddened elephant Nāḷāgiri is powerful and impressive, indeed. Yet it also suggests something about the frailty and fragility of the human project of attaining buddhahood—which finally depends, for its recognition, upon the unfortunate destinies that surround it. The Buddha's dependence upon Nāḷāgiri becomes especially clear, moreover, when we consider the episode's overwhelming concern with *public display*.

A Grand Public Spectacle

In some ways, the Buddha's taming of a wild animal by suffusing it with benevolence (P. *mettā*) is nothing remarkable. In fact, he frequently advised his own monks to practice a similar stratagem to protect themselves from wild animals when they went out into the wilderness to meditate. According to Schmithausen and Maithrimurthi, "already in the canonical texts we come across the idea that a monk can protect himself from being attacked by wild or dangerous animals by cultivating and irradiating loving-kindness (P. *mettā*, S. *maitrī*)."[39] But what distinguishes the Nāḷāgiri episode from the many passages containing this idea cited by Schmithausen and Maithrimurthi[40] are, first, the Buddha's insistence that *he alone* must tame the elephant, and, second, the episode's overwhelming emphasis on *public display*.

In the *Cullahaṃsa Jātaka*, for example, the Buddha's encounter with Nāḷāgiri is not an unexpected surprise. In fact, Ajātasattu (now the king) actually warns the entire city ahead of time that the fierce Nāḷāgiri will be let loose upon the streets and advises the city's inhabitants to stay indoors. Faithful Buddhist laypeople, upon hearing this news, go to the Buddha and urge him *not* to enter the city for alms;

instead, they will provide alms for him and his monks right there in the Bamboo Grove. In other words, why not avoid this dangerous situation altogether? The Buddha, however, while agreeing to accept alms in the Bamboo Grove, also insists upon entering the city and confronting the elephant. "Tomorrow," he declares, "I will tame the elephant Nāḷāgiri, perform a miracle, and destroy the heretics!"[41] On the following morning, moreover, he orders Ānanda to instruct all of the monks residing in the eighteen great monasteries around Rājagaha to enter the city along with him (in the *Saṅghabhedavastu*, this amounts to five hundred monks altogether).[42] Thus, in contrast to the scenario of a single monk meditating alone in the wilderness and unexpectedly encountering a wild animal, the Buddha intentionally engineers a grand public procession through the streets of the city of Rājagaha.

Once they enter the city and the monks see Nāḷāgiri rushing toward them, they again urge the Buddha to turn back, but the Buddha replies, "Don't be afraid, Monks! I am capable of taming Nāḷāgiri."[43] At this point, a number of other people attempt to save the Buddha's life by offering to confront the elephant in his place—but the Buddha makes it clear that *he alone* must do the taming. Sāriputta, seeing himself as the "son" of the Buddha and observing that "when a duty arises for the father, it is indeed the burden of the eldest son," declares, "I alone will tame him!"[44] The Buddha, however, sharply admonishes him with an aggressive statement of the absolute superiority of *his* power over that of his disciples: "Sāriputta, the power of the Buddha is one thing; the power of his disciple is something else altogether. Stop it."[45] Eighty other senior monks make the same request, but the Buddha refuses them all. Finally, Ānanda, "being unable to comply [with the Buddha's command] because of his powerful affection for the Teacher," yells out, "Let this elephant kill me first!"[46] He throws himself in front of the Buddha and refuses to move, even after the Buddha has commanded him three times, whereupon the Buddha makes use of his supernatural powers to forcibly pluck Ānanda out of the way and deposit him back among the other monks. Clearly, the Buddha is concerned that *he alone* should confront the elephant. The Buddha's insistence that his disciples get out of the way may even have been a cause of some embarrassment, for in one of the "dilemmas" posed in the *Milindapañha*, King Milinda is puzzled by this episode and wonders why all of the arhats ran away from the elephant, when arhats are supposed to be free of all fear? It is only by engaging in its usual casuistry that the *Milindapañha* is able to make sense of the Buddha's disciples retreating.[47]

These details make it clear that in addition to demonstrating Man's superiority over Beast, the Buddha is equally concerned with showcasing his absolute dominance over all other male disciples. (Perhaps this is why he is so insistent that all those monks should enter the city along with him.) There is a strongly *gendered* element to the scene, embodied by the Buddha's "macho" attitude and his aggressive belittlement of his male disciples' inferior powers. The Buddha is representative not so much of human potential as a whole, but of *male* humanity—he is the Ultimate Man, described in the *Mahāvastu* as "the Man, the True Man, the Great Man, the Bull Man, the Substantial Man, the Hero Man, the Elephant Man, the Lion Man, the Kingly Man . . . the Chief Man, the Thoroughbred Man, the Foremost Man."[48] This Ultimate Man then goes on to demonstrate his protective powers over women and children as well. For immediately following the failed interventions of Sāriputta and Ānanda, a mother carrying a baby on her hip and running away from Nāḷāgiri in a state of panic accidentally drops her baby in the path of the maddened elephant. The Buddha saves the baby by directly challenging Nāḷāgiri: "Hey there, Nāḷāgiri!," he yells, "They did not get you drunk on sixteen pitchers of liquor so that you could seize somebody else; they did it so that you could seize me!"[49] The Buddha *alone*—as Ultimate Man and Ultimate Father—*must* demonstrate his mastery over the maddened elephant.

The Buddha's highly gendered and "macho" attitude takes a slightly different form in the *Saṅghabhedavastu* version, where it is Devadatta who plays the part of the weak and inferior male. As Nāḷāgiri rushes toward the Buddha, Devadatta yells out from the top of the palace: "O Ten-Powered One, I will see you crushed by the force of the elephant! O Son of the Śākyas, today, you will no longer have any disciples!" The Buddha's pugilistic response makes him sound somewhat like a boy in a schoolyard fight:

> You are vile, Devadatta! You have uttered words of challenge without reckoning with me, the one powerful with the Ten Powers. Now see the power of the marvelous one who is powerful with the Ten Powers![50]

He then proceeds to perform a series of miracles (addressed further below) that lead directly to the taming of Nāḷāgiri. Once again, it is *he alone*, as Ultimate Man, who must dominate the maddened elephant.

Throughout this assertion of the Buddha's superior masculinity, there is also a strong emphasis on the presence of *spectators* and the element of *public display*. In the Pāli *Vinaya*, we are told that "people climbed up onto terraces, balconies, and rooftops"[51] to watch the confrontation, while the *Cullahaṃsa Jātaka* similarly refers to a "great crowd"[52] gathering at the scene. Once the elephant has been tamed, the crowd shouts, claps their hands, and "throws all kinds of ornaments, covering the body of the elephant"[53]—thus creating a spectacular visual display. Likewise, in the *Buddhavaṃsa Commentary*, the great crowds of people honor the now docile elephant "in many ways with fragrant garlands of flowers, sandalwood, perfumes, aromatic powders, ornaments, etc., and wave banners of cloth on all sides," while "the drums of the gods resound against the surface of the sky."[54] The drama of Man's instantaneous victory over Beast thus becomes a mass public spectacle and ritualistic display taking place in the very heart of the city.

Far from edifying just a single animal, moreover, the Buddha's taming of Nāḷāgiri has far-reaching soteriological reverberations that become famous in later Buddhist history. In the *Cullahaṃsa Jātaka*, it is said that as a result of the taming of Nāḷāgiri, "eighty-four thousand living beings drank the nectar of immortality," whereupon the Buddha left the city "like a warrior who has won a victory."[55] In the *Buddhavaṃsa Commentary*, "eighty hundred thousand *koṭis* [of living beings] penetrated the Dhamma," and this became the third of the "three penetrations of the Dhamma" that characterized the Buddha Piyadassin's glorious career.[56] And, in one of the dilemmas of the *Milindapañha*, when King Milinda wonders whether it is possible for laypeople to attain nirvana without becoming monks, the monk Nāgasena answers with a long list of occasions upon which this occurred—including the taming of Nāḷāgiri, when "ninety million living beings"[57] attained nirvana. The taming of Nāḷāgiri thus takes on not only public, but perhaps even *cosmic*, proportions—a far cry indeed from the scenario of a single monk meditating alone in the wilderness. Perhaps it is appropriate, then, that the Buddha's taming of Nāḷāgiri soon became one of the "Eight Great Miracles" (S. *aṣṭamahāprātihārya*) of the Buddha's life and career, and its location (Rājagṛha) a major site of pilgrimage.[58]

Finally, we should also note once again the relatively insignificant role played by the Dharma within this encounter. In the Pāli *Vinaya* and the *Cullahaṃsa Jātaka*, the Buddha's preaching to Nāḷāgiri consists of only a single stanza (the same stanza in both cases), while in the *Buddhavaṃsa Commentary*, it consists of eight stanzas that are nevertheless limited to the basic theme of nonviolence. No "higher" Buddhist doctrines are ever enunciated—certainly nothing that one might expect would result in the conversion of millions of beings throughout the universe. In the *Saṅghabhedavastu* version, it is true, the Buddha's preaching to Nāḷāgiri does include the statement that "all conditioned states are impermanent, all things are without self, and nirvana is peace"[59]—yet even here, it is limited to just a few sentences. In all four versions of the story, the elephant is tamed *before* a word of the Dharma is ever uttered, and the millions of people who are edified are clearly reacting to their *witnessing of the taming,* rather than to any content of the Dharma preached by the Buddha. In terms of the ongoing tension between the centrality of the Buddha and the centrality of the Dharma, the story comes down definitively on the side of the Buddha, being driven by an overriding concern with displaying the Buddha's majesty, charisma, and grace.

It is all of these elements taken together that lead me to view Nāḷāgiri not merely as a "double" of the Buddha, but more specifically, as a *billboard* for the Buddha's power, charisma, and masculinity. Through his instantaneous taming of Nāḷāgiri, the Buddha's absolute mastery and dominance over the forces of nature, animality, and passion are spectacularly displayed before an audience of cosmic proportions. At the same time, however, this billboard necessarily shares in the identity of the figure whose power it advertises: Man and Beast remain locked together in a symbiotic relationship.

Nāḷāgiri and the Spanish Bullfight

My interpretation of the Buddha's encounter with Nāḷāgiri has been inspired, in part, by Garry Marvin's classic analysis of the cultural significance of the Spanish bullfight (*la corrida de toros*),[60] which bears many striking similarities to the Nāḷāgiri episode. In brief, Marvin argues that the *bull* in a Spanish bullfight is a pure embodiment of Nature, while the human *matador* who confronts it is a pure embodiment of Culture. As an embodiment of Nature, the bull must be a *toro bravo*, or "wild bull," specially bred to possess the fierce and aggressive qualities of a good fighting bull and distinct from the ordinary domesticated bull subject to human control. Moreover, the bull must never before have encountered a man with the cape—thus ensuring that the animal is free of any "training" or "learning" and is acting on instinct alone. In contrast, the matador, as an embodiment of Culture, is seen as the absolute epitome of Spanish cultural values—as reflected in his regulated lifestyle and training, his elaborate, gold-embroidered "suit of lights" (which emphasizes Culture through exaggeration), and his repertoire of highly controlled and stylized movements within the bullring. The meeting of matador and bull is thus not a meeting between an ordinary human being and an ordinary animal, but is instead constructed as an encounter between paradigmatic Man and Beast.

In the drama of the bullfight, the bull is removed from his own realm of Nature (the rural countryside) and brought into man's realm of Culture; thus, the bullfighting arena (a symbolic town square) must always be in an urban location, never in a rural area. A direct confrontation between Man and Bull takes place, and—if all goes well—the man succeeds in controlling and finally killing the bull, thus demonstrating the superiority of Culture over Nature in a grand public spectacle that always involves the active participation and enthusiasm of a crowd of spectators. What do these spectators come to see? "In a sense," Marvin observes, "the *matador*, although performing as and judged as an individual, is a representative of humanity; he is a figure in whom key human qualities valued by this culture are epitomized, and it is those qualities the audience comes to see asserted."[61] In order for this display to be meaningful, however, there must be a real threat of *danger* to the man. Everybody in the audience knows that the bull is physically stronger than the man, and the only way the man can control and overcome the bull is, first, by using his human *intelligence* (which the bull lacks) and, second, by successfully suppressing his own animalistic instincts of fear and terror. "If the *matador* kills successfully he shows that he has not succumbed to the threat posed by the animal; he has dominated it and, through his mastery of it, triumphantly asserted his humanity."[62] Thus, the bullfight is "a cultural event which puts the definition of humanity . . . in jeopardy precisely so that it may be dramatically reaffirmed in the most difficult of circumstances."[63]

Though I cannot do justice here to the many details of Marvin's analysis, I hope that its possible parallels to the Nāḷāgiri episode will be obvious. Nāḷāgiri's status as an elephant in musth, further enraged by the use of intoxicating drink, runs parallel to the bullfight's insistence on a specially bred *toro bravo* who has never encountered a bullfighter before—both cases reinforcing the animal's status as a pure embodiment of the forces of Nature. Though it is perhaps more of a stretch to draw parallels between the Buddha and a Spanish matador, both figures do exemplify the human being's unique ability to *cultivate* certain culturally valued qualities (such as benevolence and compassion in the case of the Buddha), as well as constituting paradigmatic embodiments of human *intelligence* and *self-control.* In both scenarios, we see an insistence on the confrontation taking place within the very heart of human habitation (the city), as well as in the presence of a large crowd of spectators. There is also, in both cases, a necessary element of *risk,* with the spectators understanding that the Buddha might be killed, just as the matador might be gored. In both cases, therefore, we have an event "constructed in such a way that the imposition of human will is extremely uncertain because of the difficult circumstances; a situation which in turn generates tension, emotion and dramatic interest."[64] If the situation does result in human victory, the cathartic effect upon the audience is thereby dramatically intensified—as attested by the "ninety million living beings" who attain nirvana.

The *gendered* aspect I have attributed to the Buddha's contest with Nāḷāgiri is even more apparent in the Spanish bullfight. Marvin observes that "although ... the fundamental distinction in the arena is between human and animal, one cannot fully understand the *corrida* without understanding that it is a totally male-orientated event, and that the values which underlie it and give cultural sense to it are essentially masculine values."[65] Thus, matadors—like buddhas—must be men, and there is great ambivalence shown toward the few rare female bullfighters who exist. Likewise, the bull must also be male, even though females of the species (wild cows) are equally capable of showing the aggressive qualities of a good fighting bull. There is a strong feeling within the culture that the bullfight *must* pit one male against another—just as it is equally difficult to imagine Nāḷāgiri as a female elephant. Moreover, since domesticated male animals are generally castrated in order to make them more amenable to human control, the fighting bull, as a representative of pure Nature, must be left *uncastrated*—just as the elephant in musth is characterized by soaring levels of testosterone and sexual passion. Further suggesting the theme of male sexuality, the matador in Spanish culture generally has the reputation of a sexual playboy or lothario, yet he is also expected to refrain from sex in the period just before the bullfight, since the bravery he needs to face the bull is believed to reside within his testicles. Similarly, the Buddha's permanent state of celibacy suggests the enormous male sexual potency he has been able to redirect into cultivating the spiritual qualities of buddhahood. Because the gendered aspect of the bullfight is so explicit and overt, it can help us to discern a similar dynamic in the Buddha's confrontation with Nāḷāgiri—which is necessarily a contest pitting Male against Male.

Marvin's analysis of the Spanish bullfight is equally illuminating, however, when we consider the *differences* between the matador/bull encounter and the Buddha's confrontation with Nāḷāgiri. One difference is that the nature/culture, body/mind, or human/animal oppositions expressed so starkly in the Spanish bullfight are significantly weaker in the Buddha's encounter with Nāḷāgiri—for the Buddha, as we have seen, is himself celebrated for his powerful physicality, while animals in Buddhist thought possess elements of reason and rationality. This difference is reflected in the different outcomes characteristic of each scenario. While the matador expresses dominance over the bull by physically *killing* him, the Buddha expresses dominance over Nāḷāgiri by suffusing him with waves of benevolence (S. *maitrī*)—an auspicious mental quality that Nāḷāgiri, as an animal, is perhaps unable to cultivate on his own, but *can* ultimately benefit from with the help of the Buddha. Thus, rather than being vanquished and killed, Nāḷāgiri emerges from the encounter with a pacified mind and becomes "like the most well-trained disciple endowed with ethical conduct and good behavior." Human dominance over the animal world here takes the gentler form of a compassionate infusion of ideal human virtues into the recalcitrant mind of the animal. Nevertheless, the basic dynamic of simultaneous kinship and otherness is still present.

One final aspect of Marvin's analysis of the bullfight that is highly suggestive when applied to Nāḷāgiri is the contrast he draws between the bullfight and another cultural context in which an animal is brought under control: the taming and training of a horse. In Spanish culture, the taming of a horse is referred to as *desbravando*, which literally refers to the "de-wilding" of the horse, or "bringing the animal under control, making it manageable and subjecting its will to that of humanity."[66] This "breaking" of the horse's will is then followed by the process of *domando* (training), which consists of training the horse to perform certain useful functions, such as accepting a saddle and harness, responding to the will of the rider, and so forth. This entire two-step process (*desbravando* and *domando*) is highly *gradual* in nature, occurring over a significant period of time. Moreover, it takes place within a restricted context (such as a ranch), rather than being displayed for public view. It is when viewed against this context that the special nature of the bullfight becomes clear. In the bullfight, *desbravando* and *domando* are dramatically condensed into a very short period of time, as the matador simultaneously breaks the will of the bull and exerts control to make the bull do exactly what he wants it to do—with the bull being killed once this process has reached a climax. This entire spectacle, moreover, is enacted *in public,* before an enormous crowd of spectators. In the bullfight, the cultural values implicit in the taming and training of horses are thus given dramatic expression in a highly potent and public form.

Exactly the same contrast can be drawn between the Buddha's taming of Nāḷāgiri and the gradual training of an ordinary monk—which is, in fact, sometimes likened to the gradual training of a horse. In the *Bhaddāli Sutta* of the *Majjhima Nikāya,* for example, the Buddha says to Bhaddāli,

> Suppose, Bhaddāli, that a skillful horse trainer obtains a good thoroughbred horse. At first, he subjects him to wearing the bit. As he is being subjected to wearing the bit, the horse is restless, squirming and struggling because he has never been subjected to that before. But through constant and gradual practice, he comes to excel at it. When, Bhaddāli, the good thoroughbred horse, through constant and gradual practice, has come to excel at that, then the horse trainer further subjects him to wearing a harness.... [*In a similar manner, the horse trainer teaches the horse to keep in step, go in a circle, drag the hooves, race, gallop, etc.—with the horse gradually getting used to each skill.*] The good thoroughbred horse, Bhaddāli, who possesses these ten qualities is considered to be worthy of the king, the possession of the king, the mark of the king.[67]

The Buddha then compares this process to the training of a monk, saying that a monk who gradually comes to possess the ten qualities of right view, right intention, right speech, right action, right livelihood, right effort, right mindfulness, right concentration, right discernment, and right deliverance becomes "worthy of offerings, worthy of hospitality, worthy of gifts, worthy of reverential salutations, an unsurpassed field of merit for the world."[68] The *Bhaddāli Sutta* is not alone in making such a comparison; in fact, multiple passages in the *Aṅguttara Nikāya* make similar comparisons between the training of a horse and the training of a monk.[69]

It is against this larger context that the Buddha's confrontation with Nāḷāgiri takes on a greater significance. Unlike the ordinary process by which a Buddhist monk is only gradually brought under control in a step-by-step disciplinary process, the Buddha's taming of Nāḷāgiri presents the entire Buddhist path of self-transformation in a highly condensed and potent form. For as soon as he encounters the Buddha, Nāḷāgiri's will is *immediately* broken, he falls down at the Buddha's feet in complete submission, he engages in the proper ritualistic behavior (taking dust from the Buddha's feet and sprinkling it over his head), and he is instantaneously transformed into "the most well-trained disciple endowed with ethical conduct and good behavior"[70]—all before the eyes of the public. Thus, while the everyday hard work of Buddhist self-transformation may normally happen gradually and behind the monastery walls, the Buddha's taming of Nāḷāgiri broadcasts this achievement to the cosmos at large—a display made possible through the functioning of Nāḷāgiri as the Buddha's *billboard.*

Elephants, Lions, and Jackals

As noted before, the Sanskrit *Saṅghabhedavastu*'s version of this story has several unique features that distinguish it from the Pāli accounts. One major difference is the resolution of the story. Whereas the Pāli versions end with the elephant becoming tame and returning to his own stall, the *Saṅghabhedavastu* version ends quite differently. Here, the now tamed elephant (called Dhanapālaka rather than Nāḷāgiri) becomes so devoted to the Buddha that when the Buddha finally leaves Rājagṛha, the elephant dies of a broken heart and is reborn among the Cāturmahārājika gods. Following a pattern familiar to us from the animals of the *Avadānaśataka*, upon being reborn as a deity, he immediately remembers his former life as an animal and then descends from heaven to go and visit the Buddha. The Buddha gives him a discourse on the Dharma, whereupon the elephant-turned-god attains the fruit of stream-entry and gives voice to a "solemn utterance" (S. *udāna*) celebrating his permanent freedom from animality and all such unfortunate destinies (the same *udāna* also found in several tales from the *Avadānaśataka*):

> The oceans of blood and tears have dried up, the mountains of bones have been leapt over, the doors to states of suffering (S. *apāya*) have been slammed shut, the doors to heaven and liberation are flung wide open—for I am established among gods and humans![71]

The Buddha then explains to his monks the karmic causes of Dhanapālaka's changing fortunes: Long ago, under the former buddha Kāśyapa, he was a monk who continuously violated the disciplinary rules; thus, he was reborn as an elephant. But "since he gave rise to faith (S. *cittam abhiprasādya*) in my presence, when he died, he was reborn among the Cāturmahārājika gods."[72] And, since he had read and recited the sacred texts in that long-ago life as a monk, he has now attained the fruit of stream-entry. The *Saṅghabhedavastu*'s version of the story thus ends with a standard pattern characteristic of the animal stories of the *Avadānaśataka*.

Another, more interesting feature that is unique to the *Saṅghabhedavastu* account—and the one I wish to focus upon here—is its inclusion of several miracles performed by the Buddha in the process of taming the maddened elephant.[73] For rather than merely extending his right hand to stroke the elephant's forehead, as he does in the Pāli versions, the Buddha here takes a more violent and dramatic approach:

> Then the Blessed One magically created from the palm of his right hand five lions, with their manes bearing crowns. When Dhanapālaka smelled their odor, he pissed and shit on himself and began to run away. The Blessed One set all the directions on fire so that they were blazing, burning, and magically transformed into one solid flame—all except for a single spot at his own feet, which was tranquil and magically made cool. Then the elephant Dhanapālaka, rushing hither and thither, saw that everything was ablaze except for a single spot magically made cool at the feet of the Blessed One.... Then Dhanapālaka's outbreak of intoxication

> disappeared, and he approached the Blessed One with a gentle, wandering gait.[74]

It is only after this impressive display of magical power that the Buddha strokes the elephant's forehead and briefly preaches the Dharma to him, as in the Pāli accounts.

The scene painted here is similar in many respects to other occasions on which the Buddha converted fierce and recalcitrant beings through the use of his magical powers—save for the single, striking detail of *lions* emerging from his extended right hand.[75] The same detail is also mentioned by Xuanzang as he is traveling through Magadha:

> Outside the north gate of the palace city there is a stupa built at the place where Devadatta, who was on intimate terms with Ajātaśatru, let out Dhanapāla, an intoxicated elephant, in an attempt to hurt the Tathāgata. But the Tathāgata produced five lions from the tips of five fingers to tame the drunken elephant before he proceeded on his way.[76]

What is the significance of these lions, and why are they used to tame the maddened elephant?

In a wide-ranging study drawing on both textual and art-historical sources, Claudine Bautze-Picron examines the symbolic significance of the lion and the elephant in Indian tradition, and their pairing with each other in association with the Buddha.[77] In brief, she demonstrates that the lion-elephant opposition—which is pan-Indian in nature and not unique to Buddhism—is associated with an entire series of parallel oppositions, such as light/dark, fire/water, heaven/earth, and swiftness/immobility. At Hindu and Jain sites, she notes, the two animals are often depicted in hostile opposition to one another, with the lion generally dominating over the elephant. In contrast, at Buddhist sites from the Gupta period onward, the lion and the elephant tend to be depicted as complementary in nature, with both representative of the Buddha, who is equally *mahā-nāga* (Great Elephant) and *mahā-siṃha* (Great Lion).[78] The juxtaposition of lion and elephant thus becomes a way of signifying the Buddha's cosmic unification of all such opposing elements (light/dark, fire/water, etc.)—just as we also see in his famous "twin-miracle," in which he emits fire out of his shoulders and water out of his feet. Bautze-Picron further notes, however, that in an *earlier* period of Buddhist art and architecture, there is a greater tendency to *oppose* the lion and the elephant, who now stand for the Buddha (associated with the lion) overcoming Māra (associated with the elephant). Moreover, she argues, we still see "a trace of this opposition surviving till a later period in the theme of the taming of Nālāgiri"[79]—which is, as we have seen, a shadow-image of the Buddha's original victory over Māra. From this perspective, it makes sense for the Buddha of the *Saṅghabhedavastu* to tame the elephant Nāḷāgiri by shooting *lions* out of his hand.

A slightly different perspective on elephants and lions is afforded by another of Bautze-Picron's observations: while both animals are closely associated with the Buddha, the elephant is more associated with the Buddha's *awakening*, while the lion is more associated with his *preaching of the Dharma*. Since Māra rides upon an elephant in musth, the Buddha's victory over Māra at the moment of his awakening involves the taming of this elephant, which now becomes assimilated into the Buddha's own character and remains closely tied to his awakening. In contrast, the symbolic associations of the lion all pertain to the Buddha's preaching: he sits upon a "lion-throne" (P. *sīhāsana*) and preaches the Dharma with a "lion's roar" (P. *sīhanāda*). "'Lion,'" as the *Aṅguttara Nikāya* notes, "is a designation for the Tathāgata, the Arhat, the fully enlightened Buddha. And the Dhamma taught by the Tathāgata to the assembly—that is his Lion's Roar."[80] Thus, the lion—as Bautze-Picron notes—is "the *accomplished* form of the Buddha as master."[81] The taming of the elephant Nāḷāgiri thus reenacts the Buddha's own awakening, while also demonstrating the mastery involved in his subsequent preaching of the Dharma. Just as we saw earlier in connection with the Spanish bullfight, the taming of Nāḷāgiri—especially when it involves these lions—displays the entire career of the fully enlightened Buddha in a highly condensed and potent form.

Which animal, then, shall we assign to Devadatta, the wicked instigator responsible for engineering Nāḷāgiri's attack? In Buddhist sources, the lion is most commonly contrasted with the *jackal*—who lives off the lion's leavings and thus falsely comes to believe that he is just as capable as the lion. He tries in vain to hunt like a lion and roar like a lion, but soon finds that he is only a lowly jackal. Thus, heretical non-Buddhist teachers are sometimes compared to jackals. In the *Pāṭika Sutta* of the *Dīgha Nikāya,* for example, the boastful naked ascetic Pāṭikaputta challenges the Buddha to a contest of supernatural powers, but soon finds that he is unable even to rise from his seat. The Buddha and Pāṭikaputta are then compared to a lion and a jackal: The lion is truly the king of the beasts, while the jackal is a lowly creature who *tries* to roar like a lion, but can only howl and yelp like a jackal:

> Considering himself to be a lion,
> the jackal thinks, "I'm king of the beasts!"
> Even so, he howls like a jackal.
> And how can the wretched [howl of] the jackal compare to a lion's roar?
> Following after another and seeking their scraps,
> the jackal is so unaware of himself that he thinks he is a tiger.
> Even so, he howls like a jackal.
> And how can the wretched [howl of] the jackal compare to a lion's roar?
> Eating frogs and mice from the threshing-room floors,
> and corpses thrown into the charnel-ground,
> growing fat in the great and empty wilds,
> the jackal thinks, "I'm king of the beasts!"
> Even so, he howls like a jackal.
> And how can the wretched [howl of] the jackal compare to a lion's roar?[82]

Similar in many ways to these heretical non-Buddhist teachers, Devadatta, too, is a natural candidate for association with the jackal, since he, too, mistakenly thinks that he is the equal of the Buddha and worthy of taking the Buddha's place as the leader of the Sangha. In fact, if we look at the Pāli *Jātaka* collection, we find that there are at least six *jātakas* that contrast the noble lion with the miserable jackal[83]—and two of these are of special interest here. In both the *Virocana Jātaka* (No. 143)[84] and the *Jambuka Jātaka* (No. 335),[85] which tell virtually the same story, a jackal throws himself at a magnificent lion's feet and begs to be his servant in exchange for meat from the lion's prey. After living contentedly in this arrangement for a while, however, the jackal begins to grow haughty, thinking that *he* can hunt for prey just as well as the lion. He begs the lion to switch places with him and let *him* kill the prey instead. The lion warns him that jackals cannot do the work of a lion, but the jackal insists. Finally, the lion agrees. The jackal then attempts to kill an elephant—but the elephant simply steps on him, crushing the jackal's skull. Thus, the story concludes:

> He who invests himself with the pride of a lion,
> even though he's a jackal and not a lion,
> upon attacking an elephant,
> soon lies on the ground lamenting.[86]

As we would expect, the lion is a previous birth of the Buddha, while the jackal is a previous birth of Devadatta. Notice also that it is an *elephant*—the Buddha's other animal "double"—who crushes the jackal's skull.

The imagery of lions and jackals found within Buddhist sources is consistent, moreover, with the imagery found throughout Sanskrit literature as a whole: the lion is consistently seen as the noble "king of the beasts" whose roar is celebrated, whereas the jackal, as a natural scavenger, exists on the periphery of animal society and is commonly associated with carrion, death, other lowly animals (such as dogs and donkeys), and low-caste people such as *caṇḍālas*. Further, the howl of the jackal augurs doom and misfortune. In the *Mahābhārata*, for example, the evil Duryodhana howls like a jackal upon his birth, and a jackal similarly howls at the game of dice that results in disaster for the Pandava heroes. The theme of the jackal attempting to usurp the kingly position of the lion may likewise be found in a famous story from the

Pañcatantra in which a jackal falls into a vat of indigo dye and takes advantage of his novel appearance to declare himself the king of all beasts—yet is soon undone by his telltale jackal's howl.[87]

The episode involving the taming of Nāḷāgiri thus fits into a much larger web of animal associations that are omnipresent throughout Buddhist (and larger Sanskrit) literature. The Buddha's awakening and victory over Māra, his preaching of the Dharma for the benefit of all sentient beings, and even his worldly conflicts with non-Buddhist teachers and evil monks such as Devadatta—all play themselves out in the language of lions, elephants, jackals, and other beasts. Animals thus constitute a parallel language for giving voice to the Buddhist cosmic drama.

CONCLUSION

The potency of the animal as a symbol lies in humanity's dualistic relationship with the animal. On the one hand, we ourselves *are* animals; on the other hand, we define ourselves in opposition to all other animals. There is thus both kinship and otherness, identity and difference, attraction and repulsion in humanity's relationship to the animal. Through this dualistic interplay, animality becomes a fruitful resource for defining what it means to be human. As Buddhism—arguably, more so than any other major religion—is a profoundly human-centered tradition, we should not be surprised to see Buddhist texts from India making ample use of animality in expressing Buddhism's vision of the project of being human. Animality manifests itself, moreover, through an endless variety of different species (with different qualities, characteristics, and habitats), and thus presents us with an extremely rich pool of symbolic possibilities. The availability and potency of this pool in the world of premodern India is perhaps difficult to imagine from our own vantage point in the modern, industrialized West, where animals are retreating more and more from our everyday view and experience. This book constitutes a very preliminary effort to gain a glimpse of some of the ways in which this pool of symbolic possibilities was employed.

In the ongoing tension between kinship and otherness, Part I of this book leans in the direction of *otherness*, where the animal is seen as "other" to the human subject. In Buddhist doctrine and cosmology, the animal is defined in opposition to the human being, with the difference between them being the difference between bad karma and good karma—and the fruition of each in an "unfortunate" or a "fortunate" realm of rebirth (S. *durgati, sugati*). Ultimately, this distinction seems to boil down to the animal's lack of *prajñā*, or the "higher mental faculties," and its corresponding lack of moral agency—both of which serve as a means of highlighting the uniquely human ability to cultivate the mind and bring about an end to suffering. The ambitious human project advocated by the Buddha can only be envisioned, we might say, against the background of the nonhuman beings who surround it and remain incapable of carrying it out. Yet despite this dependence upon animality to highlight what it means to be human, Buddhist texts display a certain degree of anxiousness to keep the two realms solidly apart. The difference between human beings and animals must be *categorical* in nature, and the hierarchy between them must be maintained. While some provision is made for animals to escape from their unfortunate situation (through the mechanism of giving rise to *prasāda* when in the physical presence of the Buddha), the narratives in which this occurs seem equally preoccupied with limiting and constraining what the animal can achieve, as a way of safeguarding the prerogatives of being human. In Part I of this book, then, we are suspicious of the animal and wish to keep our distance.

Part II of this book moves from *otherness* to *kinship*—a move made possible by the positing of a world in which animals *speak*. Animals who *speak* are given a *voice*, and thereby turned into subjects in their own right rather than objects available for human use and consumption. Equally important, however, is what these animals choose to speak *about*: rampant cruelty, abuse, and exploitation in humanity's treatment of the animal world. Speaking animals speak *about* the suffering of animals at humanity's hands, using their voices to condemn humanity for its moral shortcomings—as well as shedding a strange and unforgiving light upon human social institutions such as marriage, caste, and kingship. Animals who speak are also necessarily endowed with reason, rationality, and moral agency, giving lie to the animal's lack of *prajñā* and bridging the unbridgeable gap between human beings and animals. Yet the animal's *prajñā* is contradictory here: on the one hand, animals who speak are capable of engaging human beings in a closely matched contest of wits; on the other hand, they use their wits to demonstrate that the *only* relevant criterion in our relationships with others—particularly in a Buddhist cosmos—is our shared ability to experience suffering. ("The question is not, Can they *reason*? nor Can they *talk*? but, Can they *suffer*?")[1] Equally contradictory is the animal's use of *language*. Using language is what allows for kinship and communication across the human-animal divide, yet in many cases, language is used to give voice to the deceptive and untrustworthy nature of human words and promises. In all of these ways, speaking animals blur and make untenable the categorical distinction between human and nonhuman beings, allowing human beings to see the world around them as "a communion of subjects rather than a collection of objects."[2]

The *otherness* of animals highlighted in Part I and the *kinship* with animals highlighted in Part II stand in a relationship of tension, but not outright contradiction. They might be seen as two alternative perspectives on the human project (as Buddhism sees it)—the former voice being more concerned with soteriology, perhaps, and the latter voice being more concerned with ethics. Thus, when the human subject ponders her own attempt to eradicate suffering and reach an ultimate goal, there is a need to distinguish herself from the beastly realm and invest herself in those capacities she possesses that are believed to be uniquely human. When she ponders her ethical relationships with other sentient creatures in the universe, on the other hand, there is a need to see the world from another being's perspective, be alive to the reality of their suffering, and shine the harsh light of truth upon one's own moral shortcomings. Ethics are the foundation for soteriology, of course, and it is perhaps for this reason that the animals of the *jātakas* featured in Part II seem to speak with special authority—pulling the human being back from her human-centered ambitions just enough to understand that they are ultimately rooted in an ethical relationship with the more-than-human world.

Kinship and *otherness* come together in Part III because both resources are needed to present a picture of the ultimate human being—the Buddha himself, whose story requires a number of opposing forces to be carefully balanced. Toward the beginning of the Buddha's life-story, the worldly ambitions of Prince Siddhārtha and his emotional ties to other people must be definitively severed from his character before buddhahood can be attained—yet this must happen without tainting the personality of the Buddha himself. I have suggested that one way in which this occurs is through the doubling of the Buddha in the character of his horse Kanthaka, and the subsequent "sacrifice" of Kanthaka upon the altar of the Buddha's impending buddhahood. As required by this sacrificial idiom, kinship and otherness here appear in a sequence, as the Buddha and Kanthaka are first closely identified with each other and later wrenched apart. In this way, Kanthaka can serve as the Buddha's *scapegoat* and bear the brunt of the negative emotions unleashed by his renunciation of familial and worldly life. Perhaps it is even possible to see in Kanthaka's death a distant echo of the Vedic *aśvamedha*, or horse sacrifice, which also features a horse whose death brings about the welfare of the human sacrificer.

Once the Buddha has attained full awakening and become a fully enlightened buddha, we need to look back and be reminded of his status as the consummate lone Renouncer, while still affirming his present status as a masterful Teacher and Tamer of others. The fractious dispute among the monks of Kosambī threatens to undermine both positions, either tainting his depiction as the original lone ascetic by immersing him within worldly strife, or calling into question his power to bring about a salutary effect within others. Here, I have suggested that both positions are reaffirmed through the functioning of the elephant Pārileyyaka as a *mirror* for the Buddha. *Kinship* and *otherness* here operate simultaneously, for, on the one hand, Pārileyyaka is the noble bull elephant who has majestically retreated from the rabble (much like the Buddha himself), while, on the other hand, Pārileyyaka is the Buddha's humble and submissive servant, who submits to the Buddha's authority and maintains his inferiority as an animal. In this way, the mirror fulfills its function, yet also remains transparent.

Toward the end of his life—and as a fitting capstone to his career—the Buddha publicly displays his absolute mastery over the forces of nature, animality, and passion through his instantaneous taming of the fierce elephant Nāḷāgiri. In this contest between Man and Beast—which is also representative of the opposition between nirvana and samsara—the Beast is wholly "other" to the Man and must be vanquished and forced to submit; the Beast serves as a mere *billboard* for the Man's unassailable power and charisma. And yet there is also *kinship* between them, since, in truth, the Beast that must be vanquished is the Beast that lies within. This truth is conveyed through the idiom of elephants: the auspicious white elephant sometimes associated with the Buddha is, in fact, the same animal as the maddened elephant in musth ridden by the deity Māra—only now, the elephant has been tamed. Nāḷāgiri's instantaneous movement from mad elephant to tamed elephant thus presents the entire Buddhist path of self-transformation—and the Buddha's entire career—in a highly condensed and potent form.

As the adherents of a profoundly human-centered religious tradition, Indian Buddhist authors made full and creative use of the simultaneous kinship and otherness experienced by humanity in its relationship to the animal, conveying their particular vision of the human project through a language offered to them by the elephants, lions, monkeys, jackals, geese, and deer that surrounded them in the Indian landscape. While animals remained distinct from human beings through their lack of language, animals themselves *became* a language through which Buddhist authors could speak—and, on occasion, animals themselves could be heard.

APPENDIX

ANIMAL REBIRTHS OF THE BODHISATTVA IN THE PĀLI *JĀTAKAṬṬHAVAṆṆANĀ*

(IN DESCENDING ORDER OF FREQUENCY)

[The first number (in bold) indicates the total number of occurrences; the subsequent numbers (in parentheses) list the relevant *jātakas* by number.]

Monkey (*kapi*) (*vānara*): **11** (20, 57, 58, 177, 208, 219, 222, 342, 404, 407, 516)

Deer (*miga*) (*ruru-miga*) (*sarabha-miga*) or Antelope (*kuruṅga-miga*): **11** (11, 12, 15, 16, 21, 206, 359, 385, 482, 483, 501)

Goose (*haṃsa*) (*cakkavāka*) or Golden Goose (*suvaṇṇa-haṃsa*) (*suvaṇṇa-cakkavāka*): **11** (32, 136, 270, 370, 379, 434, 451, 476, 502, 533, 534)

Lion (*sīha*): **10** (143, 152, 153, 157, 172, 188, 322, 335, 397, 486)

Parrot (*suka/suva*): **9** (145, 198, 255, 329, 429, 430, 484, 503, 521)

Elephant (*hatthi*) (*nāga*) (*vāraṇa*): **7** (72, 122, 221, 267, 357, 455, 514)

Pigeon (*kapota*) (*pārāvata/pārāpata*): **6** (42, 274, 275, 277, 375, 395)

Quail (*vaṭṭakā*) (*lāpa*): **5** (33, 35, 118, 168, 394)

Bull (*go*) (*goṇa*): **5** (28, 29, 30, 88, 286)

Vulture (*gijjha*): **4** (164, 381, 399, 427)

Bird (*sakuṇa*): **4** (36, 115, 133, 384)

Peacock (*mora*): **3** (159, 339, 491)

Crow (*kāka*): **3** (140, 204, 292)

Horse (*sindhava*): **3** (23, 24, 266)

Lizard (*godhā*): 3 (138, 141, 325)
Fish (*maccha*): 3 (75, 114, 236)
Partridge (*tittira*): 2 (37, 438)
Woodpecker (*rukkha-koṭṭaka*): 2 (210, 308)
Cock (*kukkuṭa*): 2 (383, 448)
Indian Cuckoo (*kuṇāla*): 2 (464, 536)
Jackal (*sigāla*): 2 (142, 148)
Mouse (*mūsika*): 2 (128, 129)
Singila Bird (*singila-sakuṇa*): 1 (321)
Flying Horse (*valāhaka-assa*): 1 (196)
Buffalo (*mahisa*): 1 (278)
Dog (*kukkura*): 1 (22)
Hare (*sasa*): 1 (316)
Pig (*sūkara*): 1 (388)
Frog (*maṇḍūka*): 1 (239)

Note: John G. Jones also provides a thorough accounting of animal rebirths of the bodhisattva in the *Jātakaṭṭhavaṇṇanā* in his book *Tales and Teachings of the Buddha* (2001, 24–28). My accounting differs from his in the following ways:

1. I have left out two *jātakas* in which the bodhisattva is born as a *garuḍa* and four *jātakas* in which he is born as a *nāga*—since these beings, in my view, are more appropriately seen as supernatural beings than as animals (although the Buddhist tradition itself does classify them as belonging to the animal realm). Thus, my total of 117 animal rebirths is slightly lower than Jones's total of 123.
2. Jones lists "Goose" separately from "Golden Goose"; I have collapsed these two categories together.
3. Jones lists "Golden Mallard" (No. 32) and "Mallard" (No. 136) separately from "Golden Goose," even though both of these stories use the same term (*suvaṇṇa-haṃsa*) as those listed under "Golden Goose."
4. Jones lists "Fowl" (No. 448) separately from "Cock," even though this story uses the same term (*kukkuṭa*) as that listed under "Cock."

5. Jones includes in the category "Bird" those stories using the term *sakuṇa* and those stories using the term *kuṇāla*. I have placed the two stories using the term *kuṇāla* under the separate category "Indian cuckoo."
6. Jones lists "Stag" separately from "Deer," but since these stories use the same terms (*miga* and various compounds involving *miga*), I have collapsed them together under "Deer." I have further placed "Antelope" (*kuruṅga-miga*) under the category of "Deer."
7. Jones lists "Bull" separately from "Ox," but since all of the stories in both categories use the terms *go* and *goṇa* indiscriminately (often switching from one term to the other within the same story), I have collapsed them together under "Bull."
8. Jones lists "Iguana" separately from "Lizard," but since all of these stories use the term *godhā*, I have collapsed them together under "Lizard."

ABBREVIATIONS

Note: All Pāli canonical and commentarial sources are cited from the Tipiṭaka (and commentaries) established at the Chaṭṭha Saṅgāyana or Sixth Buddhist Council held in Yangon, Myanmar, 1954–1956, and available online at www.tipitaka.org (this edition is abbreviated as CS). However, as is customary, the bibliographic references given are to the standard Pali Text Society editions, as noted below. Differences between the two that bear upon my translation of a passage are indicated in the notes.

Akbh	*Abhidharmakośabhāṣya*. Ed. Pradhan 1975.
AN	*Aṅguttara Nikāya*. Ed. Morris 1885–1910.
AŚ	*Avadānaśataka*. Ed. Speyer 1958 (2 vols. in one).
BC	*Buddhacarita*. Ed. Johnston, new enlarged ed. (2 vols. in one), 1984.
BHSD	*Buddhist Hybrid Sanskrit Dictionary*. Edgerton 1953, Vol. 1.
Bv	*Buddhavaṃsa*. Ed. Jayawickrama 1974.
Bv-a	*Buddhavaṃsa Aṭṭhakathā (Madhuratthavilāsinī)*. Ed. Horner 1946.
CBBS	*A Concordance of Buddhist Birth Stories*. Grey 1994.
CS	Chaṭṭha Saṅgāyana edition of the Pāli Tipiṭaka and commentaries (www.tipitaka.org).
Dhp	*Dhammapada*. Ed. Norman 1906–1915.
Dhp-a	*Dhammapada Aṭṭhakathā*. Ed. Norman 1906–1915.
Div	*Divyāvadāna*. Ed. Cowell & Neil 1970.

DN	*Dīgha Nikāya*. Ed. Rhys Davids and Stede 1890–1911.
DPPN	*Dictionary of Pāli Proper Names*. Malalasekera 1937–1938.
It	*Itivuttaka*. Ed. Windisch 1975.
It-a	*Itivuttaka Aṭṭhakathā*. Ed. Bose 1977 (2 vols. in one).
Jā	*Jātaka* and *Jātaka Aṭṭhakathā*. Ed. Fausboll 1875–1897.
LV	*Lalitavistara*. Ed. Tripathi 1987.
MN	*Majjhima Nikāya*. Ed. Trenckner 1888–1925.
MP	*Milindapañha*. Ed. Trenckner 1880.
Mv	*Mahāvastu*. Ed. Senart 1882–1897.
PTSD	*The Pali Text Society's Pali-English Dictionary*. Ed. Rhys Davids and Stede 1966.
SbhV	*Saṅghabhedavastu* of the (Sanskrit) *Mūlasarvāstivāda Vinaya*. Ed. Gnoli 1977–1978.
Skhv(L)	*(Longer) Sukhāvatīvyūha Sūtra*. Ed. Vaidya 1961.
Skhv(S)	*(Shorter) Sukhāvatīvyūha Sūtra*. Ed. Vaidya 1961.
SN	*Saṃyutta Nikāya*. Ed. Feer 1884–1904.
Thag	*Theragāthā*. Ed. Oldenberg and Pischel 1966.
Ud	*Udāna*. Ed. Steinthal 1885.
Ud-a	*Udāna Aṭṭhakathā (Paramatthadīpanī)*. Ed. Woodward 1926.
Vin	[Theravāda] *Vinaya Piṭaka*. Ed. Oldenberg 1879–1883.
Vin-a	*Vinaya Piṭaka Aṭṭhakathā* (*Samantapāsādikā*). Ed. Takakusu and Nagai 1924–1977.
Vv	*Vimānavatthu*. Ed. Jayawickrama 1977.
Vv-a	*Vimānavatthu Aṭṭhakathā (Paramatthadīpanī)*. Ed. Hardy 1901.

NOTES

NOTES TO THE PREFACE

1. I say "primarily" because a very common description of the Buddha refers to him as the "teacher of gods and human beings" (S. *śāstā devānāṃ ca manuṣyānām*). Nevertheless, as Schmithausen and Maithrimurthi have noted, "the true recipients of the Buddha's teaching are doubtless humans, the only beings capable of *actually* attaining liberating insight" (2009, 105).
2. Inevitably, there are minor exceptions—such as the *anāgamin*, or "nonreturner," a person who has eliminated many of the fetters binding one to samsara but fallen just short of attaining arhatship, or the final goal. If such a person does not go on to attain arhatship within the present lifetime, he or she is understood to be reborn as a deity in one of the very high heavens called the Pure Abodes (S. *śuddhāvāsa*)—"not returning" to the Realm of Desire (S. *kāma-dhātu*), hence the name—and to attain nirvana directly from there. Technically, then, this could be described as a deity attaining nirvana. (See Buswell and Lopez 2014, 37–38, s.v. *anāgamin*).
3. Lévi-Strauss 1963, 89.
4. Daston and Mitman 2005, 12 (emphasis added).
5. Daston and Mitman 2005, 13.
6. For further details, see Buswell and Lopez 2014, 561 (s.v. *nāga*). For two classic studies of the *nāga*, see Fergusson 1971 and Vogel 1926.
7. For further details, see Buswell and Lopez 2014, 314–315 (s.v. *garuḍa*). See also Nagar 1992.
8. Schmithausen and Maithrimurthi (2009, 102) do mention a few Buddhist texts in which animals are included in the Buddha's audience, but in general, this is not the case.
9. See the multiple sources listed in Chapter 1, note 34.
10. For a discussion of this issue, see Waldau 2013, 16–20.
11. See Kemmerer 2006.

NOTES TO PART I INTRODUCTION

1. For these passages, I rely upon the translations provided in the very useful 1967 entry on "Chikushō (Animal)" from *Hôbôgirin* (see Bareau and May 1967).

NOTES TO CHAPTER 1

1. *Majjhima Nikāya* No. 129 (MN iii, 169).
2. Some texts also posit a sixth *gati*, that of demigods (S. *asura*), who are placed in between human beings and gods but considered an unfortunate rebirth. The positing of five or six *gatis* constitutes the fully developed system, which clearly took some time to develop. For some brief remarks on its earlier stages—and when animals may have entered the picture—see Schmithausen and Maithrimurthi 2009, 78–84. For a cross-cultural study of the development of rebirth eschatologies, see Obeyesekere 2002.
3. E.g., MN iii, 165 (but repeated in many places throughout the Pāli Canon).
4. AN iii, 353.
5. In contrast, however (as John Strong has pointed out to me), in the famous account of the Buddha's smile (found in the *Avadānaśataka* and *Divyāvadāna*), the animal and ghost realms of rebirth seem to be paired together and placed slightly above a rebirth in hell—for if the Buddha wishes to predict somebody's rebirth as an animal, the rays of light emanating from his smile enter into his heels; for rebirth as a ghost, they enter into his toes (which are parallel to the heels); and for rebirth as a hell-being, they enter into the soles of his feet (slightly lower than the heels and the toes). See Strong 1983, 60, Table 2.
6. *Majjhima Nikāya* No. 12 (trans. Ñāṇamoli and Bodhi 1995, 164–178).
7. Benjamin 1997, 50.
8. MN iii, 167–169.
9. The *Saddharmasmṛtyupasthāna Sūtra* (T. 721) was translated into Chinese in 538–541 CE. For a thorough analysis of this text, see Lin 1949. For the various classifications of animals, see Bareau and May 1967.
10. On the Jain classification, see Chapple 2006 and Wiley 2006.
11. For example, those who hold wrong views and dispute with each other are reborn as animals characterized by mutual hostility, such as snakes and mongooses; those who are attached to their spouses are reborn as amorous birds, such as pheasants and ducks; those who are greedy are reborn as greedy animals, such as jackals and dogs; etc. For multiple examples, see Schmithausen and Maithrimurthi 2009, 80–83; Bareau and May 1967, 314–316; and Strong 2008, 39–40 (translated passage from the *Ṣaḍgatikārikā*).

12. SN iii, 152.
13. Mv i, 27.
14. The *Mahāsaṃnipāta Sūtra* (T. 397) was translated into Chinese in 414–426 CE (trans. Bareau and May 1967, 314).
15. Div 422.
16. *Buddhacarita*, Ch. 14, vv. 25–26 (BC i, 160).
17. The *Mahāvibhāṣā* (T. 1545) was translated into Chinese in 656–659 CE (trans. Bareau and May 1967, 313).
18. The categories of "meat-eaters" and "grass-eaters" (and the assumption that there can never be an alliance between them) are used consistently throughout the *Pañcatantra* to encapsulate the relationship between predator and prey. See Taylor 2007, 76–88.
19. It 36. See also AN i, 51 and DN iii, 71–72.
20. It-a i, 159.
21. Doniger 2005, 27–32.
22. MN iii, 169. For two slight variations, see also SN v, 455–457.
23. MN iii, 169–170.
24. MN iii, 170.
25. Mv i, 27–28.
26. Trans. Bareau and May 1967, 314.
27. Commentary on *Abhidharmakośa* 5.22 (Akbh 292).
28. Waldau 2000, 91.
29. Ryder first used the word "speciesism" in a printed pamphlet produced in 1970; for a more recent discussion by the same author, see Ryder 2000. See also Singer 2009.
30. Waldau 2002.
31. Waldau 2002, 38.
32. Waldau 2002, 16.
33. For a thorough discussion of this injunction, including a discussion of the various contexts in which the phrase "even down to an ant" is either present or absent, see Schmithausen and Maithrimurthi 2009, 48–59.
34. See, for example, Chapple 1992; Chapple 1993; Harris 2006; Harvey 2000, 150–186; Kemmerer 2012, 91–126; McDermott 1989; Perlo 2002, 115–132; Schmithausen and Maithrimurthi 2009, 47–77; Singh 2006; Story 1964; Waldau 2000 and Waldau 2002.
35. As Waldau elsewhere puts it, "Continuity . . . exists, but, again, it is overwhelmed, so to speak, by a deep conviction of an essential discontinuity" (2000, 98). Examples of greatly overemphasizing human-animal continuity over discontinuity are relatively easy to find: Lisa Kemmerer, for example, states that "Buddhist philosophies of reincarnation, oneness, and inter-being have created a sense of kinship and community across all species" (2012, 114); and Francis Story maintains that Buddhism has "more sense of kinship

with the animal world" than the West, which is "not a matter of sentiment, but is rooted in the total Buddhist concept of life" (1964, 3).

36. The rule against killing a human being is Pārājika 3, and the rule against killing a (nonhuman) living being is Pācittiya 61. Several other rules (all of the Pācittiya class) are also aimed at preventing the destruction of living beings—for example, Pācittiya 10 (against digging in the ground), Pācittiya 11 (against destroying plants or trees that tree-spirits or other beings may live in), Pācittiya 20 (against sprinkling water that contains living beings), and Pācittiya 62 (against using water that contains living beings).
37. As Waldau notes, "the acceptance of instrumental uses [of animals] is so widespread in the Pali Canon that it could fairly be called a 'background' view which was simply assumed" (2002, 104).
38. *Buddhacarita,* Ch. 14, vv. 21–24 (BC i, 159–160).
39. *parādhīnatā* (BC i, 160).
40. With regard to Japan, Barbara Ambros (2014, 252) has similarly noted of Genshin's *Ōjōyōshū* that Genshin "recognizes and empathizes with the suffering and physical exploitation of beasts, but he casts this condition as retributive, karmic justice for evil deeds committed by humans in their former lives. Thus, the occupants of the beastly realm do not exist *sui generis*, but in moral correlation to human existence."
41. See Sciberras 2008 for a refutation of Waldau's arguments—although Sciberras does accept a more limited claim of Buddhist speciesism.
42. Waldau 2002, 124.
43. See Aung and Rhys Davids 1979, 347.
44. Trans. Bareau and May 1967, 311–312. On the question of whether or not animals exist in heaven, in hell, or among the *pretas*, see also Lin 1949, 23, 38–40, and 61–63.
45. Trans. Bareau and May 1967, 312 (emphasis added).
46. Skhv(L) 225.
47. Skhv(S) 255.
48. Monier-Williams 1979, 659 (s.v. *prajñā*).
49. PTSD 390 (s.v. *paññā*).
50. Schmithausen and Maithrimurthi 2009, 87.
51. MP 32.
52. Schmithausen and Maithrimurthi 2009, 86, n. 221.
53. Jā iii, 71–74 (trans. Cowell 1895–1913, iii, 47–49) (see also CBBS 190–191, s.v. Kuṭidūsaka).
54. Jā iii, 73.
55. See *Abhidharmakośa*, Ch. 4, v. 97 (and commentary) (trans. Pruden 1988–1990, ii, 680–681).
56. *Abhidharmakośa* 4.43 and commentary (Akbh 226).
57. See translation in Horner 1938–1966, iv, 110–111 and 180.

58. Vin i, 62.
59. AN iv, 225.
60. Thomas Aquinas, *Summa Theologica*, as quoted in Hobgood-Oster 2008, 33.
61. For a concise account of predominant Western views on the moral status of animals, see Gruen 2010 and Singer 2009, 185–212.
62. Houlbrooke 1996, 124, as quoted in Fudge 2002b, 35.
63. William Perkins, *A Discourse of Conscience* (1596), as quoted in Fudge 2002b, 34 (spelling modified).
64. *Hitopadeśa*, v. 25, trans. in Jaini 1987, 169.
65. Barbara Ambros (2014, 52–53) likewise observes, "Proponents of econationalism in Japan have often pointed to Buddhism as a major reason for why Japan has supposedly fared so much better than the West in its treatment of animals; however, this assessment is usually predicated on an implicit rejection—whether by environmentalists or Buddhist apologists—of Abrahamic, particularly Christian, attitudes toward other animals. The most positive Buddhist attitudes toward animals . . . are contrasted with the most negative Abrahamic ones . . . Buddhism here serves as a reverse image of the perceived shortcomings of Western traditions, a position that Larry Lohmann (1993) has termed 'green orientalism.' "
66. Batchelor 1992, 12.
67. Phelps 2004, 33, 40.
68. Barbara Ambros (2014, 251–252), for example, cites a passage from Genshin's *Ōjōyōshū* as being characteristic of the premodern Japanese Buddhist view of animals, and it is striking to see how many echoes the passage contains with the Indian Buddhist passages cited here: "Third, I will explicate the realm of beasts . . . [In terms of species,] there are 3,400,000,000 of them. If we divide them into broad categories, there are only three: (1) birds (*chō*); (2) hairy four-legged beings (*jū*); and (3) crawlers (*chū*). Among these various species, the strong and the weak harm each other. They never have anything but temporary assurance of drink or food. Day and night they live in fear. Furthermore, aquatic beings fall victim to fishermen, and beings that walk on land fall prey to hunters. As for beings such as elephants, horses, oxen, donkeys, camels, mules, their heads are struck with iron rods, their noses pierced with hooks, or their necks tethered with reins. They bear heavy burdens and are whipped. However, they only think of water and grass and have no other knowledge. Moreover, centipedes and weasels are born in darkness and perish in darkness. Beings such as lice and fleas rely on human bodies to live and die. . . . [Animal] suffering is unfathomable. Those who are stupid and lack a conscience and those who accept alms without repaying their debt of gratitude receive this retribution. (These phrases are dispersed throughout the sūtras and śāstras.)"

69. *Mahāsaṃnipāta Sūtra* (T. 397), trans. Bareau and May 1967, 314.
70. *Mahāsaṃnipāta Sūtra* (T. 397), trans. Bareau and May 1967, 313–314.
71. MN iii, 169.

NOTES TO CHAPTER 2

1. *Avadānaśataka* No. 56 (AŚ i, 323).
2. See, for example, the story discussed in note 41.
3. Monier-Williams 1979, 696–697 (s.v. *prasāda*).
4. PTSD 446 (s.v. *pasāda*).
5. Rotman 2009, Chs. 3–6.
6. Rotman 2009, 65.
7. Rotman 2009, 67.
8. Rotman 2009, 75.
9. *Divyāvadāna* No. 4 (trans. Rotman 2008, 135–142).
10. Rotman 2009, 89.
11. *Divyāvadāna* No. 7 (trans. Rotman 2008, 161–175). See Rotman 2009, 90–97 for his analysis of this story.
12. Rotman 2009, 97.
13. Rotman 2009, 111.
14. Rotman 2009, 140.
15. Rotman 2009, 130.
16. Rotman 2009, 111.
17. Rotman 2009, 148.
18. Div 136–142 (trans. Rotman 2008, 243–252).
19. Div 136.
20. Div 136.
21. Div 137.
22. Div 137.
23. Div 137.
24. Div 140.
25. Div 141.
26. Div 142.
27. *Divyāvadāna* No. 15 (quoted in Rotman 2009, 103).
28. Rotman 2009, 103.
29. AŚ i, 319–324.
30. *tiryag-yoni-gato* (AŚ i, 321).
31. AŚ i, 321.
32. AŚ i, 322.
33. AŚ i, 322.

34. AŚ i, 322.
35. AŚ i, 323.
36. AŚ i, 323.
37. AŚ i, 341–344.
38. AŚ i, 341.
39. AŚ i, 342.
40. AŚ i, 344.
41. One story involving animal characters that I have not dealt with here is the *Śukapotaka Avadāna* (*Divyāvadāna* No. 16) (Div 198–200, trans. Rotman 2008, 333–336). I have left this story out of my discussion because it utterly fails to follow the *prasāda* pattern—although it perhaps serves to illuminate this pattern through contrast. This story involves two parrot chicks who know how to speak using human language, and who are regularly preached to by Ānanda. One day, the Buddha comes to visit. He preaches to the chicks the four noble truths and establishes them in the three refuges and the five moral precepts of the layperson. The Buddha is described as being *prāsādika*, yet the chicks are never said to give rise to *prāsāda*. When a cat suddenly snatches them, they cry out, "Praise to the Buddha, Dharma, and Sangha!" (Div 199). They die "with their mindfulness focused on Buddha, Dharma, and Sangha" (Div 199) and are thus reborn as gods in heaven. In all ways—from their use of human language to their taking of the three refuges and the five moral precepts—these chicks seem to function more like human laypeople than like animals. And—correspondingly—they win rebirth in heaven through their mindfulness (S. *smṛti*) rather than by giving rise to *prāsāda*. The story thus seems like an anomaly and is not characteristic of animals in general.
42. AŚ i, 289–294.
43. AŚ i, 331–335. In his taming of the buffalo, the Buddha performs the same miracles as he uses in the taming of Nāḷāgiri in the *Saṃghabhedavastu* of the *Mūlasarvāstivāda Vinaya*, which I will examine later; see Chapter 7.
44. Because the Buddha preaches briefly on both impermanence and no-self to the fierce buffalo, Padmanabh Jaini (1987, 173) cites the *Mahiṣa Avadāna* as evidence that "Buddhists considered animals capable of insights which normally would be considered possible only for human beings." I find this conclusion to be unwarranted, however, since the Buddha clearly states that the buffalo's rebirth in heaven is the direct result of him giving rise to *prasāda*, and no mention is made of his reaction to the Buddha's preaching.
45. This is also noted by Naomi Appleton (2014, 27), who observes that in both Buddhist and Jain narratives, "a significant part of the [animal's] success in attaining a heavenly rebirth is the animal's state of mind at the moment of death."

46. For example, the brahmin's daughter of the *Brāhmaṇadārikā Avadāna* (*Divyāvadāna* No. 4, trans. Rotman 2008, 135–142) and the monk of the *Cakravartivyākṛta Avadāna* (*Divyāvadāna* No. 15, trans. Rotman 2008, 329–331) both give rise to *prasāda* and receive a prediction from the Buddha without any mention of their deaths occurring soon thereafter.
47. For references to other versions of this story and several artistic depictions, see Zin 2006, 96–100.
48. AŚ i, 290.
49. AŚ i, 291–292.
50. The story of the fierce buffalo proceeds in largely the same manner: The Buddha tames the fierce buffalo and reminds him of his animal rebirth, which causes the buffalo to weep. The Buddha then recites the same verses to the buffalo as he recites to the venomous snake, and, once again, the buffalo comes to despise his own nature and starves himself to death. Here, we are given one additional observation, which is that "beings born as animals are like blazing fires" (AŚ 332)—which I interpret to mean that they rely on constant food just as a fire relies on constant fuel; therefore, when the buffalo stops eating, he dies "quickly" (*āśu*) and is reborn among the gods. Once again, we are reminded of the animal's constant *eating*—but here, it is of benefit to the buffalo, since the practice of abstaining from food leads to death much more quickly for him than it might for a human being.
51. The imperative verb forms are *prasādaya, virāgaya*, and *prasādyatāṃ*.
52. Wiltshire (1983), for example, argues that suicide for arhats is condoned in the Pāli Canon, but his argument is convincingly refuted by Keown (1996). See Keown 1996, 9–10, n. 2 for a bibliography of sources on Buddhist views of suicide; see also Harvey 2000, 286–310.

PART II

1. Quoted in Weil 2012, 7.
2. Trans. Olivelle 1997, 99.
3. This story appears in the *Jātakaṭṭhavaṇṇanā* (No. 316), the *Cariyāpiṭaka* (No. 1.10), Āryaśūra's *Jātakamālā* (No. 6), and the *Avadānaśataka* (No. 37); see also CBBS 338–341 (s.v. Sasa and Śaśaka). I discuss this story, along with many other stories involving the bodhisattva's propensity to sacrifice life and limb on behalf of other beings, in Ohnuma 2007.
4. Collins 1998, 72–89.
5. *Avadānaśataka* No. 56 (discussed in Chapter 2) and *Divyāvadāna* No. 16 (discussed in Chapter 2, n. 41).
6. Harris 2006, 208.

7. Jaini 1987, 170–171.
8. Deleanu 2000, 81.
9. As occurs in the *Virocana Jātaka* (No. 143) and the *Jambuka Jātaka* (No. 335), discussed further in Chapter 7.
10. Lessing 1996. My quotations are from the English translation provided by Justin E. H. Smith, available at http://www.jehsmith.com/1/2011/04/g-e-lessing-on-the-use-of-animals-in-fables-1759.html (accessed June 25, 2015).
11. Daston and Mitman 2005, 9.
12. Forsthoefel 2007, 32. In contrast to this appeal to universality, however, Patrick Olivelle (2013b, 8) believes that one of the major functions fulfilled by animal fables in India is to naturalize caste distinctions and caste hierarchies: "Animals, divided as they are into distinct species, provide a wonderful canvas to paint the picture of a society divided into distinct groups." Using animals to represent different classes of people effectively suggests that "such social classes are not contingent social formations but essentially different species." This is also the major argument offered by Taylor (2007) in regard to the *Pañcatantra*.
13. Lessing 1996 (translation by Smith, see n. 10).
14. Forsthoefel 2007, 31–32.
15. Clayton 2008, 180.
16. Clayton 2008, 182.
17. Clayton 2008, 183.
18. Clayton 2008, 196 (emphasis added).
19. Rudd 2006, 39.
20. Rudd 2006, 44.
21. Rudd 2006, 39.

NOTES TO CHAPTER 3

1. Jā iv, 261.
2. Alfred Lord Tennyson, "In Memoriam A. H. H.," Canto 56, available at http://www.online-literature.com/tennyson/718/ (accessed July 27, 2015).
3. MV i, 27.
4. Noonan 1997; King-Smith 2010.
5. Fudge 2002a, 85–92.
6. Fudge 2002a, 89.
7. Fudge 2002a, 91.
8. Fudge 2002a, 89.
9. Jā i, 196–198 (trans. Cowell 1895–1913, i, 75–76). See also CBBS 258 (s.v. Muṇika).

10. Jā ii, 419–420 (trans. Cowell 1895–1913, ii, 285–286). See also CBBS 315 (s.v. Sālūka).
11. Jā ii, 419 (*Sālūka Jātaka*).
12. Jā i, 197 (*Munika Jātaka*).
13. Jā i, 197 (*Munika Jātaka*).
14. Jā i, 197 (*Munika Jātaka*).
15. Jā ii, 420 (*Sālūka Jātaka*).
16. Jā iii, 286–293 (trans. Cowell 1895–1913, iii, 180–183). See also CBBS 415 (s.v. Tuṇḍila).
17. Jā iii, 288.
18. Jā iii, 288–289.
19. Jā iii, 289. This suggestion appears in the word commentary for the phrase "It's hopeless" (P. *attāṇosi*).
20. Jā iv, 211–218 (trans. Cowell 1895–1913, iv, 132–136). See also CBBS 119 (s.v. Javanahaṃsa).
21. Jā iv, 216.
22. Jā iv, 217.
23. Jā iv, 217.
24. Jā iv, 217. These phrases appear in the word commentary on the two verses cited above.
25. Jā iv, 255–263 (trans. Cowell 1895–1913, iv, 161–166). See also CBBS 306–307 (s.v. Rurumiga).
26. Jā iv, 261.
27. Jā v, 354–382 (trans. Cowell 1895–1913, v, 186–202). See also CBBS 210–211 (s.v. Mahāhaṃsa).
28. *manussā nāma bahumāyā kharamantā upāyakusalā* (Jā v, 357).
29. Doniger 1989, 9, 13–14.
30. This is a very common motif; see, for example, the *Lakkhaṇa Jātaka* (No. 11), *Nigrodhamiga Jātaka* (No. 12), *Kaṇḍina Jātaka* (No. 13), *Kharādiya Jātaka* (No. 15), *Tipallatthamiga Jātaka* (No. 16), *Kuruṅga Jātaka* (No. 21), *Kuruṅgamiga Jātaka* (No. 206), *Suvaṇṇamiga Jātaka* (No. 359), *Nandiyamiga Jātaka* (No. 385), *Ruru Jātaka* (No. 482), *Sarabhamiga Jātaka* (No. 483), and *Rohantamiga Jātaka* (No. 501).
31. Jā i, 145–153 (trans. Cowell 1895–1913, i, 36–42). See also CBBS 271–272 (s.v. Nigrodhamiga).
32. Jā i, 150.
33. Jā i, 150.
34. Jā iii, 182–187 (trans. Cowell 1895–1913, iii, 120–123). See also CBBS 397–398 (s.v. Suvaṇṇamiga).
35. Jā iii, 184.
36. Jā i, 142–145 (trans. Cowell 1895–1913, i, 34–36). See also CBBS 192–193 (s.v. Lakkhaṇa).

37. Jā i, 143.
38. Jā i, 143–144.
39. Jā iv, 263–275 (trans. Cowell 1895–1913, iv, 166–174). See also CBBS 334–335 (s.v. Sarabhamiga).
40. Jā iv, 268.
41. Jā i, 160–164 (trans. Cowell 1895–1913, i, 47–50). See also CBBS 411–412 (s.v. Tipallatthamiga).
42. Jā i, 163.
43. Jā i, 163.
44. Jā i, 164.
45. Jā i, 159–160 (trans. Cowell 1895–1913, i, 46–47). See also CBBS 163 (s.v. Kharādiya).
46. Jā i, 173–174 (trans. Cowell 1895–1913, i, 57–58). See also CBBS 185–186 (s.v. Kuruṅgamiga-I).
47. Jā i, 208–210 (trans. Cowell 1895–1913, i, 85–86). See also CBBS 325–326 (s.v. Sammodamāna).
48. Jā i, 432–435 (trans. Cowell 1895–1913, i, 261–262). See also CBBS 434–435 (s.v. Vaṭṭaka-II).
49. Jā ii, 76–79 (trans. Cowell 1895–1913, ii, 53–54). See also CBBS 411 (s.v. Tinḍuka).
50. Jā iii, 369–375 (trans. Cowell 1895–1913, iii, 225–227). See also CBBS 214–215 (s.v. Mahākapi-I).
51. Jā ii, 152–155 (trans. Cowell 1895–1913, ii, 106–107). See also CBBS 186–187 (s.v. Kuruṅgamiga-II).
52. Jā iv, 288–297 (trans. Cowell 1895–1913, iv, 183–187).
53. Jā ii, 266–268 (trans. Cowell 1895–1913, ii, 186–187). See also CBBS 313 (s.v. Sālaka).
54. Jā iii, 197–199 (trans. Cowell 1895–1913, iii, 130–131). See also CBBS 5 (s.v. Ahiguṇḍika).
55. Jā ii, 267–268.
56. Jā ii, 268.
57. Jā iii, 198–199.
58. Jā i, 484–486 (trans. Cowell 1895–1913, i, 300–302). See also CBBS 130–131 (s.v. Kāka-I).
59. *niccaṃ ubbiggahadayā* (Jā i, 486).
60. Jā i, 414–416 (trans. Cowell 1895–1913, i, 246–247). See also CBBS 83 (s.v. Dubbalakaṭṭha).
61. MN iii, 128–137 (trans. Ñāṇamoli and Bodhi 1995, 989–996).
62. MN iii, 132–133 (using the Sri Lankan reading of *parasatthappahārānaṃ* for CS's *sarapattappahārānaṃ* and MN's *parasattuppahārānaṃ*; and reading MN's *bheripaṇavasaṅkhatiṇavaninnādasaddānaṃ* for CS's *bheripaṇ avavaṃsasaṅkhaḍiṇḍimaninnādasaddānaṃ*). Although abusive methods

of elephant training persist throughout South Asia, the situation is slowly changing, thanks to organizations such as HELP (Human Elephant Learning Programs; see www.h-elp.org, accessed July 28, 2015) and Elephant Experts (www.elephantexperts.org, accessed July 28, 2015), which promote more humane training methods for Asia's captive elephants, making use of the science of elephant behavior and emphasizing positive rather than negative reinforcement.

63. Jā i, 415.
64. Jā i, 415.
65. Jā i, 416. This appears in the word commentary for one of the canonical verses.
66. *Dīgha Nikāya* No. 5 (DN i, 127–149) (trans. Walshe 1995, 133–141).
67. DN i, 141.
68. DN i, 147.
69. AN iv, 42–43.
70. The same is true of other anti-sacrifice passages from the *suttas*; see, for example, DN ii, 352–354 (*Pāyāsi Sutta*, No. 23); SN i, 75–76; AN ii, 42–44.
71. Jā i, 166–168 (trans. Cowell 1895–1913, i, 51–53). See also CBBS 243–244 (s.v. Matakabhatta).
72. Jā i, 167.
73. Jā i, 168.
74. Jā iii, 514–519 (trans. Cowell 1895–1913, iii, 306–309). See also CBBS 196 (s.v. Lomasakassapa).
75. Jā iii, 518.
76. Jā iii, 518.
77. Image available at https://commons.wikimedia.org/wiki/File:Elephantmary.jpg (accessed July 28, 2015).
78. Footage available at https://www.youtube.com/watch?v=Gr6xBz-h99U (accessed July 28, 2015).
79. Wood 2012, 405.
80. *New York World*, January 5, 1903, 1–2; *New York Times*, January 5, 1903, 1; *New York Herald*, January 5, 1903, 6 (quoted in Wood 2012, 406).
81. *New York Times*, May 10, 1894, 8; *New York Tribune*, May 12, 1894, 1 (quoted in Wood 2012, 413).
82. Wood 2012, 420.
83. Wood 2012, 442.
84. Burton 1971, 7 (quoted in Wood 2012, 442).
85. *Los Angeles Times*, June 29, 1899, 17 (quoted in Wood 2012, 420).
86. Wood 2012, 409. Evans (1987) is the primary source for these cases.
87. Srivastava (2007) draws a connection between medieval animal trials and modern-day pit bull legislation.

88. Jā i, 175–178 (trans. Cowell 1895–1913, i, 58–61). See also CBBS 133 (s.v. Kakkara).
89. Jā i, 175.
90. The text itself merely says "passion, etc." (P. *chandādi*), but the four "evil courses" (P. *agati-gamana*) are elsewhere listed as passion (P. *chanda*), hatred (P. *dosa*), delusion (P. *moha*), and fear (P. *bhaya*); see DN iii, 228.
91. Jā i, 176–177.
92. In addition to the abused monkey of the *Sālaka Jātaka* (No. 249) and the *Ahiguṇḍika Jātaka* (No. 465) cited above, see also the ox of the *Nandivisāla Jātaka* (No. 28) and *Sārambha Jātaka* (No. 88), and the royal elephant of the *Daḷhadhamma Jātaka* (No. 409).
93. See, for example, the *Sīlavanāga Jātaka* (No. 72) and *Chaddanta Jātaka* (No. 514).
94. See the *Sālittaka Jātaka* (No. 107), where this action is performed by a monk in the "Story in the Present."
95. This gruesome story is told several times throughout the *jātakas*; see the *Kapota Jātaka* (No. 42), *Lola Jātaka* (No. 274), *Rucira Jātaka* (No. 275), *Kapota Jātaka* (No. 375), and *Kāka Jātaka* (No. 395).
96. See the *Kuntani Jātaka* (No. 343).
97. Jā iii, 428–434 (trans. Cowell 1895–1913, iii, 256–260). See also CBBS 25 (s.v. Aṭṭhasadda).
98. Jā iii, 429.
99. *pettikaṃ bhavanaṃ* (Jā iii, 430).
100. Jā iii, 430–431.
101. Jā iii, 431.
102. Jā iii, 432.
103. This story has several parallels: In the *Mahāsupina Jātaka* (No. 77), the king has sixteen ominous dreams, and in the *Lohakumbhi Jātaka* (No. 314), the king hears four ominous sounds. In both cases, a wise ascetic (the bodhisattva) correctly interprets the dreams/sounds and thus averts the animal sacrifice. However, neither the dreams nor the sounds pertain to the human mistreatment of animals.
104. Jā iii, 432.

NOTES TO CHAPTER 4

1. No. 219 (Jā ii, 185).
2. Quoted from Ambros 2014, 254.
3. Jā i, 319–322 (trans. Cowell 1895–1913, i, 174–177). See also CBBS 352–353 (s.v. Sīlavanāga).
4. I have dealt with such "gift-of-the-body" *jātakas* extensively in Ohnuma 2007.

5. Jā i, 322.
6. Jā iv, 255–263 (trans. Cowell 1895–1913, iv, 161–166). See also CBBS 306–307 (s.v. Rurumiga).
7. Jā iv, 259–260.
8. For an interesting analysis of how the grateful deer of the *Ruru Jātaka* came into conflict with "native" Japanese conceptions of deer when this *jātaka* traveled to Japan, see Long 2005.
9. Jā i, 322–327 (trans. Cowell 1895–1913, i, 177–181). See also CBBS 308–310 (s.v. Saccaṃkira).
10. The Aarne-Thompson-Uther Tale Type Index is a cross-cultural classification system for folktales first developed by Antti Aarne, then revised by Stith Thompson and expanded by Hans-Jörg Uther. See Uther 2004.
11. Jā i, 324.
12. Jā i, 325–326.
13. Tales of grateful animals were to become popular in Japanese Buddhism through the genre of *ongaeshi* (gratefulness tales). On this genre (and its conceptions of animality), see Long 2005.
14. Jā i, 326.
15. Jā iii, 270–274 (trans. Cowell 1895–1913, iii, 171–174). See also CBBS 268 (s.v. Nandiyamiga).
16. Jā iii, 273.
17. Jā v, 67–74 (trans. Cowell 1895–1913, v, 37–41). See also CBBS 216–217 (s.v. Mahākapi-II).
18. Jā v, 70–71.
19. Jā v, 71.
20. Jā v, 71.
21. Jā v, 71.
22. Jā v, 71.
23. Jā i, 145–153 (trans. Cowell 1895–1913, i, 36–42). See also CBBS 271–272 (s.v. Nigrodhamiga).
24. Jā i, 151.
25. Jā i, 151–152.
26. Singer 2009.
27. Singer intentionally speaks of "interests" rather than "rights," which distinguishes him from several other prominent animal rights theorists, such as Tom Regan (see, for example, Regan 1983 and Regan 2007). See Singer 2007 for a discussion of his objections to the language of animal "rights."
28. Singer 2009, 18.
29. Jeremy Bentham, *Introduction to the Principles of Morals and Legislation* (quoted in Singer 2009, 7).
30. See Singer and Cavalieri 1993. The compelling nature of this argument is well-illustrated by certain famous examples, such as Koko, the sign

language-using gorilla, who is said to understand more than 1,000 modified signs of American Sign Language and over 2,000 words of spoken English, as well as exhibiting evidence of a rich emotional life. A few examples: for a clip of Koko responding to the saddest scene in her favorite movie, *Tea with Mussolini*, go to https://www.youtube.com/watch?v=EWxCM6llL6o (accessed August 17, 2015); for a clip of Koko mourning the death of her pet kitten, All Ball, go to https://www.youtube.com/watch?v=CQCOHUXmEZg (accessed August 17, 2015).

31. Jā iii, 270–274 (trans. Cowell 1895–1913, iii, 171–174). See also CBBS 268 (s.v. Nandiyamiga).
32. Jā iv, 255–263 (trans. Cowell 1895–1913, iv, 161–166). See also CBBS 306–307 (s.v. Rurumiga).
33. Jā ii, 433–436 (trans. Cowell 1895–1913, ii, 295–297). See also CBBS 385–386 (s.v. Supatta).
34. Jā i, 484–486 (trans. Cowell 1895–1913, i, 300–302). See also CBBS 130–131 (s.v. Kāka-I).
35. Jā i, 175–178 (trans. Cowell 1895–1913, i, 58–61). See also CBBS 133 (s.v. Kakkara).
36. Moreover, the fact that this can happen without making the king dependent upon or subservient to any other human being is perhaps an added benefit.
37. Jā iv, 263–275 (trans. Cowell 1895–1913, iv, 166–174). See also CBBS 334–335 (s.v. Sarabhamiga). This story, however, does not include a specific mention of the king granting security to all living beings.
38. Jā iv, 267.
39. Jā iv, 269.
40. Trans. Olivelle 2013a, 80.
41. Trans. Olivelle 2013a, 69.
42. Trans. Nikam and McKeon 1959, 58, 55–57, 55.
43. See, for example, Schmithausen and Maithrimurthi 2009, 69–77 and Southwold 1983, 65–77.
44. Southwold 1983, 66.
45. Southwold 1983, 67.
46. Jā ii, 184–186 (trans. Cowell 1895–1913, ii, 129–130). See also CBBS 93–94 (s.v. Garahita).
47. Jā ii, 184.
48. Jā ii, 184–185.
49. Jā ii, 185 (emphasis added).
50. Jā ii, 185.
51. Jā ii, 185.
52. Jā ii, 186.

NOTES TO PART III INTRODUCTION

1. Doniger 2005, 23.
2. Goldman 1984, 49–59.
3. See Goldman 2000 and Pollock 1991, 68–84.
4. Daston and Mitman 2005, 7.

NOTES TO CHAPTER 5

1. Ch. 6, v. 55 (BC i, 65).
2. *Nidānakathā* (Jā i, 62).
3. Depending upon the source, the name of the horse is variously given as Kaṇḍaka, Kaṇṭhaka, or Kanthaka. I will refer to him throughout as Kanthaka.
4. The identification of Kanthaka as a co-natal appears, for example, in the *Nidānakathā, Lalitavistara, Abhiniṣkramaṇa Sūtra, Vimānavatthu*, and *Mahāvastu*. Typical is the statement made in the *Nidānakathā*: "At the very same time as our bodhisattva was born in the Lumbinī Grove, the queen (Rāhula's mother), the elder Ānanda, the minister Channa, the minister Kāḷudāyī, the king of horses Kanthaka, the great Bodhi tree, and the four vases of treasure also came into existence.... These seven are called the co-natals" (Jā i, 54). (Ānanda is the Buddha's cousin and personal attendant, Kāḷudāyin is a royal minister who is sent into the forest to retrieve the bodhisattva after he renounces the world, and the four vases of treasure represent the worldly inheritance the bodhisattva will reject). The only inconsistency in this list is Ānanda, who is sometimes replaced by a royal elephant. On the tradition of the co-natals, see, for example, Horner 1978, xliii–xlix.
5. Ch. 5, v. 72 (BC i, 55).
6. Mv i, 156.
7. Mv i, 156.
8. Jā i, 64.
9. In canonical sources, the fully developed story of the Great Departure appears only in the *Mahīśāsaka Vinaya* preserved in Chinese (T. 1421). For a discussion of how this story developed over time out of bits and pieces borrowed from other stories (foremost among them the going-forth of Yaśas), see Bareau 1974, 246–260.
10. Jā i, 62.
11. Jā i, 62.
12. Jā i, 63. This ends up being unnecessary, since the deity dwelling at the city gate opens it. Nevertheless, the *Nidānakathā* assures us, "If the gate had not opened, the plans of one or another of those three surely would have

succeeded" (Jā i, 63). In the *Buddhacarita*, the gate opens by itself, while in the *Lalitavistara*, it is opened by Śakra.

13. LV 195.
14. Ch. 7, Story 81, v. 18 (or 1181) (Vv 119). Reading *abhisiṃsiṃ* (with Vv) for CS's *abhisīsiṃ*.
15. Vv-a 316. Reading *āsisiṃ icchiṃ sampaṭicchiṃ* (with CS) for Vv-a's *icchi sampaṭicchi*.
16. Trans. Beal 1875, 135.
17. Ch. 5, v. 80 (BC i, 56).
18. Mv ii, 160.
19. Ch. 5, vv. 75–78 (BC i, 56).
20. SbhV ii, 91.
21. Jā i, 62.
22. Jā i, 64.
23. Ch. 7, Story 81, v. 17 (or 1180) (Vv 119).
24. Vv-a 316. Reading *ekarattiṃ* (with CS) for Vv-a's *ekarattaṃ*; reading *opavuyhaṃ* (with CS) for Vv-a's *opaguyhaṃ*; reading no full stop after *payojanaṃ* (with CS) for Vv-a's full stop after *payojanaṃ*.
25. Ch. 1, v. 67 (Bv 6).
26. Bv-a 54.
27. Given Kanthaka's close association with the bodhisattva's renunciation, perhaps it makes sense that the various "White Horse Monasteries" (Baima si) of China—including the supposedly earliest monastery at Luoyang—may have been named after Kanthaka (for this speculation, see Palumbo 2003).
28. Strong 2001, 60.
29. Jā i, 64.
30. Ch. 6, v. 4 (BC i, 59).
31. Strong 2001, 60.
32. LV 186.
33. Jā i, 63. The *Nidānakathā* actually places this shrine at a different location, earlier in the bodhisattva's journey, at the place where the bodhisattva wished to take one last look at the city of Kapilavatthu, and the entire earth rotated in order to accommodate him. As Thomas has pointed out, however, it does not make sense to call this spot "The Turning Back of Kanthaka," since the text specifically tells us that neither the bodhisattva nor Kanthaka turned around toward the city; instead, it was the entire earth that rotated so that they would not have to. Thus, he concludes, "It is more likely that the place [in question] was where the charioteer with the horse finally took leave of his master, and identical with the shrine mentioned in the *Lalita-vistara*, the Turning back of Chandaka (*Chandakanivartana*), at the place where the charioteer Channa or Chandaka left the Bodhisatta and returned with the horse" (Thomas 1975, 56). I follow his conjecture here.

34. Trans. Beal 1875, 140.
35. Mv ii, 166.
36. Ch. 6, vv. 53–55 (BC i, 65).
37. Ch. 7, Story 81, vv. 21–22 (or 1184–1185) (Vv 120).
38. Vv-a 314. Reading *ummīletvā* (with CS) for Vv-a's *ummīlitvā*; reading *dassanūpacāraṃ* (with CS) for Vv-a's *dassanupacāraṃ*.
39. Jā i, 65 (emphasis added).
40. Ch. 8, vv. 3–4 (BC i, 77).
41. Trans. Beal 1875, 146.
42. Ch. 8, vv. 17–19 (BC i, 80).
43. Ch. 8, v. 20 (BC i, 80).
44. Trans. Beal 1875, 147. Interestingly enough, this is immediately followed by another episode (perhaps occurring at just the same time?) in which it is Chandaka's human voice that is misinterpreted by the animals, causing *them* to cry out in joy at the prince's return. Regardless of whether an animal's sounds are misinterpreted by human beings, or a human being's language is misinterpreted by animals, both passages speak to the frustrating inability to communicate across the human-animal divide.
45. SbhV ii, 91.
46. LV 192, 193.
47. Mv ii, 189. In the *Kinnarī Jātaka* of the *Mahāvastu*, however, the Buddha relates a *jātaka* tale in which Kanthaka (in a previous lifetime) brought about the *reunion* of the bodhisattva and Yaśodharā (in their previous lifetimes), rather than bringing about their *separation* (see trans. Jones 1949–1956, ii, 91–111). Perhaps this might be seen as a rehabilitation of Kanthaka, but removed to a previous lifetime.
48. Ch. 8, vv. 38–41 (BC i, 83–84).
49. Ch. 8, v. 74 (BC i, 90).
50. Ch. 8, vv. 75–76 (BC i, 90–91).
51. Doniger 2006.
52. Ch. 8, v. 43 (BC i, 84).
53. Ch. 8, v. 49 (BC i, 85).
54. Mv ii, 189.
55. Trans. Beal 1875, 149.
56. In the Pāli sources, for example, Channa later experiences many troubles throughout his life as a monk. See DPPN i, 923–924 (s.v., Channa).
57. Trans. Beal 1875, 151–152.
58. Mv ii, 189–190.
59. Mv ii, 190.
60. Mv ii, 192–193.
61. Mv ii, 194–195. As interesting as the final sentence may be ("See how this pure deed succeeded for one who was only a horse!"), it relies upon Jones's

conjecture that the text's *rakṣabhūtena* ("for one who was a *rakṣa*"?) should be replaced by *aśvabhūtena* (see Jones 1949–1956, ii, 186, n3).

62. Ch. 7, Story 81, vv. 18–19 (or 1181–1182) (Vv 119). Reading *abhisiṃsiṃ* (with Vv) for CS's *abhisīsiṃ*.
63. Ch. 7, Story 81, v. 23 (or 1186) (Vv 120). Reading *dibbaṃ devapuramhi ca* (with Vv) for CS's *devo devapuramhiva.*
64. Ch. 7, Story 81, v. 24 (or 1187) (Vv 120). Masefield's translation of this verse (1989, 480) is misleading; see n. 65 below.
65. Masefield's translation (1989, 480 & 483) misinterprets both the verse and the corresponding commentary to mean that Kanthaka was the first being to hear that *the bodhisattva had succeeded in attaining awakening*—an idea that does not make much sense (did he hear about this while he was a deity in heaven?), and for which there is no other evidence. I interpret the verse and commentary to mean that Kanthaka was the first being to hear the bodhisattva speak of his *intention to attain awakening*. Perhaps Masefield did not realize that the commentary's phrase *patto sambodhimuttamanti*—which indicates what Kanthaka was the first being to hear about, and which seems to be in the past tense—is actually quoting from an earlier verse of the *Vimānavatthu* (v. 1180) (Vv 119), when the bodhisattva said directly to Kanthaka during the Great Departure: *ahaṃ lokaṃ tārayissaṃ patto sambodhim uttamaṃ* ("when I have attained the highest awakening, I will carry the world across"). Thus, the phrase actually refers to something that will happen in the *future*—which means that rather than being the first being to hear that the bodhisattva had already attained awakening, Kanthaka was the first being to hear that he intended to do so.
66. Vv-a 317. Reading *kataññū katavedī* (with CS) for Vv-a's *kataññu katavedi.* The commentary notes, "These two verses have been added by the redactors."
67. SbhV ii, 92.
68. For a few representative examples, see Egge 2002; Granoff 1990; Gummer 2014; Ohnuma 2007, 249–256; Parlier 1991; and Wilson 2003. The general idea that renunciatory and ascetic traditions in India represent an "internalization" of the Vedic sacrifice is common; see, for one example, Heesterman 1985, esp. 26–44.
69. Patton 2006, 394.
70. Patton 2006, 394.
71. LV 181.
72. Trans. Beal 1875, 135.
73. Patton 2006, 396.
74. Patton 2006, 397.
75. Patton 2006, 401.

76. Patton 2006, 401.
77. *Ṛg Veda* 1.162, vv. 20–21 (Patton 2006, 401, cited from O'Flaherty 1981, 91–92).
78. LV 196.
79. See, for example, Heesterman 1987. The partial or complete identification between the sacrificer and the sacrificial offering was recognized already by Hubert and Mauss, in their classic 1898 study of sacrifice. Basing themselves on Vedic sources, they posited this identification as a fundamental feature of *all* sacrifice: "Indeed, it is not enough to say that [the victim] represents [the sacrificer]; it is merged in him. The two personalities are fused together"—and in Vedic sources, this identification becomes "complete" (Hubert and Mauss 1964, 32).
80. Doniger 2010, 42.
81. Doniger 2006, 346 (emphasis added).
82. Doniger 2010, 42.
83. See, for example, the *Bhaddāli Sutta* (*Majjhima Nikāya* No. 65) (trans. Ñāṇamoli and Bodhi 1995, 549–550) and the *Gaṇakamoggallāna Sutta* (*Majjhima Nikāya* No. 107) (trans. Ñāṇamoli and Bodhi 1995, 874). Many passages in the *Aṅguttara Nikāya* also compare the monk to a horse in some manner; see Bodhi 2012, 329–330, 365–368, 492–496, 616–617, 819, 860–862, 1136–1140, 1277–1280, 1449–1452.
84. Doniger 2006, 346.

NOTES TO CHAPTER 6

1. *Dhammapada*, v. 330 (Dhp i, 62).
2. The *Buddhavaṃsa Commentary* provides a list of each of the locations where the Buddha spent his rainy-season retreat during the first twenty years of his ministry (trans. Horner 1978, 4–5).
3. Vin i, 337–359 (trans. Horner 1938–1966, iv, 483–513); Ud 41–42 (trans. Woodward 1935, 49–50); Dhp-a i, 53–66 (trans. Burlingame 1921, i, 175–183). There is another version of the story in the *Saṃyutta Nikāya Commentary* (commentary on the *Pārileyya Sutta*), but it contains nothing that is not found in one of the other three. In addition, several texts deal with the dispute among the monks of Kosambī without relating the Buddha's sojourn in the Pārileyyaka Forest; see, for example, the *Kosambiya Jātaka* (No. 428) (Jā iii, 486–490; trans. Cowell 1895–1913, iii, 289–291; see also CBBS 170–171, s.v. Kosambī) and the *Kosambiya Sutta* of the *Majjhima Nikāya* (MN i, 320–325; trans. Ñāṇamoli and Bodhi 1995, 419–423).

4. The dispute involves the suspension of a monk from the Order at Kosambī, with one side arguing that the suspension is valid because the monk committed an offense, and the other side arguing that the suspension is invalid because the monk did not recognize his action as an offense.
5. Vin i, 349.
6. Dhp-a i, 56.
7. Ud 41.
8. In the first episode, he goes to Bālakaloṇakāra village and visits the solitary monk Bhagu, preaching to him about the virtues of solitude; in the second episode, he goes to the Eastern Bamboo Grove and visits the monks Anuruddha, Nandiya, and Kimbila, conversing with them on the topic of harmonious living. Both contexts (solitary living and harmonious dwelling) contrast sharply with the quarrelsome atmosphere of Kosambī. These two episodes are included in the *Vinaya* and *Dhammapada Commentary* versions, but do not appear in the *Udāna* version (though they do appear in its commentary).
9. Vin i, 352.
10. Vin i, 352–353.
11. Vin i, 353.
12. Vin i, 353.
13. Vin-a v, 1152.
14. Vin i, 353.
15. "Here, one should understand that the Blessed One stayed there for three months" (Vin-a v, 1152).
16. Ud-a 250–251.
17. Dhp-a i, 59.
18. Daston and Mitman 2005, 11.
19. Waldau 2002, 60.
20. Waldau 2002, 118.
21. S. *caturaṅga-bala* or *caturaṅga-senā*, consisting of infantry, cavalry, chariots, and elephants.
22. The social, cultural, and religious history of the Indian elephant is masterfully synthesized and lavishly illustrated in Sukumar 2011.
23. For references, see, for example, PTSD 349 (s.v. *nāga*).
24. On the imagery of elephants in Buddhist literature, see Sukumar 2011, 92–129; Ramanathapillai 2009; Waldau 2002, 113–136; and Deleanu 2000, 91–98.
25. Deleanu 2000, 94.
26. *Dhammapada*, v. 330 (Dhp i, 62).
27. The full verse, which is attributed to Mahāmoggallāna, reads: "Living in the forest, gathering alms, delighting with whatever gleanings come into our

bowls, let us destroy the army of death, as an elephant destroys a house of reeds!" (*Theragāthā*, v. 1147) (Thag 104).

28. Ramanathapillai 2009, 31.
29. See, for example, the quotation from the *Dantabhūmi Sutta* of the *Majjhima Nikāya* (No. 125) provided in Chapter 3.
30. Perhaps it is also significant that elephants are not truly a domesticated animal—for rather than being bred in captivity, they generally have to be captured in the wild and then forcibly tamed. Could this suggest that one is not *born* a monk, but must be "captured" and "tamed" by the Sangha?
31. *Dhammapada*, v. 326 (Dhp iv, 326).
32. *Theragāthā*, v. 1141 (Thag 103).
33. I do not see any indication (in any version of the story) that the elephant makes use of verbal language.
34. Long 2005, 24.
35. This story is technically a *jātaka*, since Prince Dīghāvu is a previous birth of the Buddha. The latter half of the story is also told in the *Dīghīti Kosala Jātaka* (No. 371) (trans. Cowell 1895–1913, iii, 139–140); see also CBBS 81 (s.v. Dīghītikosala).
36. Vin i, 345. Verse 5 of the *Dhammapada* reads: "In this world, wrath is never appeased by wrath; wrath is appeased by non-wrath—this is an eternal law" (Dhp i, 50).
37. Vin i, 348 (emphasis added).
38. Regarding the "law of the fish," Olivelle explains: "This is a well-known proverb in ancient Indian literature with reference to an anarchical society not governed by the stern rule of a king. In such a society, the strong devour the weak, as the big fish eat the smaller fish" (Olivelle 2013a, 470, n1.4.13). As we saw in Chapter 1, Buddhism shares this harsh characterization of the animal world.
39. In the *Dhammapada Commentary* version, a group of monks later says to the Buddha, "Lord, Blessed One, you are a refined Awakened One, a refined Khattiya. We think it must have been difficult for you to spend three months [in the forest] standing and sitting alone, for you had no one to perform the major and minor duties for you, and no one to give you water for rinsing the mouth, and so on" (Dhp-a i, 61). By referring to the Buddha as a "refined" (P. *sukhumālo*) human being, and automatically assuming that no other "refined" human being was present to fulfill the customary duties for him, the monks betray their limited understanding of what it means to be truly "human." The Buddha immediately corrects them: "Monks, the elephant Pārileyyaka performed all these duties for me. When one obtains such a companion as him, it is proper to live in communion, but for one who does not obtain such a companion, it is better to dwell alone" (Dhp-a i, 61–62). The Buddha thus suggests that the elephant is a more "refined" human being than the quarreling monks he left behind.

40. Dhp-a i, 59.
41. Dhp-a i, 59–60.
42. Doniger 1989, 9.
43. Waldau 2002, 119–120. See also Deleanu 2000, 103–105. Olivelle (1997, xxiv) likewise notes of monkeys in the *Pañcatantra* that they are "playful, but fickle . . . and foolish."
44. *Theragāthā*, v. 1111 (Thag 99). Similarly, in *Theragāthā*, v. 1080, the monk whose mind is agitated but who nevertheless dresses in the clothes of an ascetic is like "a monkey dressed in a lion's hide" (Thag 96); and in *Theragāthā* v. 125, the agitated human mind is compared to a monkey caged in a five-doored hut (representing the five senses), "going from door to door and knocking again and again" (Thag 18).
45. "O Monks, that which is called 'thought' or 'mind' or 'consciousness' arises as one thing and ceases as another thing, all day and all night long. O Monks, just as a monkey roaming in a forest or woodland grabs a branch, releases it and grabs another, then releases that and grabs yet another, in just the same way, Monks, that which is called 'thought' or 'mind' or 'consciousness' arises as one thing and ceases as another thing, all day and all night long" (SN ii, 94).
46. *Theragāthā*, v. 126 (Thag 18).
47. Dhp-a i, 60.
48. The monkey's gift of honey as related in the *Dhammapada Commentary* should be distinguished from the similar story of a monkey's gift of honey found in various Chinese and Tibetan translations (see Lamotte 1944–1980, iii, 1659–1661 for references) and frequently depicted in South Asian art (see Brown 2009). In that version (whose locale varies according to the source), the monkey steals the Buddha's begging bowl and uses it to retrieve honey from a tree and offer it to the Buddha. He dies not by impaling himself on a branch but by falling into a well or a pit. Rather than being reborn as a deity, he is generally reborn as a human being who becomes a monk named Madhuvāsiṣṭha. For a Sanskrit version of this story, see the *Saṅghabhedavastu* of the *Mūlasarvāstivāda Vinaya* (SbhV ii, 47–49); for Xuanzang's references to the story (which he locates at both Vaiśālī and Mathurā), see Li 1996, 123–124 (Mathurā) and 210 (Vaiśālī). This monkey's gift of honey became one of the "Eight Great Miracles" (S. *aṣṭamahāprātihārya*) of the Buddha's life and career; see Huntington 1985–1986, Part IV. For the "Eight Great Miracles" in Thai tradition, see Skilling 2010 and Skilling and Pakdeekham 2010.
49. See Book 5 (*Sundara Kāṇḍa*), Chapters 59–62 (trans. Goldman and Goldman 1996, 278–289).
50. Goldman and Goldman 1996, 4.
51. Dhp-a i, 61.
52. Dhp-a i, 61.

53. "If one finds a wise companion, a resolute friend with a virtuous life, then let one walk with him, being pleased and mindful, overcoming all dangers. But if one does not find a wise companion, a resolute friend with a virtuous life, then let one wander alone, like a king abandoning the kingdom he has conquered, like an elephant [wandering] in an elephant-forest. Living in solitude is better, for there is no companionship with a fool. Let one wander alone, not doing evil, living at ease, like an elephant [wandering] in an elephant-forest" (*Dhammapada,* vv. 328–330) (Dhp i, 62).
54. Dhp-a i, 63.
55. Dhp-a i, 63.
56. He does, however, benefit from the *prasāda* mechanism: "But because of his faith in the Teacher (P. *satthari pasādena*), he was reborn in the Tāvatiṃsa heaven, in a heavenly golden palace thirty leagues in extent, surrounded by a thousand celestial nymphs. And his name was Godling Pārileyyaka" (Dhp-a i, 63).

NOTES TO CHAPTER 7

1. (No. 533) Jā v, 336.
2. For a convenient collection of Pāli passages relating to Devadatta (translated into English), see Ñāṇamoli 1992, 257–270. For a summary of these traditions, see DPPN, i, 1106–1111 (s.v. Devadatta).
3. Ray 1994, 162–163.
4. See, for example, Mukherjee 1966; Bareau 1997; Bareau 1988–1989; Ray 1994, 162–173; and Sarao 2004. Based on the way in which Devadatta attempts to foment a schism, all four scholars are in agreement that the Devadatta legend reflects a tension in early Buddhism between more and less austere visions of the monastic life, with Devadatta representing the more austere and rigorously ascetic faction.
5. For another version of Devadatta's story that has both similarities and differences with the version found in Pāli sources, see Bareau's summary of the story as told in the *Ekottarāgama* preserved in Chinese (Bareau 1992).
6. Vin ii, 193.
7. Vin ii, 193–195 (trans. Horner 1938–1966, v, 272–274); Jā v, 333–337 (trans. Cowell 1895–1913, v, 175–186; see also CBBS 57–58, s.v. Cullahaṃsa); Bv-a 208–214 (trans. Horner 1978, 300–309).
8. SbhV ii, 186–192.
9. For a thorough accounting of all versions of the story (as well as artistic depictions), see Lamotte 1944–1980, iv, 1767–1773 (n. 4). Lamotte divides the various versions of the story into three categories: (1) those in which the Buddha tames Nāḷāgiri through his benevolence (including the Pāli sources);

(2) those in which the Buddha tames Nāḷāgiri through magic and miracles (including the *Saṅghabhedavastu* version); and (3) some later versions, in which it is Ajātasattu rather than Devadatta who bears primary responsibility for engineering Nāḷāgiri's attack. For a discussion of how the various textual versions of the story compare to the fresco in Cave 17 at Ajaṇṭā, see Mukherjee 1987. Mukherjee's Appendix also provides English translations of the episode, as it appears in various Chinese sources—including the *Mahīśāsaka Vinaya, Sarvāstivāda Vinaya, Mūlasarvāstivāda Vinaya,* and *Ekottarāgama*. For depictions of the episode in Pāla sculpture, see Bartholomew 1989.

10. Likewise, for the sake of readability, when drawing on the *Buddhavaṃsa Commentary* version, I do not always distinguish between the Buddha Gotama and the (former) Buddha Piyadassin, or between the elephant Nāḷāgiri and the elephant Doṇamukha; and when drawing on the *Saṅghabhedavastu* version, I refer to the elephant as Nāḷāgiri rather than as Dhanapālaka.
11. Jā v, 333–334.
12. Bv-a 210. Reading *viggahavantam* (with CS) for Bv-a's *vibbhamantam*.
13. SbhV ii, 186.
14. Bv-a 210.
15. Bv-a 210.
16. On *Gaja-Śāstra*, see Sukumar 2011, 48–51.
17. SbhV ii, 189.
18. Jā v, 333–334 (emphasis added).
19. See Bautze-Picron 2009.
20. Ramanathapillai 2009.
21. For the *Buddhacarita* (Chapter 13, v. 19), see trans. Johnston 1984, 192; for the *Mahāvastu*, see trans. Jones 1949–1956, ii, 364.
22. Jā i, 74.
23. Vin ii, 194–195.
24. Jā v, 336.
25. Bv-a 211.
26. Bv-a 212.
27. SbhV ii, 188. At this point, in fact, the elephant becomes so attached to the sight of the Buddha that when the Buddha enters a house and the elephant cannot see him anymore, he begins to break into the house—whereupon the Buddha magically turns the house into crystal so that the elephant's *darśan* of him can be maintained.
28. The Nāḷāgiri story was a very popular subject in Indian Buddhist art. Artistic depictions of the story are thoroughly examined in Zin 1996 and Zin 2006, 69–95.
29. See Powers 2009.
30. Ramanathapillai 2009, 32.

31. Huntington (1985–1986, iv, 33) similarly notes of the Nāḷāgiri episode that "it is the raging beast (the wild elephant) within us that must be quelled."
32. Bv-a 210.
33. Bv-a 211.
34. The terms used for "elephant" are *kuñjara* and *nāga,* respectively (Vin ii, 194). The *Saṅghabhedavastu* version has a nearly parallel verse (SbhV ii, 188).
35. Jā v, 335, 336.
36. Vin ii, 194.
37. Jā v, 335.
38. Fudge 2002b, 4.
39. Schmithausen and Maithrimurti 2009, 101. We see a further extension of this theme in the many depictions of forest hermitages where animals lose their predatory qualities and live in peace, due to the salutary influence of the ascetics who live there. In the *Temiya Jātaka* (No. 537), for example, an entire kingdom renounces the world in favor of a peaceful forest hermitage, and (in Naomi Appleton's translation) "even the animals that had gone there, the elephants and horses, inclined their hearts towards the community of sages and were reborn in the six heavens of sense desires" (Appleton and Shaw 2015, i, 78).
40. Schmithausen and Maithrimurti 2009, 62, n. 80. On this general topic, see also Schmithausen 1997.
41. Jā v, 334.
42. SbhV ii, 188.
43. Jā v, 335.
44. Jā v, 335.
45. Jā v, 335.
46. Jā v, 335.
47. MP 207–209. Nāgasena resolves the dilemma by saying that the arhats were indeed free of fear, but *voluntarily* retreated in order to showcase Ānanda's great devotion to the Buddha, and because Nāḷāgiri would otherwise not have approached the Buddha. In a larger sense, we might also note that while all such attacks upon the Buddha can be used to showcase his enormous power, the very fact that he is attacked at all perhaps threatens to weaken this same power. The *Udāna Commentary*, for example, seems embarrassed by all such episodes in which the Buddha experienced suffering, trouble, or attacks upon his character. It resolves this embarrassment by providing a list of twelve such instances—including the attack by Nāḷāgiri—and explaining that all of them were "the residual fruits of [various] deeds done in the past" (that is, in a long-ago distant life), which are referred to as "karmic remnants" (P. *kamma-pilotikāni*) (Ud-a 263). In this way, the Buddha's power *as a Buddha* remains untainted. (On this tradition of the Buddha's

"bad karma," see Walters 1990.) Why, according to this tradition, was the Buddha confronted by Nāḷāgiri? "Formerly, while mounted on an elephant, I attacked a noble solitary sage with my elephant, as he was wandering for alms. Through the ripening of that deed, the fierce and swaggering elephant Nāḷāgiri approached me in the excellent city of Giribbaja" (Ud-a 265).

48. Mv ii, 415. For a study of the Buddha's masculinity, see Powers 2009.
49. Jā v, 336.
50. SbhV ii, 188.
51. Vin ii, 194.
52. Jā v, 335.
53. Jā v, 336.
54. Bv-a 211.
55. Jā v, 337.
56. Bv-a 212.
57. MP 349.
58. On the tradition of the "Eight Great Miracles," see Huntington 1985–1986 and Huntington 1987; on the Nāḷāgiri episode specifically, see Huntington 1985–1986, iv, 33–40. On the "Eight Great Miracles" in Thai tradition, see Skilling 2010 and Skilling and Pakdeekham 2010.
59. SbhV ii, 189.
60. Marvin 1988, esp. Chs. 8 and 9.
61. Marvin 1988, 142.
62. Marvin 1988, 141.
63. Marvin 1988, 141.
64. Marvin 1988, 131.
65. Marvin 1988, 142.
66. Marvin 1988, 133.
67. MN i, 446.
68. MN i, 447.
69. See Chapter 5, n. 83.
70. Bv-a 212.
71. SbhV ii, 190.
72. SbhV ii, 192.
73. The Buddha uses exactly the same miracles in his taming of the fierce buffalo in the *Mahiṣa Avadāna* (*Avadānaśataka* No. 58); see Chapter 2, n. 43.
74. SbhV ii, 188.
75. These lions are regularly included in depictions of the episode in Pāla sculpture; see Bartholomew 1989 for several examples. On the subject of the Buddha's "difficult" conversions, see Zin 2006.
76. Trans. Li 1996, 268–269.
77. Bautze-Picron 2009.
78. Bautze-Picron 2009, 523.

79. Bautze-Picron 2009, 559 (cited from the English summary appended to Bautze-Picron's article, which is in French).
80. AN iii, 122.
81. Bautze-Picron 2009, 549 (translated from French and emphasis added).
82. DN iii, 25–26.
83. These are the *Virocana Jātaka* (No. 143), *Sigāla Jātaka* (No. 152), *Daddara Jātaka* (No. 172), *Sīhakoṭṭhuka Jātaka* (No. 188), *Jambuka Jātaka* (No. 335), and *Manoja Jātaka* (No. 397).
84. Jā i, 490–493 (trans. Cowell 1895–1913, i, 305–307). See also CBBS 450 (s.v. Virocana).
85. Jā iii, 112–115 (trans. Cowell 1895–1913, iii, 74–76). See also CBBS 117 (s.v. Jambuka).
86. From the *Jambuka Jātaka* (No. 335) (Jā iii, 114).
87. See Taylor 2007 for an interesting study of the *Pañcatantra* built upon the tale of the indigo jackal. For the jackal's associations in Sanskrit literature, see Taylor 2007, 56–63.

NOTES TO THE CONCLUSION

1. A quotation from Jeremy Bentham, cited earlier in Chapter 4 (see note 29).
2. This phrase is attributed to Thomas Berry (although without a specific citation) and serves as the epigraph to Waldau and Patton 2006.

BIBLIOGRAPHY

Ambros, Barbara. 2014. "Animals in Japanese Buddhism: The Third Path of Existence." *Religion Compass* 8 (8): 251–263.

Appleton, Naomi. 2014. *Narrating Karma and Rebirth: Buddhist and Jain Multi-Life Stories*. Cambridge: Cambridge University Press.

Appleton, Naomi, and Sarah Shaw, trans. 2015. *The Ten Great Birth Stories of the Buddha: The Mahānipāta of the Jātakatthavaṇṇanā*. Chiang Mai, Thailand: Silkworm Books.

Aung, Shwe Zan, and C. A. F. Rhys Davids, trans. 1979. *Points of Controversy or Subjects of Discourse, Being a Translation of the Kathāvatthu from the Abhidhamma-Piṭaka*. Pali Text Society Translation Series, No. 5. London: Pali Text Society. Orig. pub. 1915.

Bareau, André. 1974. "La jeunesse du Buddha dans les Sūtrapiṭaka et les Vinayapiṭaka anciens." *Bulletin de l'École française d'Extrême-Orient* 61: 199–274.

Bareau, André. 1988–1989. "Étude du bouddhisme." *Annuaire du Collège de France*, 533–547.

Bareau, André. 1992. "L'histoire de Devadatta selon l'Ekottara-Āgama." *Eurasie: cahiers de la Société des études euro-asiatiques* 2: 68–79.

Bareau, André. 1997. "Devadatta and the First Buddhist Schism." *Buddhist Studies Review* 14 (1): 19–37.

Bareau, André, and Jacques May. 1967. "Chikushō (Animal)." In *Hôbôgirin: Dictionnaire encyclopédique du Bouddhisme d'après les sources Chinoises et Japonaises*. Vol. 4, edited by Paul Demiéville and Jacques May, 309–319. Paris and Tokyo: Maison Franco-Japonaise.

Bartholomew, Terese Tse. 1989. "'Taming of the Elephant' and Other Pāla Sculptures in the Asian Art Museum of San Francisco." In *Studies in Art and Archaeology of Bihar and Bengal: Nalinīkānta Śatavārṣikī Dr. N. K.*

Bhattasali Centenary Volume (1888–1988), edited by Debala Mitra and Gouriswar Bhattacharya, 61–65. Sri Garib Dass Oriental Series, No. 83. Delhi: Sri Satguru.

Batchelor, Martine. 1992. "Even the Stones Smile." In *Buddhism and Ecology*, edited by Martine Batchelor and Kerry Brown, 2–17. New York: Cassell.

Bautze-Picron, Claudine. 2009. "Antagonistes et complémentaires: le lion et l'éléphant dans la personnalité du Buddha." In *Penser, dire et représenter l'animal dans le monde indien*, edited by Nalini Balbir and Georges-Jean Pinault, 523–571. Paris: Librairie Honoré Champion.

Beal, Samuel, trans. 1875. *The Romantic Legend of Sâkya Buddha: From the Chinese-Sanscrit.* London: Trübner & Co.

Benjamin, Walter. 1997. *One-Way Street and Other Writings*. Translated by Edmund Jephcott and Kingsley Shorter. London: Penguin Classics.

Bodhi, Bhikkhu, trans. 2012. *The Numerical Discourses of the Buddha: A Translation of the Aṅguttara Nikāya*. Somerville, MA: Wisdom Publications.

Bose, M. M., ed. 1977. *Paramattha-Dīpanī Iti-Vuttakaṭṭhakathā (Iti-Vuttaka Commentary) of Dhammapālâcariya*. 2 vols. in one. London: Pali Text Society. Orig. pub. 1934–1936.

Brown, Robert L. 2009. "Telling the Story in Art of the Monkey's Gift of Honey to the Buddha." In *Evo ṣuyadi: Essays in Honor of Richard Salomon's 65th Birthday*, edited by Carol Altman Bromberg, Timothy J. Lenz, and Jason Neelis. *Bulletin of the Asia Institute*, n.s., 23: 43–52.

Burlingame, Eugene Watson, trans. 1921. *Buddhist Legends, Translated from the Original Pali Text of the Dhammapada Commentary*. 3 vols. Harvard Oriental Series, Vols. 28, 29, and 30. Cambridge: Harvard University Press.

Burton, Thomas G. 1971. "The Hanging of Mary, A Circus Elephant." *Tennessee Folklore Society Bulletin* 37: 1–8.

Buswell, Robert E., and Donald S. LopezJr., eds. 2014. *The Princeton Dictionary of Buddhism*. Princeton, NJ: Princeton University Press.

Chapple, Christopher. 1992. "Nonviolence to Animals in Buddhism and Jainism." In *Inner Peace, World Peace: Essays on Buddhism and Nonviolence*, edited by Kenneth Kraft, 49–62. Albany: State University of New York Press.

Chapple, Christopher. 1993. *Nonviolence to Animals, Earth, and Self in Asian Traditions*. SUNY Series in Religious Studies. Albany: State University of New York Press.

Chapple, Christopher. 2006. "Inherent Value without Nostalgia: Animals and the Jaina Tradition." In *A Communion of Subjects: Animals in Religion, Science, and Ethics*, edited by Paul Waldau and Kimberley Patton, 241–249. New York: Columbia University Press.

Clayton, Edward. 2008. "Aesop, Aristotle, and Animals: The Role of Fables in Human Life." *Humanitas* 21 (1–2): 179–200.

Collins, Steven. 1998. *Nirvana and Other Buddhist Felicities: Utopias of the Pali imaginaire*. Cambridge Studies in Religious Traditions, No. 12. Cambridge: Cambridge University Press.

Cowell, Edward B., gen. ed. 1895–1913. *The Jātaka or Stories of the Buddha's Former Births*. 7 vols. Cambridge: Cambridge University Press.

Cowell, Edward B., and Robert A. Neil, eds. 1970. *The Divyāvadāna: A Collection of Early Buddhist Legends*. Amsterdam: Oriental Press. Orig. pub. 1886.

Daston, Lorraine, and Gregg Mitman. 2005. "Introduction: The How and Why of Thinking With Animals." In *Thinking with Animals: New Perspectives on Anthropomorphism*, edited by Lorraine Daston and Gregg Mitman, 1–14. New York: Columbia University Press.

Deleanu, Florin. 2000. "Buddhist 'Ethology' in the Pāli Canon: Between Symbol and Observation." *Eastern Buddhist*, n.s., 32 (2): 79–127.

Doniger, Wendy. 1989. "The Four Worlds." In *Animals in Four Worlds: Sculptures From India*, edited by Stella Snead, 3–23. Chicago: University of Chicago Press.

Doniger, Wendy. 2005. "Zoomorphism in Ancient India: Humans More Bestial Than the Beasts." In *Thinking with Animals: New Perspectives on Anthropomorphism*, edited by Lorraine Daston and Gregg Mitman, 17–36. New York: Columbia University Press.

Doniger, Wendy. 2006. "A Symbol in Search of an Object: The Mythology of Horses in India." In *A Communion of Subjects: Animals in Religion, Science, and Ethics*, edited by Paul Waldau and Kimberley Patton, 335–350. New York: Columbia University Press.

Doniger, Wendy. 2010. *The Hindus: An Alternative History*. New York: Penguin.

Edgerton, Franklin. 1953. *Buddhist Hybrid Sanskrit Grammar and Dictionary*. 2 vols. New Haven, CT: Yale University Press.

Egge, James R. 2002. *Religious Giving and the Invention of Karma in Theravāda Buddhism*. Curzon Studies in Asian Religion. Richmond, Surrey, UK: Curzon.

Evans, E. P. 1987. *The Criminal Prosecution and Capital Punishment of Animals: The Lost History of Europe's Animal Trials*. London: Faber & Faber. Orig. pub. 1906.

Fausboll, V., ed. 1875–1897. *The Jātaka Together with Its Commentary, Being Tales of the Anterior Births of Gotama Buddha*. 7 vols. London: Trübner.

Feer, Léon, ed. 1884–1904. *The Saṃyutta-nikāya of the Sutta-piṭaka*. 6 vols. London: Pali Text Society.

Fergusson, James. 1971. *Tree and Serpent Worship; or, Illustrations of Mythology and Art in India in the First and Fourth Centuries after Christ, from the Sculptures of the Buddhist Topes at Sanchi and Amravati*. Delhi: Oriental Publishers. Orig. pub. 1868.

Forsthoefel, Thomas A. 2007. "Jataka, Pancatantra, and the Rhetoric of Animalia in South Asia." In *Buddha Nature and Animality*, edited by David Jones, 23–39. Fremont, CA: Jain Publishing Company.

Fudge, Erica. 2002a. *Animal*. Focus on Contemporary Issues. London: Reaktion.

Fudge, Erica. 2002b. *Perceiving Animals: Humans and Beasts in Early Modern English Culture*. Urbana: University of Illinois Press. Orig. pub. 2000.

Gnoli, Raniero, ed. 1977–1978. *The Gilgit Manuscript of the Saṅghabhedavastu, Being the 17th and Last Section of the Vinaya of the Mūlasarvāstivādin*. 2 vols. Serie Orientale Roma, No. 49. Rome: Istituto Italiano per il Medio ed Estremo Oriente.

Goldman, Robert P., trans. 1984. *The Rāmāyaṇa of Vālmīki: An Epic of Ancient India*. Vol. 1, *Bālakāṇḍa*. Princeton Library of Asian Translations. Princeton, NJ: Princeton University Press.

Goldman, Robert P. 2000. "Rāvaṇa's Kitchen: A Testimony of Desire and the Other." In *Questioning Rāmāyaṇas: A South Asian Tradition*, edited by Paula Richman, 105–116. Berkeley: University of California Press.

Goldman, Robert P., and Sally Sutherland Goldman, trans. 1996. *The Rāmāyaṇa of Vālmīki: An Epic of Ancient India*. Vol. V, *Sundarakāṇḍa*.

Princeton Library of Asian Translations. Princeton, NJ: Princeton University Press.

Granoff, Phyllis. 1990. "The Sacrifice of Maṇicūḍa: The Context of Narrative Action as a Guide to Interpretation." In *Kalyāṇamitra: Festschrift for H. Nakamura*, edited by V. N. Jha, 225–239. Poona, India: Poona University.

Grey, Leslie. 1994. *A Concordance of Buddhist Birth Stories*. 2nd rev. & enlarged ed. Oxford: Pali Text Society. Orig. pub. 1990.

Gruen, Lori. 2010. "The Moral Status of Animals." In *The Stanford Encyclopedia of Philosophy*, edited by Edward N. Zalta. Stanford, CA: Center for the Study of Language and Information, Stanford University. http://plato.stanford.edu/archives/fall2014/entries/moral-animal.

Gummer, Natalie. 2014. "Sacrificial Sūtras: Mahāyāna Literature and the South Asian Ritual Cosmos." *Journal of the American Academy of Religion* 82 (4): 1091–1126.

Hardy, E., ed. 1901. *Dhammapāla's Paramattha-Dīpanī, Part IV, Being the Commentary on the Vimāna-Vatthu*. London: Pali Text Society.

Harris, Ian. 2006. "'A Vast Unsupervised Recycling Plant': Animals and the Buddhist Cosmos." In *A Communion of Subjects: Animals in Religion, Science, and Ethics*, edited by Paul Waldau and Kimberley Patton, 207–217. New York: Columbia University Press.

Harvey, Peter. 2000. *An Introduction to Buddhist Ethics: Foundations, Values and Issues*. Cambridge: Cambridge University Press.

Heesterman, J. C. 1985. *The Inner Conflict of Tradition: Essays in Indian Ritual, Kingship, and Society*. Chicago: University of Chicago Press.

Heesterman, J. C. 1987. "Self-Sacrifice in Vedic Ritual." In *Gilgud: Essays on Transformation, Revolution and Permanence in the History of Religions*, edited by S. Shaked, D. Shulman, and G. G. Stroumsa, 91–106. Leiden, The Netherlands: Brill.

Hobgood-Oster, Laura. 2008. *Holy Dogs and Asses: Animals in the Christian Tradition*. Urbana: University of Illinois Press.

Horner, I. B., trans. 1938–1966. *The Book of the Discipline (Vinaya Piṭaka)*. 6 vols. Sacred Books of the Buddhists, Vols. 10, 11, 13, 14, 20, and 25. London: H. Milford, and Oxford: Oxford University Press.

Horner, I. B., ed. 1946. *Madhuratthavilāsinī nāma Buddhavaṃsaṭṭhakathā of Bhadantâcariya Buddhadatta Mahāthera*. Oxford: Oxford University Press (for the Pali Text Society).

Horner, I. B., trans. 1978. *The Clarifier of the Sweet Meaning (Maduratt havilāsini): Commentary on the Chronicle of Buddhas (Buddhavaṃsa) by Buddhadatta Thera*. Sacred Books of the Buddhists, No. 33. London: Pali Text Society.

Houlbrooke, Ralph. "The Puritan Death-Bed, c. 1560–c. 1660." In *The Culture of English Puritanism, 1560–1700*, edited by Christopher Durston and Jacqueline Eales, 122–144. Basingstoke, UK: Macmillan, 1996.

Hubert, Henri, and Marcel Mauss. 1964. *Sacrifice: Its Nature and Function*. Translated by W. D. Halls. Chicago: University of Chicago Press. Orig. pub. in French in 1898.

Huntington, John C. 1985–1986. "Sowing the Seeds of the Lotus: A Journey to the Great Pilgrimage Sites of Buddhism" (5 parts). *Orientations* 16 (11): 46–61 (Part I); 17 (2): 28–43 (Part II); 17 (3): 32–46 (Part III); 17 (7): 28–40 (Part IV); 17 (9): 46–58 (Part V).

Huntington, John C. 1987. "Pilgrimage as Image: The Cult of the *Aṣṭamahāprātihārya*" (2 parts). *Orientations* 18 (4): 55–63 (Part I); 18 (8): 56–68 (Part II).

Jaini, Padmanabh S. 1987. "Indian Perspectives on the Spirituality of Animals." In *Buddhist Philosophy and Culture: Essays in Honour of N. A. Jayawickrema*, edited by David J. Kalupahana and W. G. Weeraratne, 169–178. Colombo, Sri Lanka: N. A. Jayawickrema Felicitation Volume Committee.

Jayawickrama, N. A., ed. 1974. *Buddhavaṃsa and Cariyāpiṭaka*. Pali Text Society Text Series, No. 106. London: Pali Text Society.

Jayawickrama, N. A., ed. 1977. *Vimānavatthu and Petavatthu*. Pali Text Society Text Series, No. 168. London: Pali Text Society.

Johnston, E. H., ed. and trans. 1984. *The Buddhacarita or Acts of the Buddha, by Aśvaghoṣa*. New enlarged ed. 2 vols. in one. Delhi: Motilal Banarsidass. Orig. pub. 1936.

Jones, John G. 2001. *Tales and Teachings of the Buddha: The Jātaka Stories in Relation to the Pāli Canon*. 2nd ed. Christchurch, New Zealand: Cybereditions. Orig. pub. 1979.

Jones, J. J., trans. 1949–1956. *The Mahāvastu*. 3 vols. Sacred Books of the Buddhists, Vols. 16, 18, and 19. London: Luzac.

Kemmerer, Lisa. 2006. "Verbal Activism: 'Anymal'." *Society and Animals* 14 (1): 9–14.

Kemmerer, Lisa. 2012. *Animals in World Religions*. Oxford: Oxford University Press.

Keown, Damien. 1996. "Buddhism and Suicide: The Case of Channa." *Journal of Buddhist Ethics* 3: 8–31.

King-Smith, Dick. 2010. *The Sheep-Pig*. London: Puffin. Orig. pub. 1983.

Lamotte, Étienne, trans. 1944–1980. *Le traité de la grande vertu de sagesse de Nāgārjuna (Mahāprajñāpāramitāśāstra)*. 5 vols. Bibliothèque du Muséon, Vol. 18. Louvain: Bureaux du Muséon.

Lessing, Gotthold Ephraim. 1996. "Von dem Gebrauche der Thiere in der Fabel" [1759]. In *Literaturtheoretische und ästhetische Schriften*, 43–47. Stuttgart: Philipp Reclam.

Lévi-Strauss, Claude. 1963. *Totemism*. Translated by Rodney Needham. Boston: Beacon.

Li, Rongxi, trans. 1996. *The Great Tang Dynasty Record of the Western Regions, Translated by the Tripiṭaka-Master Xuanzang under Imperial Order, Composed by Śramaṇa Bianji of the Great Zongchi Monastery (Taishō, Volume 51, Number 2087)*. BDK English Tripiṭaka, No. 79. Berkeley, CA: Numata Center for Buddhist Translation and Research.

Lin, Li-Kouang. 1949. *L'aide-mémoire de la vraie loi (Saddharma-smṛtyupasthāna-sūtra), recherches sur un sūtra développé du Petit Véhicule*. Paris: Librairie d'Amérique et d'Orient, Adrien-Maisonneuve.

Lohmann, Larry. 1993. "Green Orientalism." *Ecologist* 23 (6): 202–204.

Long, Hoyt. 2005. "Grateful Animal or Spiritual Being? Changing Conceptions of Deer in Early Japan." In *JAPANimals: History and Culture in Japan's Animal Life*, edited by Gregory M. Pflugfelder and Brett L. Walker, 21–58. Michigan Monograph Series in Japanese Studies, No. 52. Ann Arbor: University of Michigan Center for Japanese Studies.

Malalasekera, G. P. 1937–38. *Dictionary of Pāli Proper Names*. 2 vols. London: J. Murray.

Marvin, Garry. 1988. *Bullfight*. Oxford: Basil Blackwell.

Masefield, Peter, trans. 1989. *Elucidation of the Intrinsic Meaning So Named: The Commentary on the Vimāna Stories (Paramattha-dīpani nāma Vimānavatthu-aṭṭhakathā)*. With assistance of N. A. Jayawickrama. Oxford: Pali Text Society.

McDermott, James P. 1989. "Animals and Humans in Early Buddhism." *Indo-Iranian Journal* 32: 269–280.

Monier-Williams, Monier. 1979. *A Sanskrit-English Dictionary, Etymologically and Philologically Arranged, with Special Reference to Cognate Indo-European Languages*. New ed. Oxford: Oxford University Press. Orig. pub. 1899.

Morris, Richard, ed. 1885–1910. *The Aṅguttara-nikāya*. 5 vols. and Index. London: Pali Text Society.

Mukherjee, Biswadeb. 1966. *Die Überlieferung von Devadatta, dem Widersacher des Buddha, in den kanonischen Schriften*. Munich: Kitzinger in Kommission.

Mukherjee, Biswadeb. 1987. "The Nalagiri Episode: Ajanta Painting and Literary Sources." *Journal of the Asiatic Society (of Bengal)* 29 (3): 56–81.

Nagar, Shanti Lal. 1992. *Garuda, the Celestial Bird*. New Delhi: Book India.

Ñāṇamoli, Bhikkhu, trans. 1992. *The Life of the Buddha, according to the Pali Canon*. Kandy, Sri Lanka: Buddhist Publication Society.

Ñāṇamoli, Bhikkhu, and Bhikkhu Bodhi, trans. 1995. *The Middle Length Discourses of the Buddha: A New Translation of the Majjhima Nikāya*. Boston: Wisdom Publications.

Nikam, N. A., and Richard McKeon, trans. 1959. *The Edicts of Asoka*. Chicago: University of Chicago Press.

Noonan, Chris, dir. *Babe*. 1997. DVD. Universal Studios.

Norman, H. C., ed. 1906–1915. *The Commentary on the Dhammapada*. 5 vols. London: Pali Text Society.

Obeyesekere, Gananath. 2002. *Imagining Karma: Ethical Transformation in Amerindian, Buddhist, and Greek Rebirth*. Comparative Studies in Religion and Society, No. 14. Berkeley: University of California Press.

O'Flaherty, Wendy Doniger, trans. 1981. *The Rig Veda*. Harmondsworth, UK: Penguin.

Ohnuma, Reiko. 2007. *Head, Eyes, Flesh, and Blood: Giving Away the Body in Indian Buddhist Literature*. New York: Columbia University Press.

Oldenberg, Hermann, ed. 1879–1983. *The Vinaya Piṭakaṃ, One of the Principal Buddhist Holy Scriptures in the Pāli Language*. 5 vols. London: Williams and Norgate.

Oldenberg, Hermann, and R. Pischel, eds. 1966. *Theragāthā and Therīgāthā*. 2nd ed., with Appendices by K. R. Norman and L. Alsdorf. Orig. pub. 1883.

Olivelle, Patrick, trans. 1997. *The Pañcatantra: The Book of India's Folk Wisdom*. Oxford World's Classics. Oxford: Oxford University Press.

Olivelle, Patrick, trans. 2013a. *King, Governance, and Law in Ancient India: Kauṭilya's Arthaśāstra*. New York: Oxford University Press.

Olivelle, Patrick. 2013b. "Talking Animals: Explorations in an Indian Literary Genre." In *Charming Beauties and Frightful Beasts: Non-human Animals in South Asian Myth, Ritual and Folklore*, edited by Fabrizio M. Ferrari and Thomas Dähnhardt, 1–14. Sheffield, UK: Equinox.

Palumbo, Antonello. 2003. "Dharmarakṣa and Kaṇṭhaka: White Horse Monasteries in Early Medieval China." In *Buddhist Asia 1: Papers from the First Conference of Buddhist Studies Held in Naples in May 2001*, edited by Giovanni Verardi and Silvio Vita, 167–216. Kyoto: Italian School of East Asian Studies.

Parlier, Edith. 1991. "La légende du roi des Śibi: Du sacrifice brahmanique au don du corps bouddhique." *Bulletin d'Études Indiennes* 9: 133–160.

Patton, Kimberley. 2006. "Animal Sacrifice: Metaphysics of the Sublimated Victim." In *A Communion of Subjects: Animals in Religion, Science and Ethics*, edited by Paul Waldau and Kimberley Patton, 391–405. New York: Columbia University Press.

Perlo, Katherine Wills. 2002. *Kinship and Killing: The Animal in World Religions*. New York: Columbia University Press.

Phelps, Norm. 2004. *The Great Compassion: Buddhism and Animal Rights*. New York: Lantern.

Pollock, Sheldon, trans. 1991. *The Rāmāyaṇa of Vālmīki: An Epic of Ancient India*. Vol. III, *Araṇyakāṇḍa*. Princeton Library of Asian Translations. Princeton, NJ: Princeton University Press.

Powers, John. 2009. *A Bull of a Man: Images of Masculinity, Sex, and the Body in Indian Buddhism*. Cambridge, MA: Harvard University Press.

Pradhan, P., ed. 1975. *Abhidharmakośabhāṣyam of Vasubandhu*. Rev. 2nd ed. Tibetan Sanskrit Works Series, No. 8. Patna: K. P. Jayaswal Research Institute. Orig. pub. 1967.

Pruden, Leo, trans. 1988–1990. *Abhidharmakośabhāṣyam*. 4 vols. Berkeley, CA: Asian Humanities Press.

Ramanathapillai, Rajmohan. 2009. "A Forest Ride on Wild Elephants: The Philosophy of Wilderness in Buddhism." *Gajah* 30: 29–33.

Ray, Reginald A. 1994. *Buddhist Saints in India: A Study in Buddhist Values and Orientations*. New York: Oxford University Press.

Regan, Tom. 1983. *The Case for Animal Rights*. Berkeley: University of California Press.

Regan, Tom. 2007. "The Rights of Humans and Other Animals." In *The Animals Reader: The Essential Classic and Contemporary Writings*, edited by Linda Kalof and Amy Fitzgerald, 23–29. Oxford: Berg.

Rhys Davids, T. W., and William Stede, eds. 1890–1911. *The Dīgha Nikāya*. 3 vols. London: Pali Text Society.

Rhys Davids, T. W., and William Stede. 1966. *The Pali Text Society's Pali-English Dictionary*. London: Luzac. Orig. pub. 1921–1925.

Rotman, Andy, trans. 2008. *Divine Stories: Divyāvadāna, Part I*. Classics of Indian Buddhism. Boston: Wisdom Publications.

Rotman, Andy. 2009. *Thus Have I Seen: Visualizing Faith in Early Indian Buddhism*. New York: Oxford University Press.

Rudd, Gillian. 2006. "Making Mention of Aesop: Henryson's Fable of the Two Mice." *The Yearbook of English Studies* 36 (1): 39–49.

Ryder, Richard. 2000. *Animal Revolution: Changing Attitudes toward Speciesism*. Rev. and updated ed. Oxford: Berg. Orig. pub. 1989.

Sarao, K. T. S. 2004. "In-Laws of the Buddha as Depicted in Pāli Sources." *Chung-Hwa Buddhist Journal* 17: 243–265.

Schmithausen, Lambert. 1997. *Maitrī and Magic: Aspects of the Buddhist Attitude toward the Dangerous in Nature*. Österreichische Akademie der Wissenschaften Philosophisch-Historische Klasse Sitzungsberichte, No. 652. Vienna: Verlag der Österreichischen Akademie der Wissenschaften.

Schmithausen, Lambert, and Mudagamuwe Maithrimurti. 2009. "Attitudes towards Animals in Indian Buddhism." In *Penser, dire, et représenter l'animal dans le monde indien*, edited by Nalini Balbir and Georges-Jean Pinault, 47–121. Paris: Librairie Honoré Champion.

Sciberras, Colette. 2008. "Buddhism and Speciesism: On the Misapplication of Western Concepts to Buddhist Beliefs." *Journal of Buddhist Ethics* 15: 215–240.

Senart, Émile, ed. 1882–1897. *Mahāvastu avadānaṃ. Le Mahāvastu: Texte sanscrit publié pour la première fois et accompagné d'introductions et d'un commentaire*. 3 vols. Paris: Société Asiatique.

Singer, Peter. 2007. "Animal Liberation or Animal Rights?" In *The Animals Reader: The Essential Classic and Contemporary Writings*, edited by Linda Kalof and Amy Fitzgerald, 14–22. Oxford: Berg. Orig. pub. 1987.

Singer, Peter. 2009. *Animal Liberation: The Definitive Classic of the Animal Movement*. Updated ed. New York: HarperCollins. Orig. pub. 1975.

Singer, Peter and Paola Cavalieri, eds. 1993. *The Great Ape Project: Equality beyond Humanity*. London: Fourth Estate.

Singh, Arvind Kumar. 2006. *Animals in Early Buddhism*. Delhi: Eastern Book Linkers.

Skilling, Peter. 2010. "Lumbinī: Liturgy and Devotion." In *The Birth of the Buddha: Proceedings of the Seminar Held in Lumbini, Nepal, October 2004*, edited by Christoph Cueppers, Max Deeg, and Hubert Durt, 345–354, 459–460. LIRI Seminar Proceedings Series, Vol. 3. Lumbini, Nepal: Lumbini International Research Institute.

Skilling, Peter, and Santi Pakdeekham. 2010. "Imaginaires of Late Ayutthaya Pilgrimage: The Seven and Eight Great Sites at Wat Ko Kaeo Suttharam, Phetchaburi." *Aséanie* 25: 147–194.

Southwold, Martin. 1983. *Buddhism in Life: The Anthropological Study of Religion and the Sinhalese Practice of Buddhism*. Manchester, UK: Manchester University Press.

Speyer, J. S., ed. 1958. *Avadānaçataka: A Century of Tales Belonging to the Hīnayāna*. Indo-Iranian Reprints, No. 3. The Hague: Mouton. Orig. pub. 1906–1909.

Srivastava, Anila. 2007. "'Mean, Dangerous, and Uncontrollable Beasts': Mediaeval Animal Trials." *Mosaic* 40 (1): 127–143.

Steinthal, Paul, ed. 1885. *Udāna*. London: Oxford University Press.

Story, Francis (Anāgārika Sugatānanda). 1964. *The Place of Animals in Buddhism*. Bodhi Leaves, No. 23. Kandy, Sri Lanka: Buddhist Publication Society.

Strong, John S. 1983. *The Legend of King Aśoka: A Study and Translation of the Aśokāvadāna*. Princeton Library of Asian Translations. Princeton, NJ: Princeton University Press.

Strong, John S. 2001. *The Buddha: A Short Biography*. Oxford: Oneworld.

Strong, John S. 2008. *The Experience of Buddhism: Sources and Interpretations*. 3rd ed. Belmont, CA: Thomson Wadsworth.

Sukumar, Raman. 2011. *The Story of Asia's Elephants*. Mumbai: Marg Foundation.

Takakusu, J., and M. Nagai, eds. 1924–1977. *Samantapāsādikā: Buddhaghosa's Commentary on the Vinaya Piṭaka*. 8 vols. Pali Text Society Text Series, No. 167. London: Pali Text Society.

Taylor, McComas. 2007. *The Fall of the Indigo Jackal: The Discourse of Division and Pūrṇabhadra's Pañcatantra*. Albany: State University of New York Press.

Thomas, Edward J. 1975. *The Life of Buddha as Legend and History*. 3rd ed. London: Routledge & Kegan Paul. orig. pub. 1927.

Trenckner, Vilhelm, ed. 1880. *The Milindapañho, Being Dialogues between King Milinda and the Buddhist Sage Nāgasena*. London: Williams and Norgate.

Trenckner, Vilhelm, ed. 1888–1925. *The Majjhima Nikāya*. 4 vols. London: Pali Text Society.

Tripathi, Shridhar, ed. 1987. *Lalita-Vistara*. 2nd ed. Buddhist Sanskrit Texts, No. 1. Darbhanga: Mithila Institute. 1st ed. by P. L. Vaidya, published in 1958.

Uther, Hans-Jörg. 2004. *The Types of International Folktales: A Classification and Bibliography Based on the System of Antti Aarne and Stith Thompson*. 3 vols. Helsinki: Suomalainen Tiedeakatemia, Academia Scientiarum Fennica.

Vaidya, P. L., ed. 1961. *Mahāyāna-Sūtra-Saṃgrahaḥ, Part I*. Buddhist Sanskrit Texts, No. 17. Darbhanga: Mithila Institute of Post-Graduate Studies and Research in Sanskrit Learning.

Vogel, Jean Phillipe. 1926. *Indian Serpent-Lore, Or, The Nāgas in Hindu Legend and Art*. London: Arthur Probsthain.

Waldau, Paul. 2000. "Buddhism and Animal Rights." In *Contemporary Buddhist Ethics*, edited by Damien Keown, 81–112. Curzon Critical Studies in Buddhism. Richmond, Surrey, UK: Curzon.

Waldau, Paul. 2002. *The Specter of Speciesism: Buddhist and Christian Views of Animals*. American Academy of Religion Academy Series. New York: Oxford University Press.

Waldau, Paul. 2013. *Animal Studies: An Introduction*. Oxford: Oxford University Press.

Waldau, Paul, and Kimberley Patton, eds. 2006. *A Communion of Subjects: Animals in Religion, Science, and Ethics*. New York: Columbia University Press.

Walshe, Maurice, trans. 1995. *The Long Discourses of the Buddha: A Translation of the Dīgha Nikāya*. Somerville, MA: Wisdom Publications.

Walters, Jonathan S. 1990. "The Buddha's Bad Karma: A Problem in the History of Theravāda Buddhism." *Numen* 37 (1): 70–95.

Weil, Kari. 2012. *Thinking Animals: Why Animal Studies Now?* New York: Columbia University Press.

Wiley, Kristi. 2006. "Five-Sensed Animals in Jainism." In *A Communion of Subjects: Animals in Religion, Science, and Ethics*, edited by Paul Waldau and Kimberley Patton, 250–255. New York: Columbia University Press.

Wilson, Liz. 2003. "Human Torches of Enlightenment: Autocremation and Spontaneous Combustion as Marks of Sanctity in South Asian Buddhism." In *The Living and the Dead: Social Dimensions of Death in South Asian Religions*, edited by Liz Wilson, 29–50. Albany: State University of New York Press.

Wiltshire, Martin. 1983. "The 'Suicide' Problem in the Pāli Canon." *Journal of the International Association of Buddhist Studies* 6 (2): 124–140.

Windisch, E., ed. 1975. *Itivuttaka*. London: Pali Text Society. Orig. pub. 1889.

Wood, Amy Louise. 2012. "'Killing the Elephant': Murderous Beasts and the Thrill of Retribution." *Journal of the Gilded Age and Progressive Era* 11 (3): 405–444.

Woodward, F. L., ed. 1926. *Paramattha-Dīpanī Udānaṭṭhakathā (Udāna Commentary) of Dhammapālacariya*. Pali Text Society Text Series, Vol. 143. London: Pali Text Society.

Woodward, F. L., trans. 1935. *The Minor Anthologies of the Pali Canon, Part II: Udana (Verses of Uplift) and Ittivuttaka (As It Was Said)*. Sacred Books of the Buddhists, Vol. 8. London: Pali Text Society.

Zin, Monika. 1996. "Der Elefant mit dem Schwert." In *Festschrift Dieter Schlingloff zur Vollendung des 65: Lebensjahres dargebracht von Schülern, Freunden und Kollegen*, edited by Friedrich Wilhelm, 331–344. Reinbek: Dr. Inge Wezler Verlag für Orientalische Fachpublikationen.

Zin, Monika. 2006. *Mitleid und Wunderkraft: Schwierige Bekehrungen und ihre Ikonographie im indischen Buddhismus*. Wiesbaden: Harrassowitz Verlag.

INDEX

Page references followed by an "*f*" indicate figures. Citations with S. indicate Sanskrit; citations with P. indicate Pāli.